By permission of The Boston Athenæum.

JOHN MARSHALL
From the portrait by Chester Harding, painted in 1830.

THE STORY OF THE SUPREME COURT

By ERNEST SUTHERLAND BATES

"We are under a Constitution, but the Constitution is what the judges say it is."

CHARLES EVANS HUGHES

1

WITH FRONTISPIECE

THE BOBBS-MERRILL COMPANY

PUBLISHERS

INDIANAPOLIS   NEW YORK

OK
1561
.B3

COPYRIGHT, 1936
BY THE BOBBS-MERRILL COMPANY

FIRST EDITION

Printed in the United States of America

PRINTED AND BOUND BY
BRAUNWORTH & CO., INC.
BUILDERS OF BOOKS
BRIDGEPORT, CONN.

To

HARRY ELMER BARNES

CONTENTS

CONTENTS—*Concluded*

THE STORY OF THE SUPREME COURT

The Story of the Supreme Court

CHAPTER I

THE ORIGIN OF THE SUPREME COURT

1. *The Social and Political Background*

THE Supreme Court is the most distinctive feature of the
American system of government. It is, in fact, with regard
to the extent of the powers of the Court, a wholly unique
feature. The democratic nations of England and France, as
well as the non-democratic nations of Germany, Italy, and
Russia, have nothing corresponding to it. Canada, Australia,
British South Africa, and some of the South American states
have given to their courts a strictly limited right to review
legislation under certain circumstances, but no other nation has
placed the judiciary above the legislature with authority practically to nullify the acts of the latter without appeal save
through the difficult process of constitutional amendment. The
Supreme Court of the United States is the supremest supreme
court in all the world.*

It did not have this proud position in the beginning. Its
present authority, decried in many quarters even today, has
been won after nearly a century and a half of struggle with the
other branches of the government in a series of legal battles
far more intellectually thrilling than those cruder ones determined by musketry and force. To understand the Supreme
Court it is necessary to know its history. And that history
began before its birth.

The Supreme Court was but one of the many children—and
by no means a favorite child—of the Constitution. And the
Constitution in turn had many parents—the fifty-five members

---

*See Felix Frankfurter, *The Business of the Supreme Court* (1927),
pp. 4-5. For full information, consult Charles G. Haines, *The American
Doctrine of Judicial Supremacy* (1914).

of the Constitutional Convention. And those members were products of their time, which John Fiske long ago well named "the Critical Period of American History."

A few years behind them lay the American Revolution— fought, as is generally recognized today, not primarily over differences of abstract theory but to decide the very concrete question of whether the colonies should continue to be exploited for the benefit of the British merchants, manufacturers, and landholders who controlled the British Parliament. Nevertheless, abstract theories of the utmost importance were developed in support of the American cause by John Adams, Samuel Adams, and that James Wilson who will appear so prominently in the following pages. Seeking grounds on which to justify colonial resistance to Parliament, they found these in the same philosophy of natural rights by which John Locke had justified the British Revolution of 1688. In its terms, men were considered to possess as a gift from "Nature and Nature's God" the right to "life, liberty, and property" anterior to the civil rights bestowed by law; governmental enactments that violated any of these natural rights were therefore intrinsically null and void.

A further support for this position was found in the British common law which particularly safeguarded the right to private property. "So great is the regard of the law for private property," wrote Blackstone, the supreme authority on the common law, "that it will not authorize the least violation of it; no, not even for the general good of the whole community."

In the Declaration of Independence, Jefferson, less devoted to the propertied classes than were the Adamses and Wilson, substituted the natural right to "the pursuit of happiness" for the traditional right to property, and in a document designed to enlist all Americans, poor as well as rich, in the cause of the Revolution, Jefferson's more conservative colleagues allowed the innovation to pass. So also the statement that "all men are endowed by their Creator with these rights" was accepted, although it exposed the colonials to the charge of patent inconsistency in still maintaining Negro slavery—an inconsistency which British critics were not slow to point out.

Independence once gained, the doctrine of natural rights, having served its immediate purpose, tended to sink into the background while the American leaders turned their attention to more pressing problems of actual government. The notion of a higher law, behind the civil law, guaranteeing among other things the right to private property, had, however, been urged too strongly to be forgotten; it had sunk deeply into the American consciousness; and one will never do justice to the conservatives of the following generations without realizing that they sincerely believed private property to be a part of the moral order itself.

As long as the same ends could be obtained through written constitutions and laws, the doctrine of natural rights slumbered on in a state of suspended animation, but when after the Civil War further sanctions for expanding property than those afforded by statutory law seemed needed, we shall find the old notions revived under the new name of "Due Process."

This development was far in the future, however, at the time of the Constitutional Convention of 1787, called to consider immediate questions of practical government.

Prior to the Revolution, the colonies had been governed by the centralized authority of the British Parliament with only such minor diversity as was permitted by their various charters. The effect of the Revolution was suddenly to transform them into thirteen free and independent nations. For six years after the signing of the Peace of Paris on September 3, 1783, they functioned as separate autonomous states, each under its own political organization which as in colonial days in most cases embraced clearly divided executive, legislative and judiciary departments with the final authority vested in the legislatures as representatives of the people or at least that part of the people not disfranchised by the property qualifications of the suffrage.

True, the thirteen states were, under the Articles of Confederation adopted in 1781, also loosely joined in a "perpetual Union," called "the United States of America," for purposes of common defense against foreign enemies. The Articles were little more than an elaborate treaty of perpetual alliance.

The Union possessed neither executive nor judiciary, and though the Continental Congress was continued with authority to declare war and make treaties it was not authorized to regulate commerce (save with the Indians), to coin money, or to collect taxes.

Lacking the power of the purse, Congress could do little to preserve the public credit, which rapidly declined owing to the delays of the states in meeting their revolutionary debts. American commerce and industry suffered domestically through being obliged to conform to thirteen different sets of local laws and in foreign competition through being without the support of a strong central government such as Great Britain and France put behind the demands of their own merchants and manufacturers. Finally, the desperate condition of the poorer classes after the Revolution led in many states to attempts at alleviation through the issue of great quantities of paper money and through the passage of stay laws on debts ("moratoriums" they would be called today), measures which were naturally resisted to the uttermost by the wealthier classes, and were generally opposed by the courts within the limits of their power.

When in 1786 Daniel Shays raised a small army of impoverished Revolutionary veterans in open rebellion against the state of Massachusetts, although the insurrection was easily suppressed, the fears of the conservative members of society led them to foresee a possible dissolution of the whole economic order. General Knox expressed a wide-spread sentiment in writing to Washington as follows:

"The people who are the insurgents have never paid any, or but very little taxes—But they see the weakness of government; They feel at once their own poverty, compared with the opulent, and their own force, and they are determined to make use of the latter, in order to remedy the former. Their creed is 'That the property of the United States has been protected from the confiscations of Britain by the joint exertions of all, and therefore ought to be the common property of all. And he that attempts opposition to this creed is an enemy to equity and justice, and ought to be swept from off the face of the

earth.' In a word they are determined to annihilate all debts public and private and have agrarian laws, which are easily effected by means of unfunded paper money which shall be a tender in all cases whatever. . . ."

With what was considered the "natural right" to property thus endangered, a large number of prosperous Revolutionary leaders felt that there was no inconsistency with their former principles in now desiring a stronger central government. Mainly through the energetic efforts of Alexander Hamilton, Congress was led to invite the states in February, 1787, to send delegates to a Convention at Philadelphia for "the sole and express purpose of revising the Articles of Confederation."

2.   The Constitutional Convention*

After a very careful and thorough analysis of the economic interests of the fifty-five delegates to this convention, elected in every case not directly by the people but by the state legislatures, Charles Beard in his epoch-making work, *An Economic Interpretation of the Constitution* (1913), came to the following conclusions:

"A majority of the members were lawyers by profession. [Thirty-one, to be exact.]

"Most of the members came from towns, on or near the coast, that is, from the regions in which personalty was largely concentrated.

"Not one member represented in his immediate personal economic interests the small farming or mechanic classes.

"The overwhelming majority of members, at least five-sixths, were immediately, directly, and personally interested in the outcome of their labors at Philadelphia, and were to a greater or less extent economic beneficiaries from the adoption of the Constitution."†

Forty members held government securities, twenty-four had money loaned out at interest, fourteen were involved in land

---

*For an excellent account of the Convention, see Fred Rodell, *Fifty Five Men* (1936).

†Quoted by permission of the publishers, The Macmillan Company.

speculations, eleven were concerned in manufacturing or shipping, fifteen were slave-owners. Of the two classes into which American society had come to be divided after the Revolution, creditors and debtors, the creditors alone were represented in the Convention.

Of the Convention's work the essentially friendly Albert J. Beveridge writes:

"The general Federal Convention that framed the Constitution at Philadelphia was a secret body; and the greatest pains were taken that no part of its proceedings should get to the public until the Constitution itself was reported to Congress. The Journals were confided to the care of Washington and were not made public until many years after our present Government was established. The framers of the Constitution ignored the purposes for which they were delegated; they acted without any authority whatever; and the document, which the warring factions finally evolved from their quarrels and dissensions, was revolutionary."*

The revolutionary character of what they were doing was to some extent concealed from the members themselves by the methods which they were naturally led to adopt. Following the fiction that they were merely revising the Articles of Confederation they set themselves from the first to prepare a written constitution, something unknown at that time outside of this country but perfectly familiar in principle to Americans through their experience of royal charters and state constitutions. Three outlines were submitted as bases of discussion: what was known as the "Virginia Plan," largely prepared by James Madison but presented by Edmund Randolph; the "South Carolina Plan," presented by Charles Pinckney; and the "New Jersey Plan," presented by William Paterson. The Convention adopted features now from one, now from another of these plans, and applied the same process of selection to the various state constitutions. With regard to the special feature of the Supreme Court, the Convention was probably influenced not

*Albert J. Beveridge, *Life of John Marshall,* Houghton Mifflin Company (1919), Vol. I, p. 323.

only by the example of the state courts but by that of the special Court of Appeals set up by Congress in 1780 to determine the disposition of prizes captured at sea and other cases arising under international relations. In all these ways the Convention made use of a mass of American precedents in building up a governmental structure all the parts of which were familiar but which as a whole was nevertheless a new creation.

The fundamental novelty of the projected system lay in the fact that it proposed to establish a dual scheme of government, federal and state, with the sovereignty virtually divided according to the powers given to each branch. This was the Convention's answer to the main problem before it: how to create a central government strong enough to protect property, yet not so strong as to be able to interfere with property. The same consideration dictated the subdivision of the federal government into the three co-ordinate branches, executive, legislative (itself subdivided into two branches), and judiciary, with an elaborate system of "checks and balances" among them. In every department, the new government was to be one of extensive yet strictly limited powers.

Particular attention was devoted to preventing "the tyranny of the majority" over "the minority of wealth and education." "The people," even with the safeguard of the property qualifications of the suffrage then in vogue, were trusted with the direct election of only a part of a part of the government: the House of Representatives. The Senate and the executive were to be indirectly elected, and the judiciary was made appointive with life tenure except for possibility of impeachment. In the language of the debates of the time the new government was to be distinctly "representative," not "democratic."

Among the powers denied to the states were the right to "coin money," to "emit bills of credit," or to "make any thing but gold and silver coin a tender in payment of debts," thereby putting a summary stop to the issue of that fiat money so dear to the debtor class. Furthermore, in what was to prove one of the most important clauses in the Constitution, the states were

forbidden to pass any law "impairing the obligation of contracts." This last was a phrase attributed to the subtlety of James Wilson of Pennsylvania; it meant at least that debts could not be legally annulled and might mean as much more as it could be made to mean.

The practical sagacity of the framers of the Constitution is witnessed by the fact that the general framework of government which they devised has stood the test of time for nearly one hundred and fifty years. Yet they would have needed the wisdom not merely of men but of angels to have foreseen all of the issues likely to arise under a system so richly sown with the seeds of future conflict. There was, in the first place, the problem of the dual sovereignty of the Union and the states— a problem only to be settled by a civil war. And within the Union itself there was the division of powers among the three branches of the federal government, executive, legislative, and judiciary, likely to give rise to struggles between any two of them. Theoretically, all of these matters were covered by the Constitution, but who was to decide just what the Constitution meant?

Is this all-important power, enjoyed at the present time by the Supreme Court, explicitly confided to it by the Constitution itself? It is not even mentioned there.

Is it, if not explicitly mentioned, at least implied in the Constitution? Over this more difficult question historians and statesmen have long wrangled and still wrangle. According to one party, the power of "judicial review"—the technical term for the authority of the courts to nullify legislative acts—was intended to be given them by the Constitutional Convention; according to the other, it was a "usurpation" by John Marshall in the case of *Marbury* v. *Madison* sixteen years later. But both of these conclusions seem to be dictated much more by the conservative or radical inclinations of the arguers than by the evidence of the facts. There is no proof that the members of the Convention, so admirably able to express their intent in other cases, in this one instance left it to be gathered from doubtful implications. And, on the other hand, John

Marshall was very far from being the one and only original "usurper."

What actually happened was that the accepted theory of judicial review, like most accepted theories, was a gradual development. A relatively new idea when it was suggested, as it was, in the Constitutional Convention, it was discussed there in only the most cursory and inconclusive manner. In the later arguments over the ratification of the Constitution the idea was advanced by numerous influential advocates of the Constitution. In the First Congress it was accepted in principle by the majority, and was clearly implied in the Judiciary Act of 1789. During the first few years it was both asserted in theory and exercised in fact by the federal judiciary before John Marshall's enunciation of the "right" or "power," whichever it be considered, in 1803. But between 1803 and the Dred Scott decision of 1855 it was never exercised. Not until after the Civil War, did it fully emerge from the realms of disputed theory and become an increasingly important fact.

At this point in the story only the first three stages of the long evolution can be discussed: the happenings in the Constitutional Convention, in the ratifying conventions, and in the First Congress—all prior to the actual erection of the Supreme Court.

To find the probable intent of the members of the Philadelphia Convention it is necessary to look into the accepted political theories of their day. Many attempts have been made to use the argument from silence to prove that the framers of the Constitution regarded the right of judicial review as so self-evident that specific provision for it was unnecessary. Yet in 1787 nothing was less self-evident, for precedent (and it is usually precedent, not logic, that makes an idea seem "self-evident") was heavily against it.

The example of British law, always potent in America, was entirely on the side of the supremacy of the legislature over the judiciary. The final interpretation of the unwritten but recognized British constitution had always been left to king or Parliament. There were no clear examples of judicial review

in the history of other foreign countries.   Nor were there any in America during the whole colonial period.

With regard to the last point, there is indeed today a popular and widely propagated belief to the contrary.   Thus David Lawrence writes in the New York *Sun,* March 28, 1936, "For many years prior to the writing of our constitution it was the custom of the people to appeal to the courts against abusive acts by colonial legislatures."   This would indeed have been a surprising custom since it would have meant appealing from native legislation to the royal courts.   In point of fact, as even so zealous a defendant of the judiciary as Charles Evans Hughes points out, the appeals went the other way, "from the courts to the legislative assemblies: . . . As a rule, the bench was not learned and the selection of judges was largely determined by politics or favor."*   The only analogy to judicial review with which the colonists were familiar, and that in a most unfavorable sense, was the frequent annulment of colonial laws by His Majesty's Privy Council, which was one of the causes of the Revolution.

During the Revolution and afterward, popular opposition to the judiciary increased.   As Beveridge writes, "It must be carefully kept in mind that from the beginning of the Revolution most of the people were antagonistic to courts of any kind, and bitterly hostile to lawyers."   Thus the town of Dedham, Massachusetts, instructed its representatives in the legislature to strive for laws to "check" attorneys and if unsuccessful in that "to endeavor that the order of Lawyers be totally abolished."   Braintree, Massachusetts, similarly demanded the passage of laws to "crush, or, at least, put a proper check of restraint" on lawyers.   All this, Beveridge adds, "was the result of the bitter hardships of debtors," since the courts usually enforced all contracts with great rigor.

As the legislatures themselves were largely made up of lawyers there was slight chance of the enactment of such revo-

---

*C. E. Hughes, *The Supreme Court of the United States* (1928), pp. 2, 3. See also Louis Boudin, *Government by Judiciary* (1932), Appendix B, "Alleged Colonial Precedents."

lutionary measures as Dedham and Braintree desired, but instances of legislative encroachment on the courts were numerous. In Vermont, we read (D. Chipman, *Vermont Reports,* p. 21), "During the first Septenary, the legislature frequently interfered with the judiciary department. . . . They constituted themselves a Court of Chancery. They appointed a board of Commissioners with full power to decide in a summary manner all disputes relative to the title of lands. They also frequently granted new trials in cases which had been finally decided by the judiciary. The power thus exercised by the legislature, with the approbation of a majority of the people, naturally confirmed the idea that the power of the Legislature was unlimited and supreme."

In view of the possibility of just such excesses of authority, several states in their constitutions had devised certain checks upon the legislature. Thus the Pennsylvania constitution of 1776, closely followed by the Vermont constitution of 1777, provided for the election of a council of censors every seven years "to inquire whether the constitution has been preserved inviolate in every part" and to recommend the repeal of any laws in contravention of it. In the New York constitution of 1777 a different method to secure the same end was adopted, whereby a permanent council of revision was established, consisting of the governor, chancellor, and judges of the supreme court, to examine all laws about to be passed by the legislature and exercise a veto power, which could be overturned by a two-thirds vote. It will be observed, however, that in these three cases, the only ones in which any constitutional limitations were laid on the legislatures, the ultimate power was still reserved to them.

In addition to the protection against legislative encroachment afforded by such constitutional provisions, the state courts themselves now began very tentatively to assert a right of judicial review over legislation. Formerly it was believed that there were a number of instances of actual nullification of state laws by the judiciary between 1776 and 1787. Charles Haines, in his valuable work, *The American Doctrine of Ju-*

dicial Supremacy, listed no less than seven of such supposed cases, but the exhaustive study of each made by Louis Boudin in his *Government by Judiciary* showed that only one was a real instance of the exercise of judicial review and that one, the North Carolina case of *Bayard* v. *Singleton,* 1 Martin, 45, occurred so late in 1787 that it is doubtful if any reports of it could have reached the Philadelphia Convention. The other cases resolved themselves at most into badly reported instances of a more or less hesitant assertion of the right of review without attempting to put it into practice.*

At the time of the Philadelphia Convention the recognized need was to check the encroachments of the legislature on the judiciary, not the reverse. Even Jefferson, that most ardent upholder of legislative authority against the judiciary, admitted in his *Notes on Virginia* that in the pre-convention period the state legislatures had in many cases "decided rights which should have been left to judicial controversy."

As a check on the legislature the Constitutional Convention discussed the idea of a council of revision, taken over from the New York state constitution and incorporated in the Virginia Plan which suggested just such a council with the same limited veto power, to be composed of the president and two justices of the Supreme Court. The proposal was voted down on June 4, 1787, by the decisive majority of eight states to two, and though it was later again brought up by Madison and Wilson it was again defeated and the veto power was left solely to the executive without the assistance of the judiciary.

In the debates on the council of revision the larger question of judicial review in general came up quite incidentally. It became evident at once that there was no unanimity of opinion on the subject either among those who opposed the council or those who favored it.

Elbridge Gerry objected to the idea of such a council be-

---

*These other cases were: the case of Josiah Phillips in Virginia, 1778; *Holmes* v. *Walton,* N. J. 1780; *Commonwealth* v. *Caton,* Virginia, 1782; *Rutgers* v. *Waddington,* New York, 1784; *The Symsbury Case,* Connecticut, 1784-85; *Trevett* v. *Weeden,* Rhode Island, 1786. For discussion see Louis Boudin, *Government by Judiciary,* Vol. I, Ch. IV and Appendix C.

cause it would give a double negative to the Supreme Court, since the judicial function of expounding statutes would necessarily involve "a power of deciding on their Constitutionality."

Luther Martin of Maryland agreed with Gerry.

But others, without granting the inherent powers of the judges to declare laws unconstitutional, were opposed to giving them even the single negative of the veto.

Thus, Gunning Bedford, Jr., of Delaware argued that "it would be sufficient to mark out in the Constitution the boundaries to the legislative authority, which would give all the requisite security to the rights of the other departments. The representatives of the people were the best judges of what was for their interest, and ought to be under no external control whatever."

Similarly the realistic Benjamin Franklin saw that the power to negate the law is intrinsically also a power to control the law. "It would be improper," he said, "to put it in the power of any Man to negative a Law passed by the Legislature because it would give him the control of the Legislature."

John Mercer of Maryland disapproved "of the Doctrine that the Judges as expositors of the Constitution should have authority to declare a law void."

Charles Pinckney of South Carolina opposed "the interference of the Judges in the Legislative business."

John Dickinson of Delaware—that "piddling thinker" as John Adams called him—rather helplessly thought that "no such power (of judicial review) ought to exist" but was "at a loss what expedient to substitute."

The supporters of the council of revision were equally divided in their reasons. Madison, its chief proponent, who was later to write in *The Federalist* "in republican government the legislative authority necessarily predominates," took the same position in the Philadelphia Convention, denying that the courts "would be so daring as to place a veto on a Law that had passed with the assent of the Legislature." Nevertheless, he argued, not inconsistently, "Experience in all the states had

evinced a powerful tendency in the legislature to absorb all power into its vortex. This was the real source of danger to the American constitution, and suggested the necessity of giving every defensive authority to the other departments that was consistent with republican principles." Madison has often been numbered with the defenders of judicial supremacy because of his later statement in the Convention that "a law violating a constitution established by the people themselves would be considered by the Judges null and void," but Boudin shows conclusively from the context of the speech that Madison was referring to a hypothetical act of secession on the part of some individual state and not at all to laws of Congress.

If Madison thus wanted a council of revision as a milder substitute for judicial review, Wilson, on the other hand, was emphatic in desiring it as an addition to whatever other rights the courts might be supposed to possess. "It has been said," he argued, "that the judges, as expositors of the laws, would have an opportunity of defending their constitutional rights. There was weight in this observation; but this power of the judges did not go far enough. Laws may be unjust, may be unwise, may be dangerous, may be destructive; and yet not be so unconstitutional as to justify the judges in refusing to give them effect. Let them have a share in the revisionary power, and they will have an opportunity of taking notice of these characters of a law, and of counteracting, by the weight of their opinions, the improper views of the legislature."

George Mason of Virginia took exactly the same view. Although the judges could certainly declare an unconstitutional law void, he said, nevertheless, "with regard to every law however unjust, oppressive or pernicious, which did not come plainly under this description, they would be under the necessity as judges to give it free course. He wished the further use to be made of the judges, of giving aid in preventing every improper law."

Gouverneur Morris of New York and Oliver Ellsworth of Connecticut, later Chief Justice of the Supreme Court, enthusiastically endorsed the plan, presumably—in view of their

opinions elsewhere expressed—being in complete agreement with Mason and Wilson.

And this is all that is known to have been said in the Constitutional Convention on the subject of judicial review. Six members supported it, five opposed it, the rest were silent.

Charles Beard in his work *The Supreme Court and the Constitution* (1912) argues from their utterances on other occasions that at least twenty-five members of the Convention were definitely in favor of the judicial review of both federal and state legislation, but his list is considered by Corwin and Boudin extremely doubtful (Madison, for example, one of those included, being at the time of the Convention clearly on the other side), and in any event twenty-five would not have constituted a majority of the Convention. The most that can fairly be stated is that there was a brief discussion, eliciting a wide divergence of opinion on the subject, and that no action was taken on the question.

For this negative result there was the best of reasons, namely that the problem could not possibly be solved logically in terms of the accepted theory of the Convention that the national government should consist of three co-ordinate branches of equal authority each ruled by the Constitution or, in a widely quoted phrase, that the American system was to be "a government of laws and not of men."* Laws and constitutions, being inanimate, cannot possibly govern except as they are administered by men. It was perfectly true that to leave the final interpretation of the Constitution to Congress would make Congress supreme over the Constitution, but Franklin was equally correct in saying that to leave the interpretation to the courts would give the same supremacy to them, resulting in the situation tersely described by Charles Evans Hughes in his remark, when off the bench, "The Constitution is what the judges say it is." To defend "the independence" of either the judiciary or the legislature without encroachment on the other when the two should come in conflict was logically impossible.

---

*Or as the schoolboy mentioned by Corwin rendered it, "A government of lawyers and not of men."

Practically the problem could be met as the similar logical impasse between the powers of House and Senate has been met: by one or the other of the parties giving way. The American system evidently permits of various combinations: Judiciary vs. Legislative, Judiciary vs. Executive, Legislative vs. Executive, Judiciary vs. Legislative and Executive, Judiciary and Legislative vs. Executive, Judiciary and Executive vs. Legislative. Every one of these combinations has occurred repeatedly, and the history of the Supreme Court on its governmental side is just the history of the changing results of these shifting alliances.

In terms of the immediate future the indecision of the Convention meant a gain for the judiciary. As Madison wrote despondently in regard to the proposed Virginia constitution of 1788, "In the state constitutions and indeed in the federal one also, no provision is made for the case of a disagreement in expounding them (the laws), and as the courts are generally the last making the decision, it results to them, by refusing or not refusing to execute a law, to stamp it with its final character. *This makes the Judiciary Department paramount in fact to the Legislature, which was never intended and can never be proper.*"*

If any man knew the intentions of the Philadelphia Convention that man was certainly James Madison, so often acclaimed as "the Father of the Constitution." What was then considered the relative practical importance of the three departments of the national government was probably indicated by the order in which they are taken up in the Constitution and by the space given to each. Article I, dealing with the legislative department, contains 303 lines; Article II, dealing with the executive, contains 127 lines; Article III, dealing with the judiciary, contains only 51 lines.

The whole subject of the judiciary received far less attention from the Convention than did the other two departments of the government. Concentration on the latter was made inevitable by the nature of the divisions within the Convention,

---

*Italics ours.

which turned on the opposition between large and small states and between the North and the South.   More than once the debates became so violent that the Convention threatened to break up, and it was only by the utmost use of the principle of mutual concessions and compromise that the members were able finally to draw up and accept the Constitution as we have it.

Even then, its acceptance by the people was considered doubtful.   In such circumstances, to have given further importance to the unpopular judiciary would have added to the chances of rejection.   As we have seen, only the boldest and most far-sighted of the conservatives, such as Wilson, Ellsworth, and Morris, had been ready to come out openly in the Convention for the power of judicial review.

3. Ratification of the Constitution

Bitter as were the conflicts in the Convention, they were as nothing compared to those which arose when the instrument was submitted to the states for ratification.   Here the issue was once more between the debtor and the creditor classes, both groups recognizing the ways in which the Constitution benefited the latter.   The debtors were in the majority, but they lacked influence and organization, and many of them were excluded from voting by the property qualifications.   Then, too, several of the state conventions seem to have misinterpreted, to put it mildly, the mandates of the people.   Thus, though the Constitution was ratified by all of the states except North Carolina and Rhode Island, the ratification, as every historian today admits, was by a popular minority.

Charles Beard in his *Economic Interpretation* sums up the results of a very close analysis of the situation in every state in the following words:

"The Constitution was ratified by a vote of probably not more than one-sixth of the adult males."   (Hence, the phrase, "We the people" in the preamble—taken from the constitution of Massachusetts—must be interpreted in the same liberal manner as that similar phrase "all men" in the Declaration of

Independence. Literally, it should have read, "We one-sixth of the adult white males.")

"It is questionable whether a majority of the voters participating in the elections for the state conventions in New York, Massachusetts, New Hampshire, Virginia, and South Carolina, actually approved the ratification of the Constitution." (To these states Beveridge adds Pennsylvania.)

"In the ratification, it became manifest that the line of cleavage for and against the Constitution was between substantial personalty interests on the one hand and the small farming and debtor interests on the other."

During the contest, which was conducted by the Federalists—as the supporters of the Constitution now were called—with the utmost shrewdness, the ablest of their leaders decided to venture the assertion that the right of judicial review was included in that desirable "independence of the judiciary" guaranteed by the Constitution. The nature of their campaign is admirably summarized by J. Allen Smith:

"The advocates of judicial supremacy were careful to support it not as a conservative safeguard, but as a means—assumed to be necessary—of protecting popular rights and enforcing the constitutional checks on public officials. Every effort was made to create the impression that the Supreme Court of the United States was designed to protect the people, and by its position under the Constitution, was admirably fitted to serve as the authoritative interpreter of their will. . . . There is probably no other instance in the whole history of constitutional development where public opinion has been so misled as to the fundamental nature of a political arrangement. The ostensible purpose in advocating the assumption of the veto power by the courts was to provide a means of enforcing constitutional restraints; but the real purpose was to centralize political authority largely in the Supreme Court of the United States, and through the power of final interpretation, to make the Constitution an adequate bulwark of conservatism."*

*J. Allen Smith, *The Growth and Decadence of Constitutional Government,* Henry Holt and Company (1930), pp. 100-101. An interesting illus-

In the ratifying conventions, Oliver Ellsworth of Connecticut, James Wilson of Pennsylvania, Edmund Pendleton and John Marshall of Virginia took a prominent part in furthering the aim of judicial supremacy in their respective states, but the most influential of all on general public opinion was Alexander Hamilton of New York through his essays contributed to *The Federalist.*

Hamilton had been greatly disappointed in the outcome of the Convention in which he had taken little part after it summarily rejected his scheme for an autocratic government with the power centralized in a president and senate to be elected by the propertied classes alone and to hold office for life.   Privately, he affirmed the Constitution to be quite "worthless." Nevertheless, he preferred it to nothing, and once he had entered the lists in its defense, bringing to the task the talents of the ablest advocate in America, he very quickly became its foremost champion.   His argument for judicial review, in *The Federalist,* No. 78, fully bears out J. Allen Smith's description of the Federalist tactics.

"The complete independence of the courts of justice is peculiarly essential in a limited constitution.   By a limited constitution I understand one which contains certain specified exceptions to the legislative authority; such, for instance, as that it shall pass no bills of attainder, no *ex post facto* laws, and the like.   Limitations of this kind can be preserved in practice in no other way than through the medium of the courts of justice; whose duty it must be to declare all acts contrary to the manifest tenor of the Constitution void.   Without this, all the reservations of particular rights or privileges would amount to nothing. . . .

"If it be said that the legislative body are themselves the constitutional judges of their own powers, and that the con-

---

tration of Professor Smith's argument is furnished by the Republican platform of 1936 which repeats the identical Federalist assertions of 1788. The first plank reads: "We pledge ourselves: (1) to maintain the American system of constitutional and local self-government, and to resist all attempts to impair the authority of the Supreme Court of the United States, the final protector of the rights of our citizens against the arbitrary encroachments of the legislative and executive branches of the government. There can be no individual liberty without an independent judiciary."

struction they put upon them is conclusive upon the other departments, it may be answered that this cannot be the natural presumption, where it is not to be collected from any particular provisions in the Constitution. It is not otherwise to be supposed that the Constitution could intend to enable the representatives of the people to substitute their will to that of their constituents. It is far more rational to suppose that the courts were designated to be an intermediate body between the people and the legislature, in order, among other things, to keep the latter within the limits assigned to their authority. The interpretation of the laws is the proper and peculiar province of the courts. A constitution is, in fact, and must be, regarded by the judges as a fundamental law. It must therefore belong to them to ascertain its meaning, as well as the meaning of any particular act proceeding from the legislative body. If there should happen to be an irreconcilable variance between the two, that which has the superior obligation and validity ought, of course, to be preferred; in other words, the constitution ought to be preferred to the statute, the intention of the people to the intention of their agents.

"Nor does this conclusion by any means suppose a superiority of the judicial to the legislative power. *It only supposes that the power of the people is superior to both;** and that where the will of the legislature, declared in its statutes, stands in opposition to that of the people, declared in the Constitution, the judges ought to be governed by the latter, rather than the former. They ought to regulate their decisions by the fundamental laws, rather than those which are not fundamental."

Hamilton's argument, it will be seen, was simple, skillful, and sophistical. It assumed the points at issue first that the Constitution was a more direct expression of the will of the people than any act of their representatives in Congress could be, and, second that the Constitution could and would be preserved with less change if interpreted by the courts than by Congress. The first assumption, dealing with the past, was false; the second, dealing with the future, was doubtful. And on their basis he reached the paradoxical conclusion that the

---

*Italics ours.

courts, far removed from the people by the manner of their appointment, were nevertheless more representative of them than a congress which the people themselves elected.

In the light of Hamilton's general aristocratic attitude and his real opinion expressed in his oft-quoted remark "The 'People'—your 'People,' sir—is a great beast," the sudden reverence for the popular will in this article of *The Federalist* of course cannot be taken seriously.   Much more sincere was the guarded class appeal in a later paragraph of the same essay:

"But it is not with a view to infractions of the Constitution only that the independence of the judges may be an essential safeguard against the effect of occasional ill humors in the society.   These sometimes extend no farther than to the injury of the private rights of particular classes of citizens, by unjust and partial laws.   Here also the firmness of the judicial magistracy is of vast importance in mitigating the severity and confining the operation of such laws. . . . This is a circumstance calculated to have more influence upon the character of our governments than but a few may be aware of. . . ."

This is the essay always quoted even today by the advocates of judicial review.   But Hamilton added another, No. 81, on the same subject, which is less often mentioned.   As will be seen, it quite startlingly modified his earlier statements.   Its purpose was to refute an objection to the Constitution which was, namely, this: "The Parliament of Great Britain, and the legislatures of the several States, can at any time rectify, by law, the exceptionable decisions of their respective courts.   But the errors and usurpations of the Supreme Court of the United States will be uncontrollable and remediless."   This criticism he then attempted to prove was "made up altogether of false reasoning upon misconceived fact," and his proof ran as follows:

"*It is not true . . . that the Parliament of Great Britain, or the legislatures of the particular States, can rectify the exceptionable decisions of their respective courts, in any other sense than might be done by a future legislature of the United States.**

---

*Italics ours.

The theory, neither of the British, nor the State constitutions authorizes the revisal of a judicial sentence by a legislative act. Nor is there anything in the proposed Constitution, more than in either of them, by which it is forbidden.   In the former, as well as in the latter, the impropriety of the thing, on the general principles of law and reason, is the sole obstacle.   A legislature, without exceeding its province, cannot reverse a determination once made in a particular case; though *it may prescribe a new rule for future cases. . . .*"*

If, as Hamilton here claims, there was no difference between the British and American systems, so that the legislature in America as in Great Britain could "rectify the exceptionable decisions of the courts" by passing a "new law," what becomes of the finality of judicial review?   His language is, perhaps intentionally, rather vague, but apparently his position is here not far from that of Jefferson and Jackson who, as we shall see, held that the decision of the judiciary was binding upon the courts but not upon the other departments of the government.

The concessions made by Hamilton in No. 81 are plausibly conjectured by Boudin to have been owing to some protest from Madison, his colleague in *The Federalist,* to the extreme views advanced in No. 78.   Whatever he may have meant in No. 81, it is palpably out of tune with his earlier utterance. Accordingly, No. 78 was given a prominent place in the Federalist Bible while No. 81 was tacitly discarded as heretical.

4.   The Judiciary Act of 1789

The vigorous drive of the Federalist leaders to obtain recognition for the conception that questions of constitutionality should be left to the courts rather than to Congress was so successful that the doctrine was accepted by the majority of the First Congress itself.   This was shown early in the first session when in April, 1789, a bill was introduced giving the president the right to remove the secretary of foreign affairs

*Italics ours.

as a right implied, though not expressed, in his constitutional right of appointment. But did the right to appoint, necessarily carry with it the right to remove? The question was debated pro and con; already, before the Constitution was a year old, an obscurity had been discovered in it, and objection was made to the bill that in such doubtful cases Congress ought not to act until the Supreme Court had decided the question. Others held on the contrary that Congress was all the freer to act because its judgment if incorrect would be overruled by the Supreme Court. James Madison alone stoutly upheld the equal right of the legislature with the judiciary to decide questions of constitutionality.

"I beg to know," he said, "upon what principle it can be contended that any one department draws from the Constitution greater powers than another, in marking out the limits of the powers of the several departments. . . . Nothing has yet been offered to invalidate the doctrine that the meaning of the constitution may as well be ascertained by the legislature as by the judicial authority. . . . It is therefore a fair question whether this great power may not as well be decided at least by the whole legislature, as by part—by us, as well as by the executive or the judicial. As I think it will be equally constitutional, I cannot imagine it will be less safe that the exposition should issue from the legislative authority than any other. . . ."

But Madison was borne down, less by the weight of argument than numbers. On the other side were Elbridge Gerry and Fisher Ames of Massachusetts; John Lawrence and Peter Silvester of New York; William Smith of Maryland; John Page and Alexander White of Virginia; William Smith of South Carolina; Abraham Baldwin of Georgia.

Rarely in history has one seen such a spirit of abnegation in any governmental body! But the explanation of the strange phenomenon is not far to seek. The representatives of wealth and power, as overwhelmingly in control of the First Congress as they had been of the Philadelphia Convention, had nevertheless learned from the narrowness with which the Constitution itself had escaped defeat how precarious was their tenure. Congress was a semi-popular body; the executive was indi-

rectly elected; it was obvious that the judiciary being purely appointive, as well as from its whole tradition, would prove the most conservative of the three branches of the government. The political wisdom of those who reasoned thus was quickly demonstrated by future events; the Federalists lost control of the House of Representatives in 1793, and of the executive in 1801 but they would retain control of the Supreme Court until 1835.

The Judiciary Law of 1789, the enabling act which brought the federal system of courts into actual being, was essentially a Federalist measure, drawn up as it was by two of the most extreme of the party leaders, Oliver Ellsworth and William Paterson.   It established a Supreme Court consisting of a chief justice and five associate justices; a system of thirteen District Courts, one for each state; and three Circuit Courts, to be held twice a year, each composed of two justices of the Supreme Court sitting in conjunction with one district court judge.   It also in its famous twenty-fifth section extended the appellate jurisdiction of the Supreme Court far beyond anything directly provided for in the Constitution.   This remarkable section read:

"A final judgment or decree in any suit in the highest court of law or equity *of a state* in which a decision in the suit could be had, where is drawn in question the validity of a treaty or statute of, or an authority exercised under the United States and *the decision is against* their validity; or where is drawn in question the validity of a statute or an authority exercised under a state, on the ground of their being repugnant to the Constitution, treaties, or the laws of the United States *and the decision is in favor* of their validity, or where is drawn in question the construction of any clause of the Constitution, of a treaty, or a statute of, or commission held under the United States, *and the decision is against* the title, right, privilege or exemption specially set up or claimed by either party, under such clause of the said constitution, treaty, statute or commission, *may be reexamined and reversed or affirmed in the Supreme Court* of the United States upon a writ of error."*

---

*Italics ours.

The effect of this act was nothing less than to render the federal judiciary, at least by implication, superior over state courts, state legislatures, and the federal Congress. It provided for appeals from state courts to the Supreme Court; it provided that the constitutionality of state laws should be subject to the decision of the Supreme Court; and it provided that a federal law could be declared unconstitutional by a state court if this decision was upheld by the Supreme Court; and it went as far as mere logical implication without explicit statement could well go in giving the Supreme Court the direct power to declare federal laws unconstitutional.

On this last point Charles Beard writes: "It surely is not unreasonable to assume that the men who established this rule [of appeal from the state courts] believed that the Supreme Court could declare acts of Congress unconstitutional independently of decisions in lower state courts. Indeed, it would seem absurd to assume that an act of Congress might be annulled by a state court with the approval of the Supreme Court, but not by the Supreme Court directly."

Doctor Beard's logic is plainly correct, but there were other considerations than logic that impelled the Federalists to leave this ultimate power of the Supreme Court a matter of implication rather than of explicit statement as they could so easily have made it. It was one thing to uphold the supremacy of the judiciary in speeches unreported to the people; it was quite another to flaunt it before their eyes in an enactment. Hamilton's admissions in *The Federalist* themselves testify to the wide-spread opposition which the doctrine of judicial review had aroused; the Judiciary Act in any case was likely to be severely criticized; why should the Federalists, for the sake of mere theoretical consistency, have assumed the further burden of a probably unpopular and apparently unnecessary clause?

The bill, as it was, was sufficiently drastic to arouse considerable animosity in Congress. James Jackson of Georgia declared it an outrage on "the poor man"; William Sumter of South Carolina saw in it "the iron hand of power"; Samuel Livermore of New Hampshire denounced it as "a new-fangled system"; William Maclay of Pennsylvania called it "the gun-

powder plot of the Constitution" designed "to swallow all the State constitutions by degrees; and thus to swallow by degrees, all the State Judiciaries." Even Elbridge Gerry called it a tyranny, even the conservative William Smith of South Carolina declared that "this constant control of the Supreme Federal Court over the adjudication of the State Courts would dissatisfy the people." But as in the Constitutional Convention the conflict between state and national authority absorbed the attention to the neglect of possible future conflicts between the national legislature and the national judiciary.

The Federalists had little difficulty in carrying their measure. Madison, always torn between his nationalism and his love of Virginia, rather surprisingly supported it and showed later in the session by his remarks on the first ten amendments that he had at last come to accept the full theory of judicial review, apparently regarding opposition to it as a lost cause. Ellsworth defended his law, according to Maclay, "with wrath and anger," and so did those staunch Federalists, Fisher Ames, Theodore Sedgwick, Roger Sherman, and Egbert Benson. Its passage was never really in doubt, and it was finally enacted on September 24, 1789.

The First Congress had granted to the Supreme Court enormous powers, overt or implied, which seventy-three later Congresses would never have the will or courage to take away from it. Among these was the implied power to declare the acts of Congress itself unconstitutional. This was therefore no initial usurpation by John Marshall; neither was it a part of the Constitution; it was a free birthday present of Congress to the Supreme Court. The responsibility for it rests squarely upon the national legislature which acted under the authority conferred upon Congress (by Article III, Section 2, of the Constitution) to regulate the appellate jurisdiction of the Supreme Court. By the same authority under which Congress gave the Supreme Court this power, Congress could also at any time deprive the Supreme Court of the power.

True, in that case the Court might go back to Hamilton and declare the deprivation unconstitutional as violating the intrinsic nature of a written constitution. By the same logic, it

could even declare a constitutional amendment unconstitutional. But such legalistic tangles are still remote, and if they should occur they would not be wholly unlike situations that have arisen in the past and would be similarly settled, not by legal argument but by one party's giving way under the pressure brought to bear upon it.

All such problems were unforeseen when the Judiciary Act of 1789 was adopted. Then the immediate question was the important one: how far the Supreme Court would actually succeed in exercising the powers theoretically conferred upon it. And the answer to that question would largely lie with the Supreme Court itself.

Chapter II

THE COURT UNDER CHIEF JUSTICE JAY

1789-1795

John Jay, John Rutledge, William Cushing, James Wilson, John Blair, James Iredell, Thomas Johnson, William Paterson.

1. Personnel of the First Court

It is a pleasant theory still held by the naïve that the president of the United States in making his appointments to the Supreme Court is governed primarily by considerations of merit. That unfortunately has never been the case in the past and is not likely to be the case in the future. The president can hardly be expected to appoint men, however outstanding they may be, whose views on matters of public policy are known to be radically different from his own. He has personal and political obligations, which, being human, he will be tempted to fulfill through appointments to the Court. Besides being president, he is the leader of a political party, and partisan considerations will be borne in mind. So also will be the question of territorial representation. The most that can be said is that with a high-minded president merit will be one of the important qualifications for appointment to the Court; with a low-minded president it will not even be one of them. This will become abundantly clear as the story of the Court progresses.

Washington, of course, was a high-minded president. Yet Washington deemed it to be his duty to appoint only Federalists to the positions on the first Court—this excluding such critics of the Constitution as Patrick Henry and Luther Martin—and it also seemed important to him that the North and the South should be equally represented. Within these limits he made his selections on the merit basis.

Hamilton would have been an obvious first choice for the position of chief justice but that his foreign birth was felt to be an insuperable obstacle. The same disqualification applied to James Wilson, who made personal application for the post. The friends of John Rutledge of South Carolina were active in his behalf, and he considered himself thoroughly worthy of the place, as he later wrote Washington, but, after some hesitation, the President passed him by in favor of John Jay of New York, appointing both Wilson and Rutledge, however, associate justices.

John Jay was closely connected with the landed aristocracy of New York, being related by birth to the Bayards and Van Courtlandts, and having married into the great Livingston family. He was a man of unquestionable personal rectitude—during the Revolution he had advocated the destruction of the city of New York although this would also have destroyed the value of nearly all his own property—and of equally unquestionable conservatism. In the Continental Congress he had supported the famous "Olive Branch" petition to George the Third, termed by testy John Adams a "measure of imbecility," and had opposed the Declaration of Independence; in New York he had checkmated a provision for the taxation of war profits by the argument that it interfered with freedom of contract. "It was one of his favorite maxims that the people who own the country ought to govern it."* He had served for two years as chief justice of the supreme court of New York, had been minister to Spain, and at the time of his appointment to the chief justiceship was acting as United States secretary of foreign affairs. His mind was remarkably clear, calm, and firm, his disposition cold, his manner reserved but courteous.

The chief rival for Jay's position, Associate Justice John Rutledge, was probably his superior in detailed knowledge of the law. He had studied in the Inner Temple in London and on his return to South Carolina had risen almost immediately to the head of his profession. Elected president of South Caro-

---

*Frank Monaghan, *John Jay* (1935), p. 323.

lina after the Revolution, he resigned because the state constitution which was carried over his veto was too "democratic." "However unexceptionable democratic power may appear at first view," he said, "its defects have been found arbitrary, severe, and destructive." He was later, however, elected governor under the new constitution which for all its alleged democracy required the holder of that office to possess "a settled plantation . . . of the value of at least ten thousand pounds currency, clear of debt." Evidently, therefore, Rutledge was like Jay a man of some wealth. In the census of 1790 he was credited with the ownership of twenty-six slaves, a large number for one who was primarily not a planter but a lawyer. As a member of the Constitutional Convention, he was one of those responsible for the clause legalizing the slave trade until 1808, by which time the Southern States estimated that they would have a sufficient stock of slaves on hand to supply their future needs. He had much capability, marred by overweening conceit and a truculent disposition.

Next to Rutledge in distinction among the justices was William Cushing of Massachusetts, the oldest member of the Court. Descended from John Cotton of ministerial fame, Cushing had in his immediate background what might be called a judicial ancestry, both his father and grandfather having been royal judges in the colony. He had succeeded to their office in 1771, had supported the Revolution, had been elevated to the chief justiceship of his state on the resignation of John Adams, and had exercised great influence in persuading Massachusetts to send representatives to the Constitutional Convention. He was a terror to debtors and was particularly detested by Shays' rebels, but he had rendered one very notable decision to the effect that the Massachusetts Bill of Rights, through its clause declaring that "All men are born free and equal," legally operated to abolish slavery throughout the state. Although of slight build and only medium height, he affected an enormous dignity of carriage and was the last American judge to wear an English full-bottomed wig.

Washington's third appointee, James Wilson, was born and brought up in Scotland where he received an excellent classical

education, after which he came to America at the age of twenty-four, studied law in the office of John Dickinson, and achieved a lucrative practice, first at Carlisle, Pennsylvania, and then in Philadelphia. As already mentioned, he had been one of the chief theorists of the Revolution, developing, along with Samuel Adams and John Adams, the doctrine, derived from John Locke, of a natural right to "life, liberty, and property" as a suitable basis from which to resist the authority of the British Parliament.

Of the three natural rights, Wilson was especially interested in the third; in fact, his financial ventures were fully as important as his legal theories and probably influenced their character. In 1781 he was associated with William Bingham (considered by Beveridge to have been the richest man in America at that time), Robert Morris (ranked by the same author as the second richest man), Thomas Willing, George Clymer, Thomas Fitzsimons, and other leading bankers and merchants in establishing the Bank of North America, a much over-capitalized institution which made loans to the government and private individuals during the Revolution at such a high rate of interest that the dividends of its stockholders ran from twelve to sixteen per cent. In 1785 the Pennsylvania Legislature repealed its charter on the ground that "the bank established in the city of Philadelphia hath been found to be injurious to the welfare of this State and in its tendency appears to be incompatible with the public safety," but Wilson and Gouverneur Morris, as attorneys for the bank, succeeded in having the institution reincorporated on the ground that the revocation of its charter impaired the vested rights of the stockholders.

Besides being a director of the Bank of North America, Wilson was much interested in land speculations, holding numerous shares in the Holland Company of dubious repute which had obtained 464,800 acres of Pennsylvania land in contravention of a state law restricting sales to actual settlers, and he was president of the Illinois and Wabash Land Company which claimed to have bought from the Indians for "large quantities of strouds, blankets, guns, flour, beads, etc.,"

an enormous tract some two hundred miles square in the neighborhood of the Wabash River. On behalf of this latter company, Justice Wilson in 1791 submitted to the United States Congress a petition offering to convey to the government all the land of the company on condition that one-fourth of it be returned with a clear title. The House Committee on Public Lands, under the influence of Jonathan Dayton, himself a notorious speculator, was ready to agree to these terms, but the Senate Committee on Public Lands refused to have anything to do with so doubtful a transaction.

Such was the economic background of the hardy, dour, and arrogant James Wilson, a man respected for his learning and his wealth, greatly feared, and little loved.*

A complete contrast, at least in manners, was offered by the fifth member of the Court, John Blair of Virginia, a personal friend of Washington and described as one "blameless in disposition, pious and possessed of great benevolence and goodness of heart." He had studied in the Middle Temple in London, and had been a judge of the first court of appeals of Virginia and a member of the Constitutional Convention. As one of the judges in the case of *Commonwealth* v. *Caton* in 1782, he had been among the first to uphold the right of the judiciary to review legislation; he was soon to be personally interested in the success of Hamilton's financial policies through heavy speculation in the public funds whereby he would reap a small fortune; but if at heart probably fully as conservative as Rutledge and Wilson, he was at any rate a conservative of gentler mold.

The last and youngest member of the Court was James Iredell, an Englishman who had emigrated at the age of seventeen to North Carolina where in due time he became a judge of the superior court and later attorney-general. He was the acknowledged leader of the Federalist Party in North Carolina, and, although Washington had great respect for his ability, his appointment to the Supreme Court was also in the nature of a reward for having at last succeeded in swinging his recalcitrant state into line to ratify the Constitution.

---

*For a more favorable view of Justice Wilson, see Burton A. Konkle's five-volume biography published in 1934.

All the justices of the first Supreme Court were men of learning and of leadership, intimately affiliated with the Federalist Party, and identified with the propertied class which that party represented. In age they ranged from Iredell who was only 38 through Jay, 43; Wilson, 47; Rutledge, 50, up to Blair and Cushing who were both 57. The average age of the Court was 48½. Thus while in the beginning the Court was almost as conservative as in any other period, it was not at all the "gerontocracy" that it has latterly become.

2. Early Struggles of the Court

It was now to be seen how far the Supreme Court could build up its paper powers into an actuality. And before Jay would be through, the Supreme Court under his leadership would establish its control over the states, would assert its position as a purely judicial and non-political body, and in spite of that would determine the foreign policy of the nation. But all this seemed most unlikely at the outset when for two full years the Court had not a single case before it. Long after the nation had become fully conscious of the new powers of Congress and the president, it remained almost unaware of the Supreme Court's existence.

The opening sessions of the Court seemed almost ignominious. Only Justices Jay, Wilson, and Cushing troubled to attend its far from impressive ceremony of organization on February 1, 1790, in the old Royal Exchange at the foot of Broad Street, New York City. The first term of only ten days was devoted entirely to the admission of attorneys to practise before the Court when occasion should arise. And the same procedure was followed in the second term of August, 1790, which lasted but two days.

In fact, it might be said that the only achievement of the Supreme Court in its first year was not in anything it did but in something it refrained from doing. For when the Virginia House of Representatives adopted resolutions denouncing Hamilton's funding bills passed in the second session of Congress, Hamilton sent copies of the resolutions to Jay with the suggestion that the Supreme Court join "in exploding the

principles they contain." This, of course, would have been equivalent to making the Supreme Court an explicit organ of the Federalist Party—showing how little Hamilton really cared about the much talked of "independence of the Judiciary."

In his reply, Chief Justice Jay, according to Charles Warren, "evinced that comprehension of the essential functions of the judicial power of the Court and of its duty never to express its judicial opinion except in a case litigated between parties in due judicial course, which is a fundamental principle of the American frame of government." Yet all that Jay actually said to Hamilton was that his suggestion was bad politics! "Having no apprehension of such measures [as the Virginia Resolutions], what was to be done appeared to me to be a question of some difficulty as well as importance; to treat them as very important might render them more so than I think they are. . . . Every indecent interference of State Assemblies will diminish their influence; the National Government has only to do what is right, and, if possible, be silent."

The third term of the Supreme Court in February, 1791, saw the admission of many more lawyers, so that by this time the legal batteries ready for action before the Supreme Court included many of the ablest attorneys in the country, such as Alexander Dallas, Jared Ingersoll, Peter S. Duponceau, Edward Tilghman, Benjamin Chew, Elias Boudinot, James Monroe, and Luther Martin. The lawyers were ready, but still the clients did not come.

At last in the August term of 1791 a single case was called up* on writ of error, but it was at once discovered that there was an error in the writ, which had been issued by the clerk of the Circuit Court, not the clerk of the Supreme Court. The only case that the Supreme Court had even momentarily before it in the first two years of its existence was immediately dismissed.

Small wonder that John Rutledge, who had never troubled to attend a meeting of the Court, felt impelled to resign in order to accept what then seemed the much more imposing position

*West v. Barnes, 2 Dallas, 401.

of chief justice of North Carolina. Small wonder that Washington had difficulty in obtaining anyone to fill his place. The unattractive post was declined by Edward Rutledge, nephew of the retiring Justice, and by Charles Cotesworth Pinckney, both of South Carolina. Thomas Johnson, a United States district judge of Maryland and former governor of the state, only consented to accept it after much persuasion, and he resigned two years later. But then at last another permanent justice of importance was secured in William Paterson, a former merchant, connected like Jay with the Livingston family, a member of the Constitutional Convention, and United States senator from New Jersey. Paterson did not know a great deal of law, but he was an influential Federalist, henceforth much given to introducing irrelevant political questions in his charges to juries and to uttering the most thunderous opinions in the mildest and most courteous of voices.

Had the positions on the Supreme Bench been the sinecures suggested by the easy duties of the Court itself they might have been easy to fill in spite of the Court's initial insignificance, but in point of fact the justices fully earned their salaries—five thousand dollars for the chief justice and forty-five hundred dollars for the associate justices—through their arduous service in connection with the Circuit Courts which they were obliged to hold for two terms every year. When one remembers that each of the circuits included three or four states and that the justices were also supposed to attend each year two terms of the Supreme Court held after 1789 in Philadelphia, each necessitating for a justice of the Southern Circuit a trip of nearly two thousand miles, and when one recalls the terrible condition of the roads in that period, the laborious character of the justices' duties will be readily perceived. With reason, James Iredell lamented that his life was "that of a travelling post boy." The justices complained to the President and to Congress, and in 1793 obtained partial relief through a law requiring only one justice instead of two to officiate on each circuit. Even with this mitigation the life of the justices remained sufficiently unpleasant.

The Circuit Court system worked badly in other respects,

also. When as often happened the roads were utterly impassable there were long delays pending the arrival of the justices. The association of one district judge with two justices proved unsatisfactory because the district judge was usually overawed and dumb in the presence of his superiors. The fact that the justices moved from circuit to circuit in successive terms led to anomalous decisions. In a letter which forms an interesting comment on the uncertainty of legal reasoning, Justice Jay confessed to Rufus King that "It has happened in more than one instance that questions in the Circuit Court decided by one set of Judges in the affirmative had afterwards in the same Court been decided by others in the negative."

Privately, Jay and the rest of the justices declared that they considered thoroughly unconstitutional the section of the Judiciary Act of 1789 which prescribed these hateful Circuit Court duties.

Nevertheless, this clumsy and possibly unconstitutional system devised by Oliver Ellsworth was to remain in force with one slight intermission for over a century. And it was by the Circuit Courts rather than by the Supreme Court that the power of the federal judiciary was first upheld. During the decade of 1790-1800 the history of the main river was largely the history of its tributaries.

In May, 1791, before the Supreme Court had as yet decided a single important case, the Eastern Circuit Court not only set aside a Connecticut statute which invalidated interest on debts to British subjects during the Revolutionary War when the creditors were inaccessible, but the Court nullified the law not as unconstitutional but as conflicting with the common law of Great Britain. The effect of this decision was in theory to incorporate at a single stroke in American national jurisprudence the whole vast system of the British common law with its innumerable and conflicting precedents reaching back a thousand years. In practice its effect was to enable the justices to incorporate just such of those precedents as they should choose to consider binding. Thus within two years from the beginning of the federal judiciary, the process of judge-made law had begun.

In 1792, eleven years before *Marbury* v. *Madison,* the right of the federal judiciary to declare acts of Congress unconstitutional was asserted by the Circuit Court.* The Act in question, a belated pension law on behalf of disabled Revolutionary veterans, appointed the judges of the Circuit Courts to receive applications and apportion the amount of the pensions according to the degree of injury sustained, subject to review by the secretary of war and Congress. This task was plainly an extra-judicial one, and the Act was therefore declared unconstitutional by Jay, Cushing, and Duane of the New York Circuit Court who, however, in view of the beneficent intent of the law, announced their willingness to act as voluntary commissioners to carry out its provisions. In the Pennsylvania Circuit Court, James Wilson, John Blair, and Richard Peters asserted that the Act was doubly unconstitutional, first, in assigning non-judicial duties to the courts and, second, in subjecting their decisions to executive and legislative review. But ultimately all of the justices except the stubborn Wilson agreed to serve in a voluntary capacity.

Owing to the fact that this was the first instance in which a federal law was declared unconstitutional, the case attracted considerable attention. By this time, the growing Anti-Federalist minority possessed two strong newspapers, the *National Gazette,* edited by the poet, Philip Freneau, and the *General Advertiser,* edited by Benjamin Franklin's vitriolic grandson, Benjamin Franklin Bache. These papers, upholding the cause of state rights against the nationalistic tendencies of the Federalist Congress, loudly supported the ruling of the judiciary, arguing that if one law were nullified in this manner, others more objectionable might go the same way. Said the *National Gazette:*

"Whilst we view the exercise of this noble prerogative of the Judges in the hands of such able, wise and independent men as compose the present Judiciary of the United States, it affords a just hope that not only future encroachments will be prevented, but also that any existing law of Congress which may be supposed to trench upon the constitutional rights of

*Hayburn's Case, 2 Dallas, 409.

individuals or of States, will, at convenient seasons, undergo a revision."

Similarly, the *General Advertiser* used the case as a spring-board from which to attack the authority of Congress, ridiculing those who objected to the Court's decisions: "As if, forsooth, Congress were wrapped up in the cloak of the infallibility which has been torn from the shoulders of the Pope; and that it was damnable heresy and sacrilege to doubt the constitutional orthodoxy of any decision of theirs, once written on calf skin."

For this, the *Advertiser* was called to time by an anonymous writer signing himself "Camden" who asked pertinently, "While the panegyrist of the Circuit Court refuses to ascribe infallibility to Congress, is he justified in clothing the Circuit Court with that quality?"

Though the humanity of the justices in consenting to serve when not compelled to do so was highly praised in the press, the upshot of the whole matter was not calculated to impress the disabled veterans with any great respect for legal processes. In order to straighten out the legal tangle, Congress in 1793 directed the Attorney-General to bring a friendly suit to test the validity of the awards made by the justices in their capacity of voluntary commissioners.* Sitting now as the Supreme Court the justices held that what they had done as commissioners had been totally without authority and possessed no legal force. So far as actually getting their pensions was concerned the disabled veterans were just where they had been at the beginning three years before. Justice had somehow got squeezed out in the conflict over the justices' prerogatives.

Meanwhile, the absurdity of the hopes of Freneau and Bache that the federal judiciary might come forth as the champion of the states had been amply demonstrated—as well as the importance of that little clause concerning contracts inserted by the advice of James Wilson in Article II, Section 1, of the Constitution. In 1792 the Eastern Circuit Court under Justices Jay and Cushing declared unconstitutional as "impairing the obligation of contract" a Rhode Island statute that

---

United States v. *Yale Todd*, 13 Howard, 52.

granted the petition of one Silas Casey to be allowed an extension of three years' time in which to pay his debts.* In 1793 two state laws were declared unconstitutional on the same ground, one by Justice Iredell in Georgia, the other by Justice Paterson in South Carolina.† A fourth state law to go the same way on the same grounds in 1795 was a statute of Pennsylvania declared unconstitutional by Justice Paterson in *Vanhorne's Lessee* v. *Dorrance,* 2 Dallas, 304. In this case the decision would have lacked impressiveness, as the statute had already been repealed by the legislature, but for the eloquence with which Justice Paterson took occasion to defend the rights of private property:

"The Constitution expressly declares that the right of acquiring, possessing and protecting property is natural, inherent and unalienable." (This was apparently the Justice's wording of the modest Fifth Amendment prohibiting the deprivation "of life, liberty, or property, without due process of law"; at least, the reader will look in vain elsewhere in the Constitution for anything corresponding to the Justice's utterance.)

"The Constitution is the origin and measure of legislative authority; it says to legislators, thus far ye shall go and no further. Not a particle of it should be shaken; not a pebble of it should be removed. Innovation is dangerous. One encroachment leads to another, precedent gives birth to precedent; what has been done may be done again; thus radical principles are generally broken in upon, and the Constitution eventually destroyed. Where the security, where the inviolability of property, if the legislature, by a private act, affecting particular persons only, can take land from one citizen who acquired it legally, and vest it in another? The rights of private property are regulated, protected, and governed by general known and established laws; and decided upon by general, known, and established tribunals; laws and tribunals not made and created on an instant exigency, on an urgent emergency, to serve a present turn or the interest of a moment. Their operation and

---

Alexander Champion and Thomas Dickason v. *Silas Casey.* See Charles Warren, *The Supreme Court in United States History* (1922), Vol. I, p. 67.

†*Samuel Brailsford* v. *James Spalding; Higginson* v. *Greenwood.* See Warren, *op. cit.,* Vol. I, p. 66.

influence are equal and universal; they press alike on all. Hence security and safety, tranquillity and peace."

Incidentally, Justice Paterson went out of his way to refute the arguments of Hamilton in *The Federalist,* No. 81, and affirm his arguments in *The Federalist,* No. 78. "It is difficult to say what the Constitution of England is; because, not being reduced to written certainty and precision it lies entirely at the mercy of the Parliament; It bends to every governmental exigency; It varies and is blown about by every breeze of legislative humor or political caprice. . . . The power of Parliament is absolute and transcendent; it is omnipotent in the scale of political existence. . . . In America the case is widely different; Every state in the Union has its constitution reduced to written exactitude and precision. What is a constitution? It is the form of government delineated by the mighty hand of the people, in which certain first principles of fundamental laws are established. The Constitution is certain and fixed; it contains the permanent will of the people, and is the supreme law of the land; it is paramount to the law of the legislature, and can be revoked or altered only by the authority that made it. The life-giving principle and the death-doing stroke must proceed from the same hand. What are legislatures? Creatures of the Constitution; they derive their powers from the Constitution; It is their commission; and therefore, all their acts must be conformable to it, or else they will be void. The Constitution is the work, or will, of the people themselves, in their original, sovereign, and unlimited capacity. Law is the work or will of the legislature in their derivative and subordinate capacity. The one is the work of the creator, and the other of the creature. The Constitution fixes limits to the exercise of legislative authority, and prescribes the orbit within which it must move. In short, gentlemen, the Constitution is the sun of the political system, around which all legislative, executive, and judicial bodies must revolve. Whatever may be the case in other countries, yet in this there can be no doubt, that every Act of the Legislature, repugnant to the Constitution, is absolutely void."

It will be observed that in repeating and expanding Hamil-

ton's argument in *The Federalist,* No. 78, Justice Paterson added a few fallacies of his own: that the Constitution was "certain and fixed"—a static conception similar to that of the verbal inspiration of the Scriptures, and one refuted by all the countless quarrels over the interpretation of the Constitution's meaning; that the legislatures "owed their existence to the Constitution,"—which however true legalistically was false historically as both the federal Congress and the state congresses were in existence before the Constitution; that, as the whole tenor of his opinion assumed, the judiciary had been somehow made the special guardian of the Constitution as the legislature was not, whereas his very decision overruling the Pennsylvania law had been made possible only by the Judiciary Act passed by Congress in 1789.

While the Circuit Courts were thus nullifying state laws at the rate of one a year, the Supreme Court itself had also become engaged in a war with the states. The first cases to come before it were suits brought by various individuals against Maryland, New York, Virginia, and Georgia. Of these four states, Georgia, the smallest in population, was the most rebellious in disposition. Largely settled originally by deported convicts from Great Britain, given an unusually democratic colonial organization by Governor Oglethorpe, still essentially a frontier community, retaining its early traditions of lawlessness, Georgia, the most individualistic of all the states and at the same time the furthest from Philadelphia, was fully prepared to dispute the authority of the Supreme Court. When the case of *Chisholm* v. *Georgia,* 2 Dallas, 419, was brought up, in which the state was sued by two citizens of South Carolina as executors of a British creditor, Georgia local patriotism fairly boiled over. The state, through a written remonstrance presented by Alexander Dallas and Jared Ingersoll, denied the jurisdiction of the Supreme Court and refused to plead. The Court, in a decision from which Justice Iredell alone dissented, gave its verdict against the state. For the first time, national and state swords were fairly crossed.

The argument of Chief Justice Jay, which was the most elaborate of all his legal utterances, was exceedingly liberal and

convincing. He dwelt upon the difference between the conception of sovereignty in Europe, where the relation involved was that of a prince to his subjects, and in America where sovereignty was vested in the people. There was no question but that one person could sue another person or any number of persons. A citizen of Pennsylvania could sue the city of Philadelphia composed of forty odd thousand people. "In the State of Delaware, there are fifty odd thousand free citizens, and what reason can be assigned why a free citizen who has demands against them should not prosecute them? Can the difference between forty odd thousand and fifty odd thousand make any distinction as to the right? . . . In this land of equal liberty, shall forty odd thousand in one place be compellable to do justice, and yet fifty odd thousand in another place be privileged to do justice only as they think proper? Such objections would not correspond with the equal rights; with the equality we profess to admire and maintain, and with that popular sovereignty in which every citizen partakes."

But the democracy of Georgia was in no mood to listen to the democratic arguments of Justice Jay. Soon after the decision was rendered, a bill was introduced in the Georgia House of Representatives that any federal marshal or other person who attempted to execute the process of the Court should be adjudged "guilty of felony and shall suffer death, without benefit of clergy, by being hanged." And the process of the Court was never executed.

For the resistance of Georgia was supported by the sentiment in other states which foresaw a host of suits against themselves that would be validated by the precedent of *Chisholm* v. *Georgia.* Although the Constitution in Article III, Section 2, explicitly gave the federal courts jurisdiction over "controversies between a state and citizens of another State," it did not say in so many words that a state could be sued, however clearly implying it, and a number of the Federalist leaders before the Constitution was ratified had given assurance that this power would never be exercised. Thus Hamilton had written in *The Federalist,* No. 81: "To what purpose would it be to authorize suits against States for the debts they owe? How could re-

coveries be enforced? It is evident that it could not be done without waging war against the contracting State; and to ascribe to the federal courts, by mere implication, and in destruction of a pre-existing right of the State governments, a power which would involve such a consequence, would be altogether forced and unwarrantable." The same thing had been forcefully asserted by Madison and Marshall.

It was thus not entirely without reason that the states now insisted that they had been betrayed. Feeling ran so high that Congress speedily adopted an amendment to the Constitution reading: "The judicial power of the United States shall not be construed to extend to any suit in law or equity, commenced or prosecuted against one of the United States by citizens of another State, or by citizens or subjects of any foreign state." This was duly ratified by the states as the Eleventh Amendment, and, in the words of Frank Monaghan, "the sovereign irresponsibility of the states was thus reestablished."*

Meanwhile, that troublesome entity, the state of Georgia, was causing further difficulty. When one Brailsford, a British creditor, sued a Georgia citizen for a debt which the state had sequestrated, Georgia demanded the right to appear as a party defendant in order to establish its title to the property, and when this was refused by the Southern Circuit Court the state filed a bill in equity with the Supreme Court to obtain an injunction against the Circuit Court.† The case was argued for the plaintiff by Alexander Dallas and for the defendant by Attorney-General Edmund Randolph. In view of Georgia's recent intransigeance, the Supreme Court, as Warren remarks, "was evidently reluctant to rule against her a second time," and so it consented to grant a temporary injunction. This led Attorney-General Randolph, in a letter to Madison, to indulge in some caustic comments on the members of the Court: the decision, he said, "provided a demonstration to me of these facts: that the Premier [Jay] aimed at the cultivation of Southern popularity; that the Professor [Wilson] knows not an iota of equity; that the North Carolinian [Iredell] repented

*Monaghan, op. cit., p. 311.
†Georgia v. Brailsford, 2 Dallas, 402, 415, 3 Dallas, 1.

of the first ebullitions of a warm temper; and that it will take a score of years to settle, with such a mixture of Judges, a regular course in Chancery." Ultimately, the Supreme Court partly escaped from its embarrassment by having an "amicable action" brought before a special jury which in obedience to a charge from Jay gave its verdict for the defendant.

But now the federal judiciary was confronted with an even more serious issue, which involved the whole problem of international relations. The progress of the French Revolution had been watched with varying emotions in America, the Federalists coming more and more to regard it as an attack upon the basic principles of social order while the Anti-Federalists, who had taken the name "Republican," greeted the democratic successes, and even excesses, of the Jacobins with enthusiastic approval. The terms of the French Treaty of 1783 bound the United States to a defensive alliance with France, but when war broke out in 1793 between Great Britain and the French Republic the Treaty was denounced by Washington on the double ground that it had been negotiated with the French monarchy, not the Republic, and that the war itself was technically an offensive not defensive one since it had been declared by France. The President's position was legalistically correct, but it gave great offense to many who regarded it as disloyalty to the allies without whose aid the United States could never have been formed in the first place. Thus the President's proclamation of strict neutrality issued in April, 1793, found the country divided in sentiment into what quickly became pro-British and pro-French parties, and this division in sentiment was soon reinforced by a division of interest. On the one hand, adventurous Americans were eager to enter the French service as privateersmen, while on the other hand the vessels captured by these privateersmen, which were often brought into American ports, and condemned by French prize courts set up in America, were very frequently owned by American citizens. Under these circumstances the federal judiciary could not possibly avoid being drawn into the contest.

At the outset, the judiciary was itself divided. In the first

case that came up, as early as June, 1793, which was that of two American ships, the *William* and the *Fanny,* captured in American waters by a French privateersman and actually brought into an American port, the District Court of Pennsylvania under Judge Peters held, to the dismay of the Administration, that the court had no power to examine the legality of prizes. In the second case, brought in July, against an American citizen, Gideon Henfield, for serving as prizemaster on a French ship, Justice Wilson charged the jury that the prisoner was guilty "under the law of nations," but the jury, nevertheless, refused to convict.

In this perplexing situation as to what was lawful and what was not, Washington, acting on the advice of Jefferson, directed Alexander Hamilton to draw up for submission to the Supreme Court a series of questions on international law, neutrality, and the construction of the British and French treaties. Hamilton, though he disapproved of the plan as imposing extrajudicial duties on the Court, framed twenty-nine questions on which the executive sought the advice of the judiciary as a guide to its own conduct. The Court respectfully declined to consider them since they were outside of its province.

This action of the Supreme Court has been generally commended by legal writers. "By declining to express an opinion except in a case duly litigated before it," writes Charles Warren, "the Court established itself as a purely judicial body; and its success in fulfilling its function has followed its adhering to this exclusive method of deciding questions of law and of constitutionality of statutes."* Probably most lawyers would agree with Charles Evans Hughes that "It is only with the light afforded by a real contest that opinions on questions of the highest importance can be decided."†

From the point of view of the general public, however, the matter cannot be settled quite so easily. To this early decision of the Supreme Court, adhered to throughout its history, is to be attributed in no small part the intolerable delays that char-

---

*Warren, *op. cit.,* Vol. I, p. 111. Quoted by permission of the publishers, Little, Brown & Company.
†Hughes, *Supreme Court,* p. 32.

acterize the American legal system more than any other. It certainly seems strange to the layman that a law should be not fully or finally a law until or unless a case under it reaches the Supreme Court, so that after having been enforced for five, ten, or a score of years it runs the hazard of a decision that it never has legally existed. Retroactive laws have usually been regarded as objectionable, yet the principle of retroaction is enshrined at the very heart of the American system. It is almost unnecessary to point out that the law's delays, thus encouraged, bear with particular hardship on the poorer classes unable practically to carry the financial burden involved in obtaining even that belated justice which theoretically is theirs.

Furthermore, the lesson of experience is not quite so unambiguous as the eulogists of the Supreme Court would lead one to suppose. In more than one of the states advisory powers are expressly conferred upon their supreme courts—this was true in Massachusetts when the federal Constitution was adopted— and it has not been shown that this system has worked less well than that adopted by the United States Supreme Court. The only point entirely beyond dispute in the whole question is that by its refusal of Washington's request, the Supreme Court further intrenched its own power as a tribunal of last resort, unwilling to offer even in a national emergency any opinion that might be overruled by other authority than its own.

In the particular national emergency of 1793, however, it must be admitted that the Supreme Court did succeed in solving the most immediate problem in a far-reaching manner. For when in the case of *Glass* v. *Sloop Betsy,* 3 Dallas, 6, the Maryland District Court, following the precedent set by Judge Peters, ruled that it had no jurisdiction over French prizes, and the case was appealed to the Supreme Court, the whole neutrality policy of the government was at stake, as unless the tendency of the previous decisions could be checked the United States would soon be coerced by the prize courts of France into a *de facto* alliance with that country. The Supreme Court met the issue squarely in a unanimous opinion which affirmed the jurisdiction of the United States over prizes brought into American ports, and at the same time asserted that the prize courts set

up by France on American soil were totally unwarranted and "not of right." The decision was of the utmost importance in forcing foreign nations reluctantly to recognize that the United States also was a nation with a sovereignty of its own.

Nevertheless, in avoiding an ignominious submission to France, the government now came dangerously near to accepting a similar relation to Great Britain in the treaty negotiated by the same John Jay who had so stoutly asserted American rights in the case of *Glass* v. *Sloop Betsy*.

Jay had long been weary of the laborious and turbulent existence of a chief justice. In 1792, though without resigning his position on the Supreme Court, he had run for governor of New York against George Clinton and would have been elected had not his adversary, aided by the chicanery of Aaron Burr, succeeded in throwing out the entire vote of Otsego County.* When offered the critical post of special envoy to Great Britain in the spring of 1794, both duty and inclination led Jay to accept. Many felt that he should at the same time have resigned the chief justiceship, but this latter office was not yet considered sufficiently important to make such action absolutely imperative. Jay was absent for nearly a year engaged in a diplomatic game in which, holding all the weaker cards, he lost nearly every trick. Eventually he secured a treaty, such as it was, the terms of which when divulged made him for a time the most unpopular man in America. It was a lucky turn for the Supreme Court that before the storm broke, Jay, while still abroad, was elected governor of New York and so, on June 29, 1795, resigned his position as chief justice.†

---

*See Monaghan, *op. cit.*, Ch. XVI, "Clinton Filches the Governorship."
†During Jay's absence four cases were decided by the Court, of which two were of considerable importance. In *United States* v. *Judge Lawrence,* 3 Dallas, 42, the French Vice-Consul was on technical grounds refused a warrant for the arrest of a French captain who had abandoned his ship, the case seeming to testify further to the Court's anti-French bias. In *Penhallow* v. *Doane's Admrs.,* 3 Dallas, 54, a decree of the old Prize Court of Appeals which had existed under the Articles of Confederation, was upheld after being twice declared invalid by the New Hampshire courts and against the formal protest of the New Hampshire Legislature. The decision elicited from even a Federalist newspaper in the state the heated criticism that it had "completely annihilated the Sovereignty of New Hampshire."

His reasons for thus accepting what would today be regarded as an inferior position appear plainly in a letter written to President Adams when in 1800 Adams begged him to return to his old place. The union of Supreme Court and Circuit Court duties, Jay thought, so hampered the efficiency of the judiciary that the latter could not hope to "acquire the public confidence and respect which, as the last resort of the nation, it should possess." There had been expectations that the system would be changed but "those expectations have not been realized nor have we hitherto seen convincing indications of a disposition in Congress to realize them." Hence, he doubted "both the propriety and the expediency of returning to the Bench, under the present system."

Nevertheless, could Jay have foreseen the future he might have looked back upon his achievements as head of the Supreme Court with considerable satisfaction. Under his capable direction the institution had certainly begun to develop its potentialities. He had kept it in close alliance with the other branches of the government, yet had maintained its independence. The federal judiciary had been successful in its conflicts with the states except in the single instance of Georgia. It had established its authority to judge the meaning of treaties. It had exercised without challenge its doubtful right to refuse to obey an act of Congress. It had added the British common law to the Constitution as a second and broader authority for its actions. Justice Jay had found the Supreme Court nothing, he left it the head of a definitely functioning branch of the government only a little inferior to the others and already beginning to exercise the wide powers which the Federalist leaders desired it to have.

CHAPTER III

THE COURT UNDER CHIEF JUSTICE ELLSWORTH

1796-1801

OLIVER ELLSWORTH, WILLIAM CUSHING, JAMES WILSON,
JOHN BLAIR, JAMES IREDELL, WILLIAM PATERSON,
SAMUEL CHASE, BUSHROD WASHINGTON, ALFRED MOORE.

1. *New Appointments*

IN THE five years between 1796 and 1801 the federal judiciary
became openly, what it had always been at heart, a political
organ of the Federalist Party. The discretion shown by John
Jay was abandoned in a series of despotic rulings which rendered the courts more unpopular than they have ever been
since that time. The period began badly with most unfortunate
appointments to the Supreme Court; it continued with a demonstration that the federal judiciary afforded no protection
whatsoever to individual liberty; and it ended with attempts to
extend the authority of the judiciary which for the first time
brought it into real conflict with the other departments of the
federal government.

Even before Jay's resignation had been offered as chief
justice, Washington received a letter from that former member of the Supreme Court, John Rutledge, suggesting that he
himself would be a most appropriate person for the position.
Rutledge hinted broadly that he would have been more suitable
for it in the first place than John Jay. "Several of my friends
were displeased at my accepting the office of Associate Judge
(although the senior) . . . conceiving (as I thought very
justly) that my pretensions to the office of Chief Justice were
at least equal to Mr. Jay's in point of law-knowledge, with the
additional weight of much longer experience and much greater
practice." Should the position now become vacant, "I feel,"

Rutledge said, "that the duty which I owe to my children should impel me to accept it, if offered. . . ." In conclusion he wished it clearly understood that he was not applying for the post. "I never solicited a place, nor do I mean this letter as an application."

Washington replied on July 1, 1795, appointing the haughty Southerner to the "unsolicited" position. But before the prospective Chief Justice arrived in Philadelphia to open the August term of the Supreme Court he committed a *faux pas* that made him most obnoxious to all good Federalists. Jay's Treaty, ratified by the Senate on June twenty-fourth, was being everywhere attacked by the Republicans because of its ignominious concessions to Great Britain and especially because it granted that monarchist and reactionary nation more favorable trade relations with the United States than those that were permitted to the democratic Republic of France. And into the camp of the opposition at this moment blundered John Rutledge in a speech delivered in Charleston, violently denouncing the Treaty. On this account Rutledge is eulogized as a great liberal leader by Claude Bowers in his *Jefferson and Hamilton,* but in point of fact the South Carolinian's objection to the Treaty was merely because it did not provide compensation for the slaves carried off by the British during the Revolution, such compensation having been one of the numerous American claims for which Jay had failed to secure recognition.

But the pro-British Federalists were not concerned with the grounds of Rutledge's opposition to the Treaty; it was enough that he opposed it. In Washington's Cabinet, Timothy Pickering and Oliver Wolcott, Secretaries of State and the Treasury, seriously alleged that Rutledge's speech was a proof that he was insane; Pickering thought that the commission of the "driveller and fool," as Wolcott called him, ought certainly to be withheld. Hamilton more moderately was moved to "pain, surprise, and mortification" by the published parts of the speech which he thought did no credit either to "Mr. Rutledge's head or heart."

Meanwhile, the disgraced head of the Supreme Court arrived quietly in Philadelphia, opened Court, and presided at the hear-

ings of two cases in which British and French claims were neatly balanced, the restitution of a prize captured by a French privateer being ordered in the one instance while in the other a French warship illegally fitted out in the United States was held immune to seizure because it was not a privateer but a part of the French Navy.*

Happily Rutledge went through the term, apparently deaf to the criticism that surged about him, though the rumors of his mental derangement started by the Federalists circulated freely. But that one session was his last. As soon as Congress met, the Federalist Senate rejected his appointment. And then Rutledge, who had not been insane before, proceeded actually to go insane! It seemed almost as if Nature itself had become Federalist and was determined to punish any infraction of party discipline.

Patrick Henry, who had become more conservative in his latter years, was now offered the vacant position, but he declined because of ill health. Next it was tendered to William Cushing the oldest member of the Court, but he too rejected it. This left Wilson as next in seniority and easily the ablest member of the Court. Wilson's reputation, however, was a little clouded from his recent part in a transaction that was later to give rise to one of the most significant of John Marshall's decisions. This was the famous case of the Yazoo Land Frauds which began in the following manner.

On January 7, 1795, an act was passed by the Georgia Legislature, over the Governor's veto, selling to four associated land companies a tract of some thirty-five million acres, embracing practically all of Georgia's public lands and including most of the present states of Alabama and Mississippi; for this vast territory, known as the Yazoo Region from the river of that name, the companies paid at the rate of twenty-eight and one-half cents an acre. Proof soon accumulated that the companies had bought the legislators before buying the land, and eventually it was shown that all but one of those who voted for the measure had been bribed. The citizens of Georgia wrath-

---

*Talbot v. Jansen, 3 Dallas, 133; United States v. Richard Peters, 3 Dallas, 121.

fully elected a new legislature which in the ensuing year rescinded the grant that had been obtained so fraudulently.

One of the four companies involved was the Georgia Company, of which Justice James Wilson was the chief promoter, contributing one hundred and twenty-five thousand dollars, for which he received seven hundred and fifty thousand acres. He was present during the meeting of the Georgia Legislature and though there is no sufficient proof that he personally took part in the bribery, he certainly knew what was going on and was willing to profit by it. Such a man, whatever his legal attainments, seemed hardly the fittest person to be appointed chief justice of the Supreme Court.

Washington finally went outside of the Court altogether and selected Oliver Ellsworth, one of the wealthiest, most conservative, and most powerful of Connecticut politicians. Connected by marriage with the family of Oliver Wolcott, friend of Robert Morris, influential in the Continental Congress in pushing the charter of the Bank of North America, attorney-general of Connecticut, judge on the state supreme court, member of the Constitutional Convention, United States senator and chief author of the Judiciary Act of 1789, Ellsworth was a perfect representative of the propertied class that formed the back-bone of the Federalist Party. A shrewd money-lender, reputed to be miserly in the management of his fortune, a profiteer from the rise of federal securities, he was also intensely pro-British, fond of eulogizing the ideal of monarchy, the senator who had supported most ardently that absurd title suggested for the President—"His Highness, the President of the United States and Protector of their Liberties." And with all this he was a brilliant and experienced lawyer. No appointment could have been made more certain to delight the Federalists or to enrage their opponents.

Between the Rutledge and Ellsworth appointments, blameless John Blair resigned as associate justice, and Washington chose as his successor Samuel Chase of Maryland, a recent convert to the Federalist cause. Was this selection a far-sighted recognition of the truth that converts are likely to be the most enthusiastic of partisans, did it emanate from the President's

personal loyalty to one who had been a helper in a time of need, or was it finally simply an acknowledgment of Chase's unquestionable intellectual ability? Perhaps all of these conflicting motives were present to Washington or to those who recommended an appointment which was to prove one of the most important ever made to the Supreme Court.

Already, at 54, Chase had behind him a varied and turbulent career. Although the son of a respectable Episcopal clergyman of Baltimore, he became in his twenties one of the most violent of those "Sons of Liberty" who rioted against the Stamp Act. At that time he was characterized by the mayor and alderman of Annapolis as a "busy, restless incendiary, a ring-leader of mobs, a foul-mouthed and inflaming son of discord." He soon became a leader in the Maryland council of safety and was appointed by the Continental Congress, together with Benjamin Franklin and Charles Carroll of Carrollton, on the commission that was sent to Canada in the vain attempt to obtain Canadian assistance against Great Britain. Chase was instrumental in bringing Maryland to vote for independence, and rode a hundred and fifty miles in two days to bring to Philadelphia the instructions which enabled him to be one of the signers of the Declaration. Later, in the Continental Congress, he was active in defeating the cabals against General Washington. But in 1778 his reputation as a patriot suffered considerably from an attempt on his part, making use of information secured as a member of Congress, to establish a corner on flour before the coming of the French fleet. In an open letter in the New York *Journal* addressed to "The Honorable ———— Esquire," Alexander Hamilton under his nom de plume of "Publius" said to him: "It is your lot to have the peculiar privilege of being universally despised. . . . Were I inclined to make a satire upon the species I would attempt a faithful description of your heart." With the same penchant for speculation in land as James Wilson, Chase was less lucky or less shrewd, for in 1789, admitting his insolvency, he was obliged to seek from the legislature a kind of private bankruptcy law, enacted on his behalf, whereby he was discharged from all debts on turning over to one of his partners several thousand acres of land, sixty

slaves, houses, furniture, etc.—exactly the type of law that was declared unconstitutional by the federal Circuit Court in 1792.

Chase's temporary financial embarrassment did not interfere with his political advancement: he rose to be chief judge of the general court of Maryland, voted against the Constitution in the ratifying convention, and was one of a committee which insisted upon amendments to protect trial by jury and freedom of the press. But at the time of his appointment to the Supreme Court, these Anti-Federalist "errors" had been abandoned by him—so his chief sponsor, Secretary of War James McHenry of Baltimore, assured Washington—and in fact Chase himself had already applied to the President for a position under the Administration.

This newest and, as was soon to be seen, most forceful of the justices, was described by Joseph Story as a "living image" of Doctor Johnson, a man of great bulk, an enormous red face, bushy white hair, and excessively rude manners.*

In an important case which came before the Supreme Court in February, 1796, Justice Chase immediately showed his mettle in rendering an opinion which was to have lasting influence on the jurisprudence of the nation. It was that of *Ware, Administrator* v. *Hylton et al.,* involving the question of whether state laws, sequestrating debts contracted before the Revolution to British creditors, were valid as against the provisions of the two treaties with Great Britain. The decision of the Circuit Court of Virginia in favor of the debtors was reversed by Chase, Cushing, Wilson, and Paterson, Chase's opinion, according to Corwin, remaining to this day "the most impressive assertion of the supremacy of national treaties over state laws."

But the case of *Ware, Administrator* v. *Hylton et al.* is of almost greater interest because of the argument presented during the hearing by John Marshall, in his first appearance as an attorney before the Supreme Court. Representing the debtors, Marshall referred scornfully to "those who wish to impair the sovereignty of Virginia" and went on to express views regard-

---

*See the excellent sketch of Chase by E. S. Corwin in the *Dictionary of American Biography,* Vol. IV.

ing judicial review which were directly opposite to those which he had advanced in the Virginia Ratifying Convention and to which he would return in *Marbury* v. *Madison:*

"The legislative authority of any country can only be restrained by its own municipal constitution. This is a principle that springs from the very nature of society; and *the judicial authority can have no right to question the validity of a law, unless such a jurisdiction is expressly given by the constitution.*"*

The day after *Ware, Administrator* v. *Hylton et al.* was settled, the Court decided another important case, that of *Hylton* v. *United States,* which was of a most extraordinary character in that the attorneys on both sides were paid by the government and the facts alleged in it were admittedly fictitious. The case concerned the constitutionality of a carriage tax passed by Congress which imposed a tax and penalty of sixteen dollars for every "chariot" kept exclusively for personal use. The government brought the amazing charge that Hylton possessed one hundred and twenty-five chariots "exclusively for defendant's own private use and not to let out to hire;" Hylton, who in reality had only one chariot, stated that his object in contesting the case was "merely to ascertain a constitutional point and not by any means to delay the payment of a public duty"; it was agreed that if the suit were won by the government judgment should be entered against Hylton "for $2,000 to be discharged by the payment of sixteen dollars."

This incredible case was probably instigated by Alexander Hamilton, who assisted Charles Lee, the Attorney-General, in presenting the government's argument. Hamilton when secretary of the treasury had been the original proponent of the carriage tax, which was supported by the Federalists, who had less use for "chariots" in the limited areas of the North and were therefore willing to make a democratic gesture, the cost of which would be borne mainly by their Republican opponents in the wide territories of the South where carriages were in great demand, while for the same reason the tax was resisted

*Italics ours. *Ware, Administrator* v. *Hylton et al.,* 3 Dallas, 199.

by the Republicans who denounced it as a direct tax and therefore unconstitutional. The case gave Hamilton who had argued against direct taxes in *The Federalist* an opportunity to show that his measure did not come under this opprobrious head, and it was also a case from which the Federalist Party would derive advantage whatever the decision: for either the tax would be upheld and their Republican adversaries put to shame, or the law would be declared unconstitutional and the favorite Federalist principle of the right of judicial review would at last be clearly established by a decision of the Supreme Court itself. Hence the anomaly of the government's arguing on both sides of the same question. The fictitious allegations of fact were brought in order to make the issue one of sufficient magnitude to come within the jurisdiction of the federal judiciary.

The judges of the Circuit Court being divided, the case, as was probably originally intended, was carried to the Supreme Court where it was decided by only three justices, Chase, Iredell, and Paterson, who upheld the constitutionality of the law. Again it was Chase who rendered the most vigorous opinion in a definition of "direct tax" which was to be accepted for exactly ninety-nine years until reversed by the Supreme Court in the famous "Income Tax Case" of *Pollock* v. *Farmers' Loan and Trust Company*.*

2.   The Court as Agent of the Federalist Party

In the August term of 1796 the question of the inclusion of the British common law in American national jurisprudence again came up. The case, that of *United States* v. *La Vengeance,* concerned the libel of a vessel for exporting arms to the French dominions from Sandy Hook, New Jersey, and it was argued that under the common law there was no admiralty jurisdiction over acts that were not committed on the high seas but within the confines of a state. Under the lead of Justice Ellsworth the Court held that the common law did not

Hylton v. *United States,* 3 Dallas, 171. *Pollock* v. *Farmers' Loan and Trust Company,* 157 U. S., 429; 158 U. S., 601.

apply in this instance and thus boldly extended federal jurisdiction over a new field. It seemed evident that this mysterious common law was authoritative when it could be used to support the federal judiciary against the states but was of no weight when cited on the other side.*

But there was a limit beyond which the Supreme Court justices dared not extend their jurisdiction. In the case of *Calder* v. *Bull,* 3 Dallas, 386, in 1798, it was decided that the Court had no power to declare a state law unconstitutional because of its being repugnant to the state constitution. No other decision would have been possible without authorizing the most gross interference of the national judiciary in the internal affairs of the states, but how difficult the Court found it to relinquish any chance of increasing its authority was seen in a long and irrelevant discussion between Justices Iredell and Chase in which they solaced themselves by reasserting—though on entirely different grounds—the right of the Court to nullify acts of Congress. Chase asserted that regardless of the Constitution any law contradicting "the great first principles of the social compact" or "against all reason and justice" could and must be nullified by the Courts; Iredell, on the other hand, was unwilling to give the Courts such a boundless latitude of discretion and was content with their "unquestionable" right to declare void all laws violating the provisions of the Constitution. Thus in less than ten years after its establishment the Supreme Court was seriously discussing the question, no longer of its supremacy over Congress but of whether its powers were limited even by the Constitution!

During 1797-1798 the once doughty Justice Wilson, now superseded by the doughtier Chase, ended his long career under a total eclipse. He was heavily involved in the financial failure of the house of Robert Morris, warrants for his arrest for debt were issued, and he managed to avoid these only by moving rapidly from state to state in pursuance of his Circuit Court duties. This was a new use to which to put the Circuit Court, and the spectacle of a Supreme Court justice dodging about to escape

United States v. *La Vengeance,* 3 Dallas, 297.

arrest did not augment popular respect for the judiciary. Wilson's health giving way under the strain of his embarrassments, he died on August 21, 1798.

The vacancy was offered by President Adams to John Marshall, newly returned from a diplomatic mission to France in association with Elbridge Gerry and C. C. Pinckney during which his reputation had been greatly enhanced by his firmness in resisting the bribery demands of Talleyrand in the X.Y.Z. correspondence. An associate justiceship in the Supreme Court did not yet carry with it sufficient prestige to tempt a Marshall, and he declined the offer. The position was then accepted by Bushrod Washington, the thirty-six-year-old nephew and heir of George Washington, who had studied law in the office of James Wilson and had had, with his connections, no difficulty in being elected to the Virginia House of Delegates and the Virginia Ratifying Convention. He was not particularly eminent as a lawyer and was quite without judicial experience, though, on the other hand, he was a careful and laborious student, having even become blind in one eye through excessive devotion to his books. Of slight stature and insignificant appearance, his neglected clothes stained from the snuff in which he indulged immoderately, Bushrod Washington was in every way an unimpressive successor of the domineering Justice Wilson.

Ever since the passage of Jay's Treaty with Great Britain the United States and France had been slowly but very steadily drifting toward war. The initial grounds of complaint belonged to France: the discriminatory trade relations established by the Treaty and the superseding of the popular American Minister James Monroe by the Anglophile C. C. Pinckney; but when the French Government proceeded to insult Pinckney and to demand "douceurs" before dealing with the additional American envoys the weight of grievance shifted to this side of the Atlantic. When the attempt of the French Directorate to bribe the envoys became known through the publication of the X.Y.Z. correspondence, a wave of indignation swept the country. The always pro-British Federalists found themselves suddenly riding high in the popular favor while the Repub-

licans, owing to their pro-French leanings, were now regarded at least in the North as an unpatriotic and almost treasonable party. It is not surprising that the Federalists sought unwisely to make the most of the apparent opportunity to annihilate their political opponents and to silence all criticism of the Federalist government.

Among other injudicious measures regretted by the cooler heads like Hamilton and Marshall was the Sedition Act of 1798 which penalized by fine and imprisonment any one who should "write, print, utter or publish any false, scandalous and malicious writing or writings against the government of the United States, or either house of the Congress of the United States, or the President of the United States, with intent . . . to bring them . . . into contempt or disrepute." The one concession to freedom of criticism made by the Act—a concession omitted in the similar Espionage laws during the World War—was that it permitted the truth to be introduced as a defense.

The constitutionality of this Act was immediately challenged by Jefferson and Madison in the famous Kentucky and Virginia Resolutions on the double ground that it went beyond the enumerated powers permitted to Congress and that it violated the First Amendment prohibiting any laws "abridging the freedom of speech or of the press." These Resolutions after adoption by the two states in question were sent to the others with an invitation to join in some effective action to prevent the law from being carried into execution.*

All the Federalist state legislatures roundly condemned the Resolutions. That of Massachusetts attempted to answer the Madison-Jefferson appeal to the First Amendment by resurrecting the definition of free speech under which John Winthrop a hundred and fifty years before had justified the execution of Quakers. Said the legislature:

"The genuine liberty of speech and the press is the liberty to utter and publish the truth; but the constitutional right of the citizen to utter and publish the truth is not to be confounded with the licentiousness, in speaking and writing, that

---

*The Resolutions also condemned the Alien Act, with which we are not here concerned as it did not come before the Courts.

is only employed in propagating falsehood and slander. This freedom of the press has been explicitly secured by most, if not all of the state constitutions; and of this provision there has been generally but one construction among enlightened men— that it is a security for the rational use, and not the abuse of the press; of which the courts of law, the juries and people will judge; this right is not infringed, but confirmed and established, by the late act of Congress."

The fallacy here, an exceedingly obvious one, lies in an assumption, the falseness of which was recognized as early as Milton's *Areopagitica,* that "the truth" is absolutely known, whereas in point of fact newly discovered truths are usually considered falsehoods when first enunciated. "The truth" of which the Massachusetts Legislature was speaking was, of course, simply the Federalist interpretation of truth, and it was this interpretation which was now about to be enforced by the Courts in a series of decisions unequaled in vindictive harshness for over a century to come. They upheld the constitutionality of the Sedition law in the most effective manner possible by simply refusing to allow its constitutionality to be questioned.

The first victim of the Sedition Act was a United States congressman, Matthew Lyon of Vermont. In a Republican paper which he owned and edited he had accused President Adams of showing "a continual grasp for power, . . . an unbounded thirst for ridiculous pomp, foolish adulation and selfish avarice," and he had also published a letter from the poet, Joel Barlow, in which the latter referred to a warlike address of the President to the Senate and the latter's favorable reply as "a bullying speech" and "a stupid answer" and expressed surprise that the Senate had not issued "an order to send him [Adams] to the mad-house." Barlow was safe in Paris among his French friends, but Lyon was at hand to bear the penalty for the reckless remarks of both. By a hand-picked jury of his enemies, and under the charge of Justice Paterson, he was duly convicted, and was sentenced by the Justice to a fine of one thousand dollars and four months in prison. Having the misfortune to fall into the hands of a

particularly sadistic United States marshal, Lyon was treated with great cruelty from the moment of his conviction. As he was poor and therefore liable to be kept in custody beyond the term of his sentence through inability to pay the fine, his friends attempted to raise the amount through a lottery, and then discovered that in doing so they had themselves fallen into sedition.

The *Vermont Gazette,* published at Bennington, having printed an advertisement of the lottery, the editor, Anthony Haswell, was indicted because the advertisement referred to Fitch the marshal as a "hard-hearted savage," and also because the *Gazette* reprinted a passage from Bache's *Aurora* which declared that "Tories" now enjoyed "the confidence of the government." Haswell, during his trial, proceeded to prove that the description of Fitch was quite accurate and proposed to prove that the remark about Tories was equally correct by the statements of two absent witnesses, General James Drake of Virginia and Secretary of War McHenry. Justice Paterson ruled that such evidence was inadmissible and reminded the jury (contrary to the terms of the Sedition Act itself) that the question before them was not of the truth of Haswell's statements but simply of their defamatory intent. The prisoner was convicted, and the Justice sentenced Lyon's champion to pay twice the amount of Lyon's fine and to serve two months' imprisonment.

More severe still was the treatment of Dr. Thomas Cooper of Pennsylvania, the ablest American philosopher of the period, tried before Justice Chase and Judge Peters for remarks hostile to the President in a paper which Cooper was then editing—remarks much less severe than are now habitually uttered by American editors during the election season. When Cooper applied for a subpœna *duces tecum* to compel the attendance of President Adams with certain papers necessary to the defense, Chase became enraged at such impertinence— though seven years later the legality of such an application was to be upheld by no less a person than John Marshall. In his charge to the jury, Chase alleged that it was essentially seditious to attempt "to destroy the confidence of the people in

their officers"; Cooper had unquestionably intended, he said, "to censure the conduct of the President!" Had not the defendant written, "Our credit is so low that we are obliged to borrow money at eight per cent in time of peace"? Was not that seditious? The statement, of course, was true, but it was the misconduct of France that had reduced the United States to such a pass. "I cannot suppress my feelings at this gross attack upon the President," cried the outraged Justice.

Cooper was convicted and sentenced to be fined four hundred dollars, to be imprisoned for six months, and then to post sureties for good behavior to the amount of two thousand dollars. With each case the penalties were mounting. But nothing had as yet been seen or would be seen again—at least to the date of the present writing—like the case that was to follow.

John Fries, a Pennsylvania farmer who ventured to resist a United States tax collector, was indicted on the charge of Justice Iredell, not for "resisting an officer of the law," not for "inciting to riot," and not even for "sedition" but for "treason." The reasoning whereby Iredell showed that resisting a tax collector was treasonable was somewhat involved. Among all the nations of the world only in the United States was there no "grievance to complain of"; yet people did complain and even resisted the laws; whence then could such resistance arise? . . . From the evil influence of France, that nation where "Liberty, like the religion of Mahomet, is propagated by the sword," that nation in whose bosom "a dagger was concealed." Fries was convicted, but a new trial was granted because one of the jurors confessed to having had a violent prejudice against the prisoner.

Justice Chase, presiding over the second trial, opened the case by presenting three papers, one each for the prosecution, the defense, and the jury, which set forth the Court's very loose interpretation of the law of treason. Fries's attorneys, William Lewis and Alexander J. Dallas, refused to go on with the case under this irregular procedure of a "prejudicated opinion," whereupon Chase, instead of assigning the prisoner other counsel, grimly assured him that the judges themselves would see

that he received full justice. This justice consisted in a second conviction on the charge of the Court and a sentence to be "hanged by the neck until dead," words said to have been pronounced by Chase in "an aweful and affecting manner." Thus the federal judiciary decided that resisting a tax collector was an act of treason and this in the face of Article III, Section 1, of the Constitution which expressly provides that "Treason against the United States shall consist only in levying war against them, or in adhering to their enemies, giving them aid and comfort." It is safe to say that in all the seventy-seven laws of Congress which have now been declared unconstitutional by the Supreme Court there cannot be found a single instance of such flat violation of the Constitution as was offered in the *Fries Case* by the federal judiciary itself. President Adams finally pardoned the luckless Fries, but the two Justices of the Supreme Court can receive no credit for the good sense and humanity of John Adams.

The *Fries Case* was one of the last in which Iredell officiated as he died suddenly on October 2, 1799, to be replaced by Alfred Moore, for five years attorney-general of North Carolina and latterly a judge of the state supreme court, but for all that a relatively mediocre individual whose appointment was probably due to a desire to have one North Carolinian succeeded by another.

The next victim on the sedition list was James Callender of Virginia whose Anti-Federalist pamphlet, *The Prospect Before Us,* had been written with the secret encouragement of Thomas Jefferson. Justice Chase, before trying the case, was given by Luther Martin a copy of the pamphlet with all the most violent passages underscored. On his way to Richmond the Justice boasted that he was going to teach the Virginians—if a respectable jury could be found there—the difference between the liberty and the licentiousness of the press. During the trial he so bullyragged Callender's attorneys, George Hay and William Wirt, that they withdrew from the case. When Colonel John Taylor of Caroline, Virginia, one of the best-known patriots and political thinkers of the period, began to substantiate a part of Callender's statements, Chase cut short

his testimony by a ruling that the prisoner's utterances could not be substantiated in detail but only as a whole. Callender was convicted and sentenced in a trial that was almost more of a farce than the others over which Chase had presided.

And these were only the most prominent of the cases that occurred during the "White Terror" enforced by the judiciary. Probably the height of tragic absurdity was reached in the instance of Abijah Adams, imprisoned because his elder brother, editor of a Massachusetts newspaper, had dared to remark concerning the Federalist theory of popular sovereignty, "It is difficult for the common capacities to conceive of a sovereignty so situated that the Sovereign shall have no right to decide on any invasion of his constitutional powers." The actual editor being fatally ill, his brother, who had merely been in mechanical charge of the printing, was indicted as "the only person to whom the public can look for retribution," and was convicted under the charge of Samuel Dana, Chief Justice of Massachusetts.

Oliver Ellsworth was lucky enough not to be involved in any of the sedition trials, but he managed to get into the political fray nevertheless through what was one of the most unpopular decisions ever rendered by a justice of the Supreme Court. This was in the case of *United States* v. *Isaac Williams** brought before the Circuit Court of the District of Columbia against a native-born American, who had been for years a naturalized citizen of France. The charge was that Williams had served as a French naval officer and had thereby violated his American obligation to remain neutral. The case turned entirely on the question of whether he was an American or a French citizen. Under the British common law, Ellsworth instructed the jury, there was no such thing as expatriation; "once a subject, always a subject"; since the common law was a part of American jurisprudence,—as had been maintained by Jay, Cushing, Iredell, and Wilson,—evidently Williams was still an American citizen. An American he was born, an American he must remain, and now as an American he should be punished. The expatriate naval officer was accordingly

---

*Federal Case 17,708; 2 Cranch, C. C. 82 *n.*

convicted and sentenced to four months' imprisonment and a thousand-dollar fine.

This at last was going too far. The pro-British bias of the federal judiciary had hitherto been tolerated because of their anti-French sentiment which was shared by a majority of their countrymen. But a long-standing grievance against Great Britain, going back to the beginning of the Napoleonic wars, had been the British impressment of American sailors who had been born on British soil, impressment based on that very rule of non-expatriation which Justice Ellsworth now upheld. The tables suddenly were turned. Instead of its being the Republicans who were betraying their country it proved to be the Federalist Chief Justice of the Supreme Court of the United States!

It had been natural in the beginning for Jay and his associates to accept the authority of the British common law, as it had been accepted, of course, in colonial jurisprudence, but it comported ill with their contention that all the powers of the national government were derived from the Constitution. In fact, the acceptance of the common law was disputed even in the judiciary. Curiously, among the justices, Chase refused openly to sanction it, though his rulings during the Sedition trials were much like those of the British Judge Jeffreys of evil fame. In New Hampshire, where the Republicans controlled the judiciary, the Supreme Court ruled out the citation of British precedents from "musty, old, worm-eaten books." And only a few years later John Randolph in Congress was effectually to ridicule the whole idea by asking "which common law" it was that the Courts had adopted for the United States—that "of the reign of Elizabeth and James the First or . . . that of the time of George the Second," that "of Sir Walter Raleigh and Captain Smith" or that of "Governor Oglethorpe," that including the law of libel "laid down by Lord Mansfield or that which has immortalized Mr. Fox"? The common law was thus proving a dangerous weapon for the Courts to wield, only too likely to wound those who attempted to use it. And the popular reaction to Ellsworth's unfortunate decision was that if the acceptance of the common law gave Great Britain the

right to impress American seamen, then away with the common law!

Ellsworth was glad enough to escape from the wrath at home by accepting an appointment as special envoy to France to carry out the pacific negotiations that Adams had begun. And when in the next term, that of August, 1800, the question of expatriation again came up in the case of *Talbot* v. *Ship Amelia,* 4 Dallas, 34, the Court was glad to use the absence of the Chief Justice as an excuse for postponing its decision.

During this session, the Court was but half itself. Ellsworth was in France, Cushing was too ill to attend, and Chase was away for the whole term electioneering for Adams in the approaching election.

Chase's political activities were only a little more blatant than those of other members of the federal judiciary who took every opportunity in their jury charges to proclaim that they were really a Federalist judiciary. Thus, for example, Justice Paterson was approvingly cited in the Federalist press as having in one of his charges set politics "in their true light by holding up the Jacobins [i.e. the Republicans] as the disorganization of our happy country." Iredell and Cushing had made similar utterances. There was no longer even a pretense of political independence on the part of the judiciary.*

In the one important decision rendered in 1800, that of *Bas* v. *Tingy,* 4 Dallas, 37, the Supreme Court once more took the unpopular side. Depredations upon French American commerce had been carried on for some time by each nation and in determining the status of a prize the Court announced that

---

*At this point it may be interesting to compare two statements by Charles Warren in his *The Supreme Court in United States History.* On p. 165 of Vol. I he quotes with approval an Anti-Federalist attack on the Court: "We have seen judges who ought to be independent, converted into political partisans and like executive missionaries pronouncing political harangues throughout the United States"—to which he adds, "This language was surely justified." But on p. 420 of the same volume we find the following: "Time and again it has been proved—and to the great honor of the profession—that no lawyer, whose character and legal ability would warrant his appointment to that lofty tribunal, would stoop to smirch his own record by submitting his judgment to the political touchstone; and no President has dared to appoint to that Court a lawyer whose character and ability could not meet the test." It may be left to the eminent historian of the Supreme Court to reconcile the two passages.

a state of "limited, partial war" with France existed. The war hysteria in America was now dying down, and it was popularly felt to be somewhat inconsistent for the Supreme Court to usurp the function of Congress and declare war at the very time when the Chief Justice was in France negotiating a treaty to prevent hostilities.

Ellsworth's easy success in his mission, for which the President had fully paved the way, spelled the ruin of his party; with the disappearance of the French quarrel the Federalists' chief lien on popularity was gone—something which Hamilton and the other militarists had foreseen. Unable to forgive the President for preventing a French war which would have kept the Federalists in power, the party leaders knifed Adams in the election of 1800 and thereby lost the executive as well as the legislature. Thomas Jefferson, their bitterest foe, was elected president of the United States.

In the light of what was to come it is difficult for us to realize the horror with which Jefferson's election was regarded by the conservatives. It was quite as if today a Communist were to be elected president. The notorious profiteer, Theodore Sedgwick, Speaker of the House, wrote dramatically to Rufus King, "The aristocracy of virtue is destroyed!" And that usually sober thinker, John Marshall, wrote to C. C. Pinckney: "The Democrats are divided into speculative theorists and absolute terrorists. With the latter, I am disposed to class Mr. Jefferson."

But the Federalists still had the "lame duck" session of Congress in their hands before the Reign of Terror could begin, and they made use of it to intrench themselves behind the only part of their lines that still held. By the Judiciary Act of 1801 they established sixteen new federal Circuit Courts, at the same time relieving the Supreme Court justices of their circuit duties. No law could have been wiser, and no law could have been passed with more ignoble motives. The combination of Supreme Court and Circuit Court functions had never worked well; it had been condemned in a report to Congress by Attorney-General Randolph as early as 1791; the justices themselves had frequently pointed out its de-

fects; yet in all the years of Federalist power the party had not seen fit to change the system; only when going out of office did the Federalists grasp at the chance to enlarge the one department of the government which they still controlled, and the relief of the justices was purely incidental to that larger end. The partisan character of the Judiciary Act was practically admitted by a provision that on the death of the next justice of the Supreme Court the number of the justices should remain at five, a clause aimed to prevent the incoming president from being able to appoint a successor to the old and enfeebled Cushing whose death seemed imminent.

Was it not foreseen that the Republican Congress might repeal this Judiciary Act? In that case there was still another string to the Federalist bow—the Constitutional provision that "the judges, both of the supreme and inferior courts, shall hold their offices during good behavior; and shall, at stated times, receive for their services, a compensation, which shall not be diminished during their continuance in office." If the Republicans should dare defy the Constitution, would not their act be held unconstitutional? Far more than ever before the Federalists pinned their hopes on the Supreme Court.

It was not to be Justice Ellsworth who would lead their forces. He had opportunely resigned owing to ill health, while still in France, and the position had then again been offered to John Jay, who declined to resume a station that had proved so irksome. The claims of Paterson were urged upon the President, but Adams would have none of Paterson. Instead, he insisted upon nominating his old favorite, John Marshall, who after a term in Congress was now secretary of state. The appointment was opposed in the Senate by Paterson's friend, Jonathan Dayton, the political boss of New Jersey, who privately said that Marshall's nomination, like others by Adams, indicated "debility or derangement of intellect." Marshall, it was pointed out to the President, had had the slenderest of legal training; his time had latterly been devoted to politics rather than the law; he had had no judicial experience. Paterson was sound on the Constitution; Marshall had vacillated. For

a week the Federalist senators clamored for Paterson, but the President stood firm and at last the Senate capitulated. The appointment of the man who is generally regarded today as the greatest of American justices was reluctantly confirmed. Jefferson was to have an opponent worthy of his steel.

CHAPTER IV

THE COURT UNDER CHIEF JUSTICE MARSHALL

1801-1835

JOHN MARSHALL, WILLIAM CUSHING, WILLIAM PATERSON, SAMUEL CHASE, BUSHROD WASHINGTON, ALFRED MOORE, WILLIAM JOHNSON, BROCKHOLST LIVINGSTON, THOMAS TODD, JOSEPH STORY, GABRIEL DUVAL, SMITH THOMPSON, ROBERT TRIMBLE, JOHN McLEAN, HENRY BALDWIN, JAMES MOORE WAYNE.

1. The Supreme Court at War with the President and Congress

DESPITE the growing importance of the Supreme Court, it was not yet deemed necessary to give it a local habitation and a home. In laying out the elaborate public buildings in the new city of Washington, which became the seat of the national government in 1800, the Supreme Court seems actually to have been entirely forgotten. The White House for the President; the Capitol for the Senate and the House of Representatives; but no provision whatsoever for the housing of the Supreme Court which only at last obtained, through the kindness of the Senate, permission to use one of its vacant committee rooms. In this insignificant chamber, twenty-four by thirty feet, Marshall was sworn into office on February 4, 1801.

JOHN MARSHALL

No man was less like the conventional conception of a judge than this greatest of American judges. Indeed, no man was less like the conventional conception of John Marshall. A judge, such a judge as Marshall above all, should be a picture of austerity: Marshall was gentle and genial, fond of cards, wine, and good living; a judge's eye should be severe, rebuking

familiarity: Marshall's was merry and affectionate; the man popularly credited with first raising the Supreme Court to its awful dignity, had no more conscious dignity than Lincoln or Jefferson. Tall, gangling, careless of clothes as they, Marshall was like them a product of the frontier, his birthplace not a hundred miles from Jefferson's. But from that same environment the two men drew opposite lessons: where the frontier taught Jefferson its dogmas of democracy and equality, it showed Marshall an example of individual conflict from which a natural aristocracy emerged. He admired efficiency, and he admired success. As an officer in the Revolution, he observed with indignation the ineptitudes of Congress, and his distrust of legislators was increased by closer familiarity with them during his own terms as assemblyman and congressman. With but two months' legal training at William and Mary College, he learned the law through his cases as they came up, and learned it so well that he was soon attorney for the great Robert Morris. With a loan from Morris, he purchased a part of the Fairfax estate making him a landed gentleman on a small scale. Closer and closer became his ties with the Federalists. His mission to France where he encountered in its decadence the Revolution that had influenced Jefferson in its first flush of hope completed the making of the master conservative.

The man destined to carry on the Hamiltonian policies through dark days ahead was better fitted than Hamilton himself for such a task. Equally bold, when the times favored boldness, he also possessed a quality unknown to Hamilton— that of discretion. He was, as Corwin says, "a supreme debater," but he was likewise a supreme tactician and strategist. John Marshall gave his decisions as Shakespeare wrote the separate scenes of his plays—each for its own immediate effectiveness—yet as with Shakespeare the main plot flowed onward somehow through all the eddies and meanderings. When to assume jurisdiction and when to disclaim it; when to interpret a law broadly and when narrowly; which precedents to cite and which to forget: these were all matters of detail wherein the law permitted, to an alert mind, a considerable

choice of weapons. Marshall was no superstitious pedant to regard the law as something sacred in itself; he understood thoroughly that it is and must be a servant of economics and politics; his office was to see that it remained a servant of what he regarded as good economics and good politics.

And now in the presidency was a man with a set of democratic theories that Marshall particularly detested, yet no mere dreamer but on the contrary a sagacious leader quite as resourceful as the Chief Justice in choosing among the legal means available the one best adapted to his ends. Tactician against tactician, strategist against strategist. The warriors were well matched.

JEFFERSON'S THEORY OF CONSTITUTIONAL INTERPRETATIONS

In the original draft of Jefferson's first message to Congress was included a long paragraph in which the President set forth his own theory of constitutional interpretation. "Our country has thought proper to distribute the powers of its government among three equal and independent authorities, constituting each a check on one or both of the others, in all attempts to impair its constitution. To make each an effectual check, it must have a right in cases which arise within the line of its proper functions, *where, equally with the others, it acts in the last resort and without appeal, to decide on the validity of an act according to its own judgment,* and uncontrolled by the opinions of any other department."*

This revolutionary theory Jefferson at the last minute deleted from his message as, in his words, "capable of being chicaned." The shrewdest politician ever in the White House realized that it would be better if possible to have the first gun fired by the enemy so that the issue might be that of judicial "encroachment" rather than judicial "independence."

In the message as it was actually delivered, no cat about to swallow a canary ever looked so innocent as did Jefferson with his casual reference to the Judiciary Act of 1801: "The Judiciary system . . . and especially that portion of it recently en-

---

*Italics ours. The entire paragraph is given in Beveridge, *op cit.,* Vol. III, Appendix A.

acted, will, of course, present itself to the contemplation of Congress." Could there be any sinister design in Jefferson's submitting together with the message "an exact statement of all the causes decided since the first establishment of the courts and of the causes which were pending when additional courts and judges were brought to their aid"? If the additional courts had really been needed, what had the Federalists to fear?

MARBURY V. MADISON

Not knowing exactly how or when the blow would fall, the Federalists were worried and nervous. On the principle that the best defense is to attack, Marshall took advantage of an early opportunity to begin the battle. In addition to the sixteen Circuit Court judges, Adams, under a supplementary law to the Judiciary Act of 1801, had at the last minute appointed forty-two justices of the peace for the District of Columbia. These appointments had been confirmed by the Senate, but there had been no time to send out the actual commissions. Jefferson, on his accession to office, instructed Madison as secretary of state to issue twenty-five of these commissions but to withhold the other seventeen which had been intended for particularly obstinate focs of the new Administration. Now four of these rejected aspirants for office, William Marbury, Dennis Ramsay, Robert Townsend Hooe, and William Harper, came into the Supreme Court and demanded a mandamus compelling Madison to deliver their commissions. Marshall issued an order to Madison to show cause why this should not be done. Thus began the famous case of *Marbury* v. *Madison,* 1 Cranch, 137, which ere its completion was to prove almost equally embarrassing to everyone concerned.

The order was really directed at the President as everyone understood, and this unprecedented action would have unified the Republicans, if they had not been unified before. The expected motion to repeal the Judiciary Act of 1801 was made on January 6, 1802, by Senator John Breckinridge of Kentucky. There followed a month's debate in the Senate followed by another month's debate in the House, during which

the whole theory of the judiciary was at last thoroughly discussed.

The main reliance of the Federalists, led by Senator Gouverneur Morris, was on their contention that the repeal if passed would be declared unconstitutional by the Supreme Court. To this, Breckinridge replied that the Constitution nowhere gave the Supreme Court any such authority. "Is it not extraordinary," he said, "that if this high power was intended, it should nowhere appear? . . . Never were such high and transcendent powers in any Government . . . claimed or exercised by construction only." The threat of nullification through the action of the Supreme Court was met by a counter-threat of impeachment in that case. By a strict party vote of sixteen to fifteen the repeal bill passed the Senate.

In the House also the debate turned on the constitutional powers of the Courts and Congress. Here the claims of the Federalists were answered still more defiantly by John Randolph of Roanoke in a ringing denunciation of the judiciary. "The decision of a Constitutional question," he said, "must rest somewhere. Shall it be confided to men immediately responsible to the people, or to those who are irresponsible?" Back of the supremacy of legislature or judiciary lay the sovereignty of the people. Which branch better represented that ultimate sovereignty had been shown by the actions of the federal courts. When Thomas Cooper, a Republican, in a criminal suit and in defense of his liberty, sought a writ against an officer of the government, it had been denied, but when William Marbury, a Federalist, in a civil suit and merely for the sake of a coveted office, demanded a similar writ it had been immediately granted.

What folly to pretend that the judiciary was a defender of the liberty of the people. "No, sir," Randolph went on, "you may invade the press; the courts will outstrip you in zeal, to further this great object; your citizens may be imprisoned and amerced, the courts will take care to see it executed; the helpless foreigner may, contrary to the express letter of your Constitution, be deprived of compulsory process for obtaining witnesses in his defense; the courts in their extreme humility cannot find authority for granting it."

A judicial check upon the legislature is needed? Why so? "Are we not as deeply interested in the true exposition of the Constitution as the judges can be? Is not Congress as capable of forming a correct opinion as they are? Are not its members acting under a responsibility to public opinion which can and will check their aberrations from duty?" The ballot box, Randolph asserted, was the real "Constitutional corrective. That is the true check; every other is at variance with the principle that a free people are capable of self-government."

Thus at last there were two definitely opposed theories of Constitutional interpretation fully set forth: what may be called the Hamilton-Ellsworth-Paterson theory (asserted, disavowed, and about to be re-asserted by John Marshall), and the Madison-Jefferson-Breckinridge-Randolph theory, now supported by a majority of Congress. Both rested ostensibly upon the same fundamental assumption, that of the sovereignty of the people as expressed in the Constitution. But after this assumption had been accepted, there was a complete parting of the ways. For the Federalists there was only one correct interpretation of the Constitution, determined by the majority of the Supreme Court; for the Republicans there were many interpretations, which might equally well be offered by the legislature or executive, subject to the verdict of the people themselves.

Behind the clash of theories was the clash of interests of which the theories were largely rationalizations, between the large property owners who looked to the courts for salvation and the small property owners who trusted in the legislature and the voters. The large property owners had hitherto had everything their own way; they were first in the field and had established their theory of constitutional interpretation which now had ten years of precedents behind it. Would the Republicans be able to overcome the ten years' handicap?

For the moment, the victory was theirs. Their opponents, outnumbered and outargued, ended by resorting to threats of violence if the Judiciary Act should be repealed. The foppish Federalist leader, James A. Bayard, arbiter of fashion in clothes and wine and women, issued a call to arms on behalf of the imperiled Constitution. "There are many now willing to

spill their blood to defend that Constitution. Are gentlemen disposed to risk the consequences?"

Undaunted by the luxurious hedonist's display of military ardor, the Republicans went straight on to carry out their policies. First, the Judiciary Act was repealed, and then to prevent the Supreme Court's declaring the repeal unconstitutional, the Court was suspended for the year 1802 and its next term of meeting set for February, 1803.

Although no constitutional question had been settled, except by inference, the outcome was a mighty victory for the Republicans. They had succeeded in limiting the power of the judiciary in the most practical way possible by decreasing the number of the judges. They had ventured to pass their law in the face of declarations by those who presumably represented the views of the judiciary that the law was utterly unconstitutional. Not only that, they had denied the authority of such declarations if made by the judiciary itself. If all this were left unquestioned by the courts, Congress would have taken a long step toward annulling the whole theory of judicial supremacy. This was the situation which confronted John Marshall when the Supreme Court resumed its sessions in February, 1803.

Still on its docket was the unfinished case of *Marbury* v. *Madison*. The issue involved in it had become academic so far as Marbury was concerned, for the term of office to which he had been appointed was almost over. But to Marshall the case now presented the most awkward of dilemmas. Madison had totally ignored the order of the Court, and there was no doubt whatsoever that if the Court's decision were given in favor of Marbury it too would be ignored by the triumphant Administration. In that event, the Court would merely put itself in the humiliating position of issuing a second order which it had no means of enforcing. On the other hand, to decide in favor of Madison would be still worse as it would give the sanction of the Court itself to the Administration's pretensions. The skill with which Marshall managed to extricate himself from this dilemma, and at one and the same time vindicate yet discard Marbury, condemn the President, and uphold the right of judicial review, can hardly be too much admired from the

purely technical viewpoint. Never was a strategic retreat conducted in so victorious a manner.

Marshall's great coup consisted in boldly declaring unconstitutional Section 13 of Ellsworth's Judiciary Law of 1789, under which the mandamus against Madison was sought; wherefore, the Court had no jurisdiction in the case. This accomplished at a single stroke two of Marshall's purposes: to establish the rule of judicial review and to get rid of that white elephant, Marbury's suit; but it would not of itself have enabled him to fulfill his third and dearest purpose of condemning Thomas Jefferson. If the usual and logical order of procedure had been followed by beginning with the question of jurisdiction, that once determined in the negative the case of course would have been closed and the verbal victory over the Republicans left sadly incomplete. So Marshall in rendering the decision of the Court adopted a new and remarkable order of his own, taking up three questions:

"First. Has the applicant a right to the commission he demands?

"Second. If he has a right, and that right has been violated do the laws of his country afford him a remedy?

"Third. If they do afford him a remedy, is it a mandamus issuing from this court?"

By giving an affirmative answer to the first two questions and a negative answer to the third, the Court was able to uphold Marbury, maintain that the President had violated the law, and yet avoid all responsibility for enforcing the law. In other words, Marshall's extraordinary line of procedure enabled the Court both to decide the case and assert that it had no jurisdiction to decide it.

Questions one and two were easily answered. Marbury had been duly appointed and commissioned for five years; his appointment was not revocable by the President; "to withhold his commission, therefore, is an act deemed by the court not warranted by law, but violative of a vested legal right." And the President, like other men, "is amenable to the laws for his conduct; and cannot at his discretion sport away the vested rights of others."

Question three was more difficult. Section 13 of the Ju-

diciary Act of 1789 explicitly authorized the Supreme Court "to issue writs of *mandamus,* in cases warranted by the principles and usages of law, to . . . persons holding office, under the authority of the United States." The constitutionality of this section had never hitherto been questioned. The Act had been drawn up by Ellsworth and Paterson, both of them members of the Constitutional Convention and later justices of the Supreme Court. The Congress that passed it included eleven other members of the Constitutional Convention, not one of whom perceived any constitutional defect in the law. The validity of Section 13 had been repeatedly recognized by both Circuit and Supreme Court.* John Marshall himself was later, by implication, to grant its validity in another case.† If there were any section of any law on the statute books constitutionally impregnable it would seem to have been Section 13 of the Judiciary Act of 1789.

At the moment, however, it was politically incumbent upon Marshall to find some reason for declaring it unconstitutional, and Marshall was equal to the emergency. The jurisdiction conferred by the Constitution upon the Supreme Court, he pointed out, was both original and appellative; the former was explicitly limited to cases "affecting ambassadors, other public ministers and consuls, and those in which a State shall be a party"; only the appellate jurisdiction was left to be determined by laws of Congress such as the Judiciary Act. Under which head did the granting of a writ of mandamus belong? "To issue such a writ to an officer for the delivery of a paper, is in effect the same as to sustain an original action for that paper, and, therefore, seems not to belong to appellate, but to original jurisdiction." From this it followed that Section 13 was not "warranted by the Constitution."

Having thus already declared the law unconstitutional, Marshall went on to consider as a final point the question whether the Supreme Court had authority to make such a declaration.

United States v. *Ravara,* 2 Dallas, 297; *United States* v. *Lawrence,* 3 Dallas, 42; *United States* v. *Peters,* 3 Dallas, 121.

†See E. S. Corwin, *Doctrine of Judicial Review* (1914), pp. 8-9

As we have seen, he had absolutely denied this authority when he appeared as an attorney in the case of *Ware, Administrator* v. *Hylton et al.* seven years before. And he could not well assert that the authority had been conferred upon the Court by Congress in the Ellsworth Act when he was engaged in nullifying a part of that very Act. Hence he resorted to the familiar argument of Hamilton in *The Federalist,* No. 78, and further supported it by Paterson's distinction between written and unwritten constitutions. "All those who have framed written constitutions contemplate them as forming the fundamental and paramount law of the nation, and consequently, the theory of every such government must be, that an act of the legislature, repugnant to the constitution, is void. . . . If an act of the legislature, repugnant to the constitution is void, does it, notwithstanding its invalidity, bind the courts . . . ? This would be to overthrow in fact what was established in theory. . . ."

The theory to which Marshall appealed was established only in the United States and, since the Republican revolution, was no longer fully established here. His universal affirmative in regard to other countries was untrue at the time he asserted it, since the written French constitution of 1791 particularly disavowed any such theory.

Marshall himself seems to have been conscious of some weakness in his inferential argument for at the very end of his long opinion he sought to bolster it up by a somewhat casual reference to the direct language of the Constitution. "It is also not entirely unworthy of observation, that in declaring what shall be the *supreme* law of the land, the *Constitution* itself is first mentioned; and not the laws of the United States generally, but those only which shall be made in *pursuance* of the Constitution, have that rank." But this obviously is quite different from saying that the Supreme Court alone shall have the power to determine which laws are in pursuance of the Constitution.

Such was the decision in the case of *Marbury* v. *Madison,* a decision every item of which revealed its political and oppor-

tunistic background.* It was significant as the first decision
of the Supreme Court to declare a law of Congress unconstitutional, but it was also significant as the last decision of that
kind for over fifty years. When the doctrine of judicial review
was revived after the Civil War it became the fashion to hark
back to Marshall's opinion as a mighty precedent, but to his
contemporaries it did not seem particularly important. The
law annulled was a piece of Federalist legislation which the
Republicans were not sorry to see abolished. The attack on
Jefferson intensely annoyed the President, and of course de-
lighted his opponents but most of Jefferson's followers regarded
it not incorrectly as an impotent gesture. The leading Republican papers, such as the *National Ægis, National Intelligencer,
Aurora,* and the *American Citizen* did not even trouble to
criticize the decision.

STUART V. LAIRD

Having made this gesture and safely asserted the power of
judicial review in a case where it would not be challenged, the
Supreme Court did not choose to exercise it in another case,
Stuart v. *Laird,* 1 Cranch, 299, decided six days later, a really
important case, in fact the most important that could possibly
be brought before them, for it involved the constitutionality of
the repeal of the Judiciary Act of 1801. Here was the chance
for which the Federalists had been waiting. Their leaders in
Congress had all insisted that the repeal was unconstitutional;
on the day of its passage the *Washington Federalist,* with which
Marshall's relations were very close had announced as with
full conviction, "By the judges this bill will be declared null
and void." Such was the decision expected by the country.

---

*Readers who find it difficult to believe that the most celebrated opinion
of the most celebrated Chief Justice of the Supreme Court could really
have been of so extraordinary a character are invited to peruse the detailed accounts in Beveridge, *op. cit.,* Vol. III, pp. 100-56; Boudin, *op. cit.,*
Vol. I, pp. 195-233; Corwin, *John Marshall and the Constitution* (1919),
pp. 64-70; Warren, *op. cit.,* Vol. I, pp. 231-68. The opinion is reprinted in
full in Ambrose Doskow, *Historic Opinions of the United States Supreme
Court* (1935), pp. 3-31.

And instead, the Supreme Court actually upheld the hated bill. And it did so, as Boudin remarks, "in the most ignominious way possible."

Stuart v. *Laird* raised two separable issues: that of the constitutionality of the Judiciary Act of 1801 in abolishing the Circuit Courts and that of the constitutionality of the Ellsworth Act in imposing Circuit Court duties upon the justices of the Supreme Court. As counsel for the plaintiff, Charles Lee, former Federalist attorney-general, laid most of his emphasis upon the former point, but the Supreme Court virtually ignored it and pretended that the second question was the only important one of consequence. In doing so, it did not entirely escape embarrassment, however, for this second question was in itself sufficiently troublesome. The union of Circuit and Supreme Court duties prescribed in Ellsworth's Judiciary Act, although originally a Federalist measure, had been discarded by the Act of 1801 and then reinstated by the repeal of that Act. It had now become a Republican measure almost as dangerous to attack as the repeal itself.

As early as 1790, Chief Justice Jay in a letter to Washington had asserted the unconstitutionality of imposing Circuit Court duties on the justices. Marshall himself felt particularly bitter on the subject because he had only accepted his appointment as chief justice on the understanding that the justices would be relieved of their onerous circuit tasks by the Judiciary Act of 1801. As Beveridge tells us, "When the Republicans repealed the Federalist Judiciary Act of 1801, Marshall had actually proposed to his associates upon the Supreme Bench that they refuse to sit as circuit judges, and 'risk the consequences.' By the Constitution, he said, they were judges of the Supreme Court only; their commissions proved that they were appointed solely to those offices; the section requiring them to sit in inferior courts was unconstitutional. The other members of the Supreme Court, however (with the exception of Chase), had not the courage to adopt the heroic course Marshall recommended. They agreed that his views were sound, but insisted that, because the Ellsworth Judiciary Act had been acquiesced

in since the adoption of the Constitution, the validity of that act must now be considered as established."*

Marshall, himself, did not sit in *Stuart* v. *Laird,* having been a member of the Circuit Court from which the case was appealed, where he had decided against the plaintiff on a purely technical point. The other Justices, however, made use of their doctrine of acquiescence to uphold the Ellsworth Act.

After summarizing Lee's argument against its constitutionality, the decision of the Court read, "To this objection, which is of recent date, it is sufficient to observe, that practice and acquiescence under it for a period of several years, commencing with the organization of the judicial system, affords an irresistible answer, and has indeed fixed the construction. It is a contemporary interpretation of the most forcible nature. This practical exposition is too strong and obstinate to be shaken and controlled. Of course, the question is at rest, and ought not now to be disturbed."

On this decision two comments must be made. In the first place, it was in flat contradiction of that of a week earlier nullifying another section of the same Ellsworth law, also supported by "practice and acquiescence." If one section were valid for that reason, why not the other? The second and more important comment is admirably put by Boudin:

"A law may . . . become constitutional by *prescription,* as was the Ellsworth Judiciary Law according to the decision in *Stuart* v. *Laird.* The judges acted under it for a number of years, either through wilfulness or ignorance. They either knew it was unconstitutional and wilfully ignored that fact. Or they did not know about it—such a thing being evidently quite possible under our system. But whether they acted from ignorance or wilfulness, their action became binding upon their successors—the law having become constitutional by lapse of time. In view of what Mr. Beveridge tells us as to the real opinion of the judges on this point, their official excuse about the 'contemporary interpretation of the most forcible nature' is mere camouflage. Evidently this contemporary interpretation was not of a sufficiently forcible nature to influence the

*Beveridge, *op. cit.,* Vol. III, p. 122.

actual opinion of the judges. For Mr. Beveridge assures us that, notwithstanding this alleged 'contemporary interpretation,' the judges really believed the law to be unconstitutional, and Marshall actually favored their refusal to act under it because of its alleged unconstitutionality. The actual decision in *Stuart* v. *Laird* was therefore either sheer pretense born of cowardice; or it means that the judges believed that, notwithstanding their own opinion as to its unconstitutionality, the law had actually *become* constitutional by lapse of time or 'prescription.' "*

WILLIAM JOHNSON

The Supreme Court was now plainly in full retreat before the Republicans, whose threats of impeachment seemed to have had effect. And in 1804 the Jeffersonians were lucky enough to obtain a footing in the institution itself. Justice Cushing had disappointed them by recovering from his illness, lingering on in a half-senile condition until 1810, but meanwhile Justice Moore fell seriously ill and resigned. Moore having been from North Carolina, it was necessary to replace him from the South; territorial considerations thus eliminated the foremost candidates, Judge McKean and Cæsar Rodney of Pennsylvania as well as John Taylor of Virginia, Jefferson's own state already possessing two representatives on the Bench, Marshall and Bushrod Washington, both ironically Federalists; so in the present emergency the President's choice fell on William Johnson of South Carolina, who was then but 32, the youngest man ever appointed to the Supreme Court. He was an honest and talented judge of the state court of common pleas and before that had been speaker of the lower house in the state legislature, but his Republicanism was a trifle suspect, owing to his having studied law in the office of C. C. Pinckney, that stoutest of Federalists and intimate friend of John Marshall.

Johnson undertook to reform a practice that had latterly grown up in the Court of having the chief justice alone deliver the opinion of the Court instead of having all the justices give

---

*Louis Boudin, *Government by Judiciary*. Quoted by permission of Godwin, Publishers.

their opinions *seriatim.* as had originally been the custom. He wrote amusingly some years later in a letter to Jefferson of his utter failure to accomplish anything:

"When I was on our State Bench, I was accustomed to delivering *seriatim* opinions in an Appellate Court, and was not a little surprised to find our Chief Justice in the Supreme Court delivering all the opinions. . . . But I remonstrated in vain; the answer was, he is willing to take the trouble, and it is a mark of respect to him. I soon, however, found out the real cause. Cushing was incompetent, Chase could not be got to think or write, Paterson was a slow man and willingly declined the trouble, and the other two judges [Marshall and Bushrod Washington] you know are commonly estimated as one judge."

IMPEACHMENT OF CHASE

Justice Chase might no longer be able to write or think, but he could still feel. Irritated beyond measure by the success of the Republicans, he took occasion in a charge to the grand jury in Baltimore, two months after *Stuart* v. *Laird,* to burst out in an intemperate harangue on the evils of democracy in general and the Republican Party in particular, assailing universal suffrage as something which would "rapidly destroy all protection to property," and asserting that "the independence of the National Judiciary" had been destroyed by the Repeal Act—which he himself had so recently joined in declaring constitutional.

The Constitution provided that judges were to hold office during "good behavior"; was it good behavior to indulge in such utterances as those of Chase? His remarks, together with his tyrannical rulings in the *Fries* and *Callender Cases* and his misconduct in trying to secure sedition indictments in Delaware when none was forthcoming, all taken together seemed to the Republicans sufficient justification for impeachment.

Urged on by Jefferson, John Randolph of Roanoke undertook the task, and impeachment was voted in the House. By the time the trial occurred, however, Randolph had broken with

both his party and the President over another incident, that of the old Yazoo land frauds which were still vexatiously alive. The original speculators, foreseeing the passage of the Georgia rescinding law that annulled their claims, had made sure of their profits by selling the lands beforehand to another group of speculators, chiefly in New England, who were willing to assume the risk because it was known that Georgia was going to deed the lands in question to the federal government, which was counted upon to make some favorable adjustment. Such was attempted by Jefferson's Administration which proposed to compromise with the "innocent" purchasers by giving them five million dollars to extinguish their claims. Randolph, because of his outraged sense of justice, was so imprudent as to sacrifice both energy and popularity in defeating this Administration measure just before the Chase trial. The result was that the Republicans, entering into the new duel with the Federalists, were divided in their own counsels and sympathies.

Nevertheless, it was universally expected that Chase would be convicted. The Republican theory of impeachment held it to be an "inquest of office" rather than necessarily a criminal trial. Few lawyers would have maintained that Chase had "behaved well" in office; if "misbehavior," as one clause of the Constitution seemed to imply, was ground for removal, Chase was doomed. And not only Chase but the whole Federalist Court with its attacks upon the President and Congress!

Marshall, summoned as a witness for Chase, was, according to his own friends, very badly scared. His hesitant testimony as to Chase's conduct in the Fries trial was more harmful than helpful to the defendant. He actually suggested in an amazing letter to Chase that "the modern doctrine of impeachment should yield to an appellate jurisdiction in the legislature. A reversal of those legal opinions deemed unsound by the legislature would certainly better comport with the mildness of our character than [would] a removal of the Judge who has rendered them unknowing of his fault."* In other words, he was willing to throw overboard the doctrine of judicial review, together with his own opinion in *Marbury* v. *Madison,* and

*Entire letter quoted in Beveridge, *op. cit.,* Vol. III, pp. 176-77.

accept a more complete legislative supremacy than even Jefferson demanded, if only he and his fellow justices would be permitted to retain their offices.

From such total surrender the Supreme Court was saved by the skill of Chase's lawyers and the dissension among his prosecutors. The former, Luther Martin, Charles Lee, Robert Goodloe Harper, Francis Hopkinson, and Philip Barton Key, stood on the letter of the Constitution specifically which mentioned only "treason, bribery or other high crimes and misdemeanors" as grounds for impeachment. With iteration and reiteration they enforced the point until the House managers were fairly groggy. Joseph Nicholson incautiously admitted his opponents' interpretation and then too late tried to retract his admission; the other managers in attempting to extricate their luckless colleague floundered into the bog themselves; Randolph in his final speech broke down and wept; and a sufficient number of Yazooist Republicans were so eager to humiliate their recent adversary that they went over to the Federalists. Justice Chase was acquitted. The Supreme Court was saved, and Jefferson prophetically declared that impeachment was "a farce which would not be tried again."

The outcome of the case enormously strengthened the morale of the Supreme Court. If the vulnerable Chase could not be impeached, certainly none of the other justices could be. John Marshall in particular soon recovered from his mood of dejection and was ready to do battle for the Lord more stoutly than before. The orthodox account is that that battle was waged solely on behalf of Nationalism. But to Marshall, as to Hamilton, Nationalism was based on the assumption that his class ought to rule the nation. Little enough support did the national government of Jefferson receive from him. He took indeed every opportunity to hamper it, and a first great opportunity came to him in the trial of Aaron Burr for treason.

TRIAL OF BURR

That Burr's gathering of an insignificant force on the Ohio in 1806 was intended to serve as the nucleus for some vast

enterprise is certain but whether this was to be a grandiose colonization scheme, an expedition for the conquest of Mexico, or an actual attempt to arouse insurrection in the western territory of the United States has never been fully determined. With the revelation of Burr's treasonable overtures to the British and Spanish Ministers together with his recently discovered later endeavor to enlist Napoleon's aid for an attack on Boston, it is no longer possible to take the once fashionable attitude of regarding Burr as an innocent and much-wronged victim of Jefferson's malignity. On the other hand, Jefferson trusted too hastily, if naturally, in the unverified reports of the ranking officer of the American Army, General James Wilkinson, a most untrustworthy individual who had long been secretly in the pay of the Spanish Government. The President stated to Congress that there was "no doubt" of Burr's guilt, when as a matter of fact there was the greatest doubt of it; he endorsed Wilkinson's defiance of the civil courts in seizing Burr and two of his assistants and sending them back to Virginia; and he used all of his influence during the trials to have the alleged conspirators convicted.

Since Burr, originally a Republican, had of recent years coquetted with the Federalists, the latter thronged to his support so that the trial before Marshall in the Circuit Court at Richmond became still another incident in the prolonged party struggle.

The trial was in ironical contrast to that of Fries. The Federalists were now as eager for acquittal as they had then been for conviction. But the rulings of the judges in the two cases were directly opposed. Where Chase had excluded what was regarded as important evidence for the defendant, Marshall excluded what was regarded as important evidence for the prosecution; where Chase made the law of treason as broad as a river, Marshall made it as narrow as a mountain stream. In spite of these differences, however, the rulings of each judge were equally in their party's interest at the time; Chase secured the desired conviction, Marshall the desired acquittal. Even Warren admits that "the belief held by Jefferson and his followers that Marshall had been influenced by personal and

partisan feeling in some of his rulings had considerable justification."*

During the trial, however, Marshall committed an error which robbed him of much of his triumph over Jefferson. Yielding to Burr's demand, he issued a subpœna to the President to appear in Court with certain documents necessary for the defense. When Madison as secretary of state had defied a similar writ with impunity, how could Marshall expect the President of the United States to be terrorized into submission? Jefferson neither appeared in person nor sent the papers, and when Burr audaciously asked that the President be sentenced for contempt of court Marshall did not respond. Although Jefferson is usually considered to have been a poor lawyer, in this instance he proved himself a better lawyer than the Chief Justice. His reply was irrefutable that the executive would be made subordinate to the judiciary "if he were subject to the commands of the latter and to imprisonment for disobedience; if the several courts could bandy him from pillar to post, and withdraw him from his constitutional duties." Marshall discreetly dropped the whole matter, and presidential immunity from witness duty has never since been questioned.

During these years various amendments to the Constitution for the purpose of bringing the Supreme Court under popular control were proposed in Congress. Immediately after the Chase trial, Randolph introduced the first of these, providing that "The Judges of the Supreme and all other courts of the United States shall be removed by the President on the joint address of both Houses of Congress." After the Burr trial an amendment was prepared with Jefferson's approval limiting the tenure of all United States judges to a term of years and providing for their removal by the president on petition by two-thirds of both houses. When these amendments failed, there was a momentary reversion to the idea of impeachment: as late as 1808 John Quincy Adams in a Senate report went over Marshall's rulings in the *Burr Case* and strongly intimated that the judge who made them ought to be impeached.

*Warren, *op. cit.*, Vol. I, p. 315. See also Corwin, *John Marshall and the Constitution*, p. 111.

But this threat, like the proposed amendments, came to nothing.

The chief reason why the Republicans did not continue to push their attacks on the judiciary was that in the meantime Jefferson had had the opportunity to make two further appointments to the Supreme Bench. In 1806 the death of Justice Paterson enabled him to appoint Brockholst Livingston, 49 years old, Judge of the New York supreme court, and member of the one American family of great wealth that had upheld Republican principles from the beginning. And in the ensuing year the addition of a new Circuit for Kentucky, Tennessee, and Ohio increasing the membership of the Supreme Court to seven, Thomas Todd, Chief Justice of Kentucky, was appointed.

JEFFERSON'S JUSTICES

The results optimistically expected from the influence of three Republicans on the Bench were not forthcoming. The members of the Supreme Court had taken to living and dining together in the same boarding-house—a custom continued until 1845—and more and more came to be a kind of club, the most exclusive in the world, where the jovial justices would sit for long hours sipping their Madeira—the best brand was labeled "the Supreme Court"—and discussing their cases, the nature of American institutions, and the ways of the world in general. In such surroundings, the genial charm of the Chief Justice was exercised to full advantage, and after a few months of exposure to it the most hardened Republicans succumbed. Thus during Marshall's long tenure of office president after president had the mortification of seeing his own appointees go over to the enemy.

Jefferson himself drank of this cup of disappointment in full measure. His famous Embargo of 1807, suspending all shipping to Great Britain, was a premature attempt, over a century before its time, to apply the principle of the boycott as a substitute for war. When nevertheless, the constitutionality of the Embargo was upheld by Judge John Davis of the District Court of Massachusetts, the New England States turned to the doctrines of the Virginia and Kentucky Resolutions which

they had so decisively rejected a decade earlier, namely, that the states themselves had a right to determine the constitutionality of law. The Embargo was constantly evaded by illegal shipping from the New England ports and by smuggling into Canada. What was now Jefferson's humiliation to find his efforts to enforce the law thwarted by the judicial decisions not merely of Marshall but also of Livingston and Johnson!

The Embargo was violently attacked by the New England shipping interests whose chief representative in Congress, Senator Timothy Pickering, emitted a speech against it which, as Beveridge says, "might well have been delivered in Parliament." He sent a copy of the speech to his friend John Marshall who replied enthusiastically, commenting upon its "excellence," its "sound argument," its "correct reasoning."*

Marshall discovered in the Embargo enactments technical defects which would not permit criminal indictments under them according to their undoubted intent. He validated a circumvention of a Virginia stay law which was designed to assist debtors during the period of the Embargo, by allowing claims to be transferred to citizens in other states who could then sue in the federal courts. Jefferson was not surprised at such rulings from a Marshall, but what of a Livingston who refused to indict the murderers of three Vermont militiamen for treason after Jefferson had officially proclaimed that part of Vermont to be in "a state of insurrection"! What of a Johnson who ruled that the President had exceeded his authority in issuing an order to collectors to detain all vessels loaded with provisions whereas the law vested a power of discretion in the collectors to decide such cases? Technicalities everywhere invoked to defeat a great and beneficent purpose.

There were still other cases in which Jefferson's appointees were of no service to the Administration. In *McIlvaine* v. *Coxe's Lessee,* 2 Cranch, 280; 4 Cranch, 209, the question was again the old one of expatriation which had by now become a burning issue between Great Britain and the United States. Was one Coxe, a native of New Jersey who had joined the British cause in 1776 to be regarded as an American or British

*Beveridge, *op. cit.,* Vol. IV, p. 14.

citizen in matters of property inheritance? The absurdities involved in such a question were pointed out by Jared Ingersoll: "That the French who aided us are called aliens, while the British loyalist refugees may hold lands as a citizen, is a language I do not understand. If the law is so, it is strange, and I must abandon an idea I have always cherished, that the rules of law were founded in sound sense." Nevertheless, according to the Supreme Court, the law was so, or nearly so. Coxe had been a citizen of New Jersey under its statutes in 1776 and was therefore "incapable of throwing off his allegiance to that State." As to whether the same rule applied to all Americans under the common law the Court declined to express an opinion as that question was not involved. Thus the Court was able to take the British side without expressly adopting the British point of view. Had Marshall himself not avoided taking part in the decision it might have been even more overtly pro-British as he fully accepted the doctrine of perpetual allegiance—"a question," as he wrote to a friend, "upon which I never entertained a *scintilla* of doubt."*

In *Croudson* v. *Leonard,* 4 Cranch, 434, the Court went over bag and baggage to the foe by upholding as final the decisions of the notoriously unfair British prize courts. "If the injustice of the belligerent powers and of their Courts should render this rule oppressive to the citizens of neutral nations," added Justice Washington piously, "let the government in its wisdom adopt the proper means to remedy the mischief." It is hardly remarkable that Jefferson should have been enraged by the Court's Olympian attitude of irresponsibility at the same time that it was thwarting every effort of the government to find the "proper means" for solving the truly desperate international problem.

In 1809 Jefferson at last went out of office, and his long war with the Supreme Court was over. The tide of battle had flowed back and forth, but in the end the Court was left in possession of the field. For this result, Jefferson himself was in large part responsible. Had he, after his initial victories, instead of wasting his strength in trying to pick off individuals

*Beveridge, *op. cit.,* Vol. IV, p. 54.

like Chase and Burr concentrated it all behind the constitutional amendment which he advocated, had he not trusted to his own appointees on the Court to overcome the redoubtable Marshall, had he thought more of measures and less of men, had he in a word been still the statesman of 1776 rather than the politician of 1800-1810, he might have carried out his program, and the whole subsequent history of America might have been different.

2.   *The Supreme Court at War with the States*

With the departure of Jefferson, Marshall's troubles with the national Administration were over for many years. The succeeding presidents were not inclined to renew the conflict: Madison was a man of essentially pacific disposition; Monroe, by the time he became president, had disowned his radicalism; the later views of John Quincy Adams were akin to Marshall's own. Hitherto, the Chief Justice had been fighting with his back to the wall; henceforth, he could take the offensive. The details of Hamilton's scheme of government by "the aristocracy of talents, of reputation, and of property," as Senator William Plumer called it, had been hopelessly shattered, but its general framework, though badly shaken, still stood. To strengthen this by a reassertion of Hamiltonian principles was the great task to which the last twenty-seven years of Marshall's career were devoted. In carrying it out, his chief opponents were to be the radically insurgent states, Pennsylvania, Ohio, Virginia, Kentucky, and Georgia.

HOLLAND COMPANY CASE

Difficulties with Pennsylvania had already begun in 1807 with the Supreme Court's decision in the case of *Huidekoper's Lessees* v. *Douglass,* 3 Cranch, 1. This involved the notorious Holland Company, in which it will be recalled, Robert Morris and Justice Wilson, those early patrons of Marshall and Bushrod Washington, had been so largely interested. As the company had made no attempt to fulfill its legal obligation to

settle the lands obtained from the state, an action of ejectment was brought against it, but the Supreme Court decided in the company's favor by adopting, in Charles Warren's words "an exceedingly strained construction of the statute." In high indignation, the state legislature adopted resolutions denying the jurisdiction of the Court, a bold move that came to nothing when it was vetoed by the Governor.

OLMSTEAD CASE

In 1809 came another ruling against the states, in a case* now interesting chiefly as an illustration of the law's delay. During the Revolution a stout American sailor named Gideon Olmstead had managed with the assistance of only three comrades to capture the British sloop *Active* but the victors had then been overtaken and brought into port with their prize by a ship belonging to the state of Pennsylvania accompanied by a privateersman. The Philadelphia prize court awarded Olmstead and his companions only one-fourth of the prize money, dividing the rest between the state and the other claimants. The Continental prize court overruled this decision, awarding the total amount to Olmstead and his crew. But the state of Pennsylvania had the actual money and kept it. For thirty years the sailor engaged in a vain litigation to reap the fruits of his deed of valor. In 1803 he obtained an order from Judge Richard Peters for the money but the state refused to deliver it and Judge Peters, fearful of impeachment, did nothing to enforce his decision. When in 1808 the Supreme Court issued a similar order, the federal Marshal found a company of militiamen drawn up around the state treasury under orders from the Governor and legislature to prevent his access. Pennsylvania patriotism was absurdly aroused by what was one of the most unquestionable of the Court's decisions, and the Governor wrote to Madison to enlist national support. Receiving instead a stern rebuke from the President, the state abruptly abandoned its defiant pose. Olmstead, now an octogenarian, at long last obtained his dues.

United States v. *Judge Peters,* 5 Cranch, 115.

YAZOO LAND FRAUDS

In 1810 the fifteen-year-old Yazoo land frauds came before the Supreme Court in one of its most celebrated cases, that of *Fletcher* v. *Peck*, 6 Cranch, 87. The claimants, after six years of efforts in Congress that were always successfully thwarted by John Randolph, decided if possible to obtain a clear title from the Supreme Court. A suit was accordingly "arranged"* between a vendor and vendee of a portion of the lands in question. The case was twice argued, the Yazoo claimants being first represented by John Quincy Adams, who made a botch of his argument, and by Robert Goodloe Harper, the noted Federalist politician, and on the second occasion by Joseph Story, also assisted by Harper. Story based his contentions, which were accepted by the Court, on James Wilson's clause in the Constitution forbidding "the impairment of contracts" which now began to reveal its full potency. Though, as Marshall was later to admit in the *Dartmouth College Case,* this clause was inserted in the Constitution to prevent the impairment of private debts, it applied equally, the Chief Justice held, to grants by a state legislature which once made could not be revoked. What of the accepted legal principle that a contract is vitiated by fraud? The admitted bribery of the Georgia legislators had been the basis of the revocation. But, Marshall said, it would not be proper for the Supreme Court to go into such questions; it must assume the incorruptibility of every department of the government—even though confessions of the bribery were on file with the grand jury. The effect of the decision was henceforth to validate every grant or franchise from a governmental agency no matter how fraudulently obtained. A result more satisfactory to American capitalism could not possibly have been secured.

The decision, of course, aroused violent criticism. Justice Johnson, in a separate opinion, while concurring in Marshall's reasoning, said pointedly, "I have been very unwilling to proceed to a decision of this cause at all. It appears to me to bear strong evidence upon the face of it, of being a mere feigned

*Warren, *op. cit.,* Vol. I, p. 393.

case. . . . My confidence, however, in the respectable gentlemen who have been engaged for the parties, has induced me to abandon my scruples, in the belief they would never consent to impose a mere feigned case upon this Court." For a justice of the Supreme Court even to suggest that that body had lent itself to a collusive action was sufficiently startling.* Congressman Farrow of South Carolina asserted roundly: "The case before the Court was a feigned issue made up between Fletcher and Peck, with the aid of their counsel, for the purpose of obtaining a judgment of the Court against Fletcher, the plaintiff. . . . Notwithstanding the great zeal of plaintiffs to gain their suits they oftentimes are disappointed; but I never did hear of one who wished to lose his suit, but what he was by some means accommodated. I never did see a Judge who had talents and ingenuity enough to overrule and defeat both parties and their attorneys, and award judgment to the plaintiff, contrary to their united efforts." The decision of the Supreme Court did the Yazoo claimants no good as long as John Randolph was in Congress, but in 1814 Randolph had lost his seat and a bill was pushed through awarding five million dollars to the four land companies.

The principle of the Yazoo decision was reaffirmed a few years later by Marshall in *New Jersey* v. *Wilson,* 7 Cranch, 164, in which a pre-Revolutionary grant to certain Delaware Indians of land exempt from taxation was held to carry the exemption with the title when the land was later sold to white settlers. The exemption applied to the land, not the Indians, Marshall said, and constituted an inviolable contract.

JUSTICE DUVAL

In 1811 two new appointments to the Supreme Court were made possible by the long awaited deaths of Cushing and Chase. One of these new members, Gabriel Duval of Maryland, Comptroller of the Treasury under Madison, was probably the most insignificant of all Supreme Court judges; 58 years old at the time of his appointment, he became a few

---

*Cf. however the account of *Hylton* v. *United States* on p. 69.

years later so deaf that he could not hear a word said in Court—an impediment which did not, however, suggest itself to him as a reason for resignation. The other new appointee, on the contrary, was one of the great historic justices—the same Joseph Story who had recently secured the validation of the Yazoo frauds.

JUSTICE STORY

Belonging to a wealthy Boston family, educated at Harvard, witty, handsome, clubbable, a fluent and fascinating conversationalist, Story was born for success. After a brief term in the national Congress he was elected to the Massachusetts Legislature where he was instrumental in obtaining a charter for the Merchants' Bank of Salem of which he was immediately afterward chosen a director and later president. Although he was nominally a Republican, his associations were now mainly with the Federalists, and Jefferson warned Madison against him. But the position must go to a New Englander, and after it had been declined by Levi Lincoln and John Quincy Adams, and Alexander Wolcott had been rejected by the Senate, it was given to Story as fourth choice. Within three months Jefferson's prophecy had come true; always a conservative at heart, Story at 32 was easily captivated by Marshall's charm and became his right-hand man. Coming when it did, the appointment was most fortunate for the Court, as Marshall knew little of admiralty law of which Story was a master, so when during the War of 1812 the Court was flooded with prize cases it was the new Justice who wrote most of the opinions.

THE COMMON LAW

With the country actually at war, ostensibly at least, over a point of common law—the question of expatriation and impressment—it became difficult to uphold the common law any longer as a settled part of American national jurisprudence. Retreat was made easy for the Federalists by the fact that the

question came before the Court through proceedings instituted five years before, without Jefferson's knowledge, to secure indictments for libel on account of various Federalist attacks upon him. The Court through Justice Johnson denied that it had any jurisdiction under the common law, the question "having been long since settled in public opinion."* In this casual and easy manner was overturned the established theory and practice of the federal judiciary under Jay and Ellsworth.

Story, rightly foreseeing immense difficulties in the absence of any regular code of criminal laws from Congress, struggled valiantly to have the common law maintained, but in 1816 the Court reaffirmed Justice Johnson's decision.† It was not, however, until 1825 that Congress adopted a definite Crimes Act, prepared by Story and sponsored by Daniel Webster.

THE LIVINGSTON CASE

In the year 1812 two of the Justices of the Supreme Court were themselves directly or indirectly involved in cases brought before the Court—in which needless to say they did not sit themselves. The case first settled was that of *Livingston and Gilchrist* v. *The Maryland Insurance Company,* 4 Cranch, 508. In 1804, two years before his appointment to the Court, Brockholst Livingston made a contract with one Baruso, a Spanish merchant trading between Boston and Peru, for the transportation of goods to South America in a ship owned by Livingston. War breaking out between Spain and Great Britain their supercargo was equipped with two sets of papers: one—for production in case of capture by the British—representing the cargo to belong to Livingston; the other—for use in the eventuality of Spanish capture—representing it to be the property of Baruso. Unluckily the British who made the capture found the wrong set of papers, and the ship was taken to Halifax and condemned. Then the American insurance company refused to pay on the ground that it had insured American property which turned out to be according to the prize court Spanish property.

United States v. *Hudson and Goodwin,* 7 Cranch, 32.
†*United States* v. *Coolidge,* 1 Wheaton, 415.

Undoubtedly it was Livingston who had lost the money; on the other hand, his venture had been in violation of both British and Spanish laws, and in order to give him the judgment it was necessary for the Court to make an extraordinary ruling which went to the opposite extreme from that adopted in *McIlvaine* v. *Coxe* four years before, a ruling, namely, that a Spanish merchant residing in America and doing business in American goods must be considered an American.

THE MARSHALL CASE

The other case, that of *Fairfax's Devisee* v. *Hunter's Lessee,* 7 Cranch, 602, concerned a part of the tract of land bought years before from the Estate of Lord Fairfax by the brothers, John and James Marshall. The entire Fairfax holdings having been confiscated by Virginia during the Revolution, a section of the same land had been granted by the state to one David Hunter. Decisions were rendered against Hunter in the state courts in 1794 and 1796, but in 1810 he obtained a reversal of them in the Virginia Court of Appeals from which the case was carried on writ of error to the Supreme Court. It has been contended that John Marshall's own land as well as that of his brother was involved and that he furnished the arguments to Story who pronounced the decision in favor of the Marshall claims.* Both of these contentions, however, have been successfully controverted,† and in any case the opinion of the Court in holding the Virginia acts of confiscation invalid under the British treaties was in entire harmony with all its previous decisions.

The Virginia court of appeals dominated by Marshall's personal enemy, Judge Spencer Roane, now took the bold step of refusing to obey the order of the Supreme Court on the ground that the right of appeal from the state courts granted by the Ellsworth Judiciary Act was wholly unconstitutional. New cause of argument was here presented, and the case once more went to the Supreme Court, this time as *Martin.* v. *Hun-*

---

*Gustavus Myers, *History of the Supreme Court* (1912), pp. 231-41, 270-73, 278-82.

†Beveridge, *op. cit.,* Vol. III, pp. 145-67.

ter's Lessee, 1 Wheaton, 304, where Story reaffirmed his former opinion in a constitutional argument of great weight. Indeed, it would seem to have only been necessary to point to the language of the Constitution itself which in Article III, Section 1, in so many words bestows on the Supreme Court the appellate power in such cases as the one in question. The Virginia court of appeals whether convinced or no, was silenced.

THE WAR OF 1812

The War of 1812 was one of the most perfect examples of human folly that history can show. Though nominally caused by the British impressment of American sailors and interference with American trade, it was violently opposed by the New England States engaged in that trade and was forced upon the country over their objection by the Western and Southern States eager for the conquest of Canada and Florida. Yet in the outcome it was the New England States that gained and the others that suffered. The war led to a tremendous development of Northern manufacturers to supply the domestic market cut off from foreign goods; profiteering and speculation resulted on a huge scale, in which the poorer citizens of the West and South had little share; when this period of over-expansion was followed by the inevitable collapse, it was, as always, those who had benefited least from the period of prosperity who bore the brunt of the disaster. The United States as a nation had its first experience of a great financial depression which steadily deepened from 1817 to 1819, recalling the situation immediately before the adoption of the Constitution. Like causes producing like results, there was once more resort to a mass of stay laws and a flood of paper money. Like causes producing like men, in the new emergency John Marshall came forward to take the place of Alexander Hamilton.

THE DARTMOUTH COLLEGE CASE

The year 1819 was Marshall's *annus mirabilis,* bringing three exceedingly important decisions: those of the *Dart-*

*mouth College Case,** *Sturges* v. *Crowninshield,* and *McCul-loch* v. *Maryland.* The first and third, particularly, revealed his full stature as a political philosopher, for in them the Chief Justice utilized the specific issues before him merely as points of departure for the enunciation of certain broad and fundamental principles, governing a multitude of other cases, and vitally affecting the entire course of American economic and social development.

No one could have guessed that a squabble among the trustees of a tiny college in the forests of New Hampshire, far removed from contact with the business world, would have consequences affecting the very innermost structure of that world. Sixty-five years before, one Eleazar Wheelock who had been conducting a little missionary school for American Indians had sent a fellow-missionary accompanied by a native convert to England in the hope of raising funds. Succeeding beyond their expectations, through the support of the Earl of Dartmouth, they returned with eleven thousand dollars. A charter was then obtained from George the Third for the establishment of "Dartmouth College" for both Indians and whites; by the terms of the charter a self-perpetuating board of twelve trustees was constituted to be "forever hereafter . . . in deed, act and name a body corporate and politick" with absolute authority over the college, including the power to remove the president by majority vote.   With the passage of time the Indians vanished before the incoming white students, and the institution became a college like others; the original trustees died and were succeeded by new ones, mostly Federalists, but with a few Republicans gradually creeping in among them; the first Wheelock died and was succeeded by his son John who became a convert to Jefferson's liberal educational ideas. The younger Wheelock's efforts to modernize the college led to a factional quarrel among the trustees and to his dismissal by the majority. The Reverend Francis Brown of Maine, safe, sane and conservative, was elected in Wheelock's place.

Then the Republican Legislature of New Hampshire took a hand in the proceedings. The revolt was instigated by Gover-

Dartmouth College v. *Woodward,* 4 Wheaton, 518.

nor William Plumer who denounced the provisions of George the Third's old charter as "hostile to the spirit and genius of a free government." In this he was encouraged by a letter from Jefferson in which the ex-President pointed out the absurdity of thinking that "preceding generations . . . had a right to impose laws on us, unalterable by ourselves; . . . in fine, that the earth belongs to the dead, and not the living." An act was passed which changed the name of "Dartmouth College" to "Dartmouth University," increased the number of trustees from twelve to twenty-five, and placed above them a board of twenty-five overseers appointed by the governor and council of state. This new governing body immediately dismissed Brown and reinstated Wheelock.

But the old trustees refused to submit: ousted from the campus, the college authorities took quarters near by where they continued to conduct their classes; a struggle began between Dartmouth College and Dartmouth University as to which was the real Dartmouth; and most of the pupils, with the conservatism which has until very recently been characteristic of American college students, supported the original institution.

What had been an educational question now became a political question between Federalists and Republicans. The case for the college was presented in the state court by Jeremiah Mason, Jeremiah Smith, and Daniel Webster, all of them prominent Federalist politicians; but it was decided by a Republican court. Chief Justice Richardson, in giving judgment for the university denied the validity of the argument of Mason, Smith, and Webster that a charter constituted an inviolable contract. Charters were not contracts at all and had never been held to be such. The constitutional clause regarding the impairment of contracts "was obviously intended to protect private rights of property. . . ." There were no such rights involved in the present case. "Who has any private interest either in the objects or the property of this institution?" If its property were destroyed, "the loss would be exclusively public." In fine, "a corporation, all of whose franchises are exercised for public purposes, is a public corporation."

It is evident that Chief Justice Richardson was here bringing

educational institutions under the police powers of the state as being in present-day language "affected with a public interest." His logic was considered so irrefutable that the university assuming its case before the Supreme Court to be already won, engaged a cheap and mediocre lawyer, John Holmes, assisted by William Wirt who did not even trouble to prepare his speech beforehand. On the other side, Webster made one of his greatest efforts, in which the reasoning was taken from the arguments of Mason and Smith before the state court, as Webster privately though not publicly admitted, but in which the language and superb manner of delivery were all his own. He cited *Fletcher* v. *Peck,* and *New Jersey* v. *Wilson* to prove that a grant was also a contract, and supplemented this by an appeal to abstract justice and "common right." Dartmouth College was an "eleemosynary institution," a "private charity"; the fact that the trustees generously gave their services for nothing increased rather than lessened the moral value of their claims. Did the law recognize "no rights but the rights of money and of visible tangible property?" "Who ever appointed a legislature to administer his charity? Or who ever heard, before, that a gift to a *college* or *hospital,* or an *asylum,* was in reality nothing but a gift to the State?"

Webster closed his written argument with a long and sonorous Latin quotation but seeing from the blank faces of the Court that the meaning had not been understood, he paused a moment and then delivered extemporaneously that emotional peroration which was to be quoted in rhetorical textbooks for half a century with its famous concluding words, "It is, Sir, as I have said, a small College. And yet there are those who love it."

On the Supreme Court, the two avowed Federalists (Marshall and Washington) and the one virtual Federalist (Story) were without difficulty persuaded by Webster's oratory; Duval and Todd, two of the four Republicans remained obdurate; the other two, Johnson and Livingston, could not make up their minds. The case was accordingly continued. During the interim of nearly a year before it was again called up the

university authorities, realizing their mistake in underrating Webster's prowess, engaged the services of William Pinkney, the acknowledged leader of the American bar whose high-flown rhetoric was more persuasive in his day than even Webster's. But meanwhile Livingston and Johnson were induced to consult the conservative Chancellor James Kent of New York by whose weighty arguments they were converted. When at the opening of the February session, 1819, Pinkney arose to address the Court, Marshall quickly announced that the judges had already reached a decision which he proceeded to read.

That the charter was a contract, he said, required "no argument to prove." Through trust in its provisions, large funds had been donated to a corporation established by it. True, no ordinary individual now had property rights involved; but the corporation had, and it too was an individual though of special type. "A corporation is an artificial being, invisible, intangible, and existing only in contemplation of law. . . . It possesses only those properties which the charter of its creation confers upon it. . . . Among the most important are immortality and individuality." In a corporation "a perpetual succession of individuals are capable of acting . . . like one immortal being."

Beveridge points out that the immediate effect of Marshall's authoritative opinion was to reassure "investors in corporate securities" and to give "confidence . . . to the business world." And he quotes with approval Sir Henry Maine's statements that the principle enunciated by Marshall "is the basis of credit of many of the great American Railway Incorporations" and, is in fact, when taken with the rest of Marshall's decisions, the very "bulwark of American individualism against democratic impatience and Socialistic fantasy." Well might business feel renewed confidence when through the mere act of legal incorporation it could put on immortality. Not until seventy years later when a still better defense of business—Big Business especially—would be discovered in the "due-process" clause of the Fourteenth Amendment, would the *Dartmouth College Case* lose its importance as a precedent.

STURGES V. CROWNINSHIELD

The second of the 1819 cases, that of *Sturges* v. *Crownin-shield,* 4 Wheaton, 122, is considered by Boudin to have been "the principal cause of the Jacksonian Revolution." But it was so only as supplemented by later cases, because the full meaning of the decision in *Sturges* v. *Crowninshield* was shrouded in obscurity. The main problem involved was whether state bankruptcy laws violated the provision in Article II, Section 8, of the Constitution giving Congress the power "to establish . . . uniform laws on the subject of bankruptcies throughout the United States"—a power of which Congress had never availed itself. In this situation were the separate states debarred from passing bankruptcy laws of their own? In addition, the issue of retroactive legislation was raised by the particular bankruptcy law in question, that of New York, which explicitly covered debts contracted before the law was passed. On this latter count the law was declared unconstitutional, as impairing the obligation of contracts, by an apparently unanimous Court speaking through Justice Marshall. Was it unconstitutional on the former count as well? Here Marshall's language was far from clear. Nor was the ambiguity removed when in a case immediately following, that of *McMillan* v. *McNeill,* 4 Wheaton, 209, the Chief Justice, again apparently speaking for the full Court, in declaring that one could not be released from the obligations of a contract made in America by the operation of the English bankrupt laws, added that this case did not differ in principle from that of *Sturges* v. *Crowninshield.* When the question was whether that principle applied to all American state bankruptcy laws, to know that it applied to English bankruptcy laws was not particularly helpful.

Justice Marshall's reasoning was sometimes involved, but his meaning was never in doubt whenever he desired it to be clear. The secret reason behind the deliberate obscurity of the Sturges decision was revealed eight years later by that Justice Johnson who was so given to telling tales out of court. In his partly dissenting opinion in the similar case of *Ogden* v. *Saun-*

ders (discussed later) Justice Johnson referred to *Sturges* v. *Crowninshield* as follows:

"If it be objected to these views of the subject that they are . . . inconsistent with the decision in the case of *Sturges* v. *Crowninshield,* my reply is, that I think this no objection to its correctness. . . . The court was, in that case, greatly divided . . . and the judgment partakes as much of a compromise, as of a legal adjudication. The minority thought it better to yield something than risk the whole."

In other words, as appeared in the later cases, the Federalist judges wanted to rule out all state bankruptcy laws and the Republicans wanted to retain them all; being in a minority, the Republicans drove the best bargain they could by agreeing to sacrifice the New York law if the rest were left untouched. It would be interesting to know how many other unanimous decisions of the Court have been reached through this extralegal but most useful method of compromise.

MC CULLOCH V. MARYLAND

In nearly all of Marshall's cases up to this time, including *Sturges* v. *Crowninshield,* the effect of the decisions of the Supreme Court was to prevent governmental interference with private business. In *McCulloch* v. *Maryland,* 4 Whcaton, 316, the effect was to increase the power of government to assist private business. The constitutionality of the United States Bank, a privately administered institution handling governmental and other funds, had been severely challenged in Congress by Madison and others at the time of the establishment of the first bank in 1791. Nevertheless, the bank ran its chartered course of twenty years without the question's ever being brought up in the federal courts. The bank, though an unpopular monopoly, had been honestly and efficiently conducted. The second National Bank, established in 1816 after the state banks had failed to function satisfactorily during the War of 1812, was the opposite of its predecessor in both these respects. Its branches made extravagant loans to their own officials, encouraged rash speculation during the prosperity

of the first years, and then at the beginning of the depression of 1819 called in their loans with the utmost rigor thus increasing the depression,—in a word the Bank of 1819 acted almost exactly as did the banks of 1929. In retaliation, most of the states began to pass laws heavily taxing the branches of the Bank. One of the worst administered of these, the Bank of Maryland, being on the brink of insolvency, decided to test the Maryland law in the courts.*

The case was argued for the Bank by Pinkney, Webster, and Attorney-General Wirt; for the state by Luther Martin, over seventy years old but still hale and hearty after a lifetime of hard drinking, together with Joseph Hopkinson and Walter Jones. There was a magnificent display of oratory on both sides—Pinkney's speech taking three days to deliver—but it is doubtful how far it influenced the decision of the Court. Marshall's opinion, one of his longest and generally considered his ablest, was probably written before the case was heard.

E. S. Corwin's eulogy of the Chief Justice's opinion from the viewpoint of legal style is amply justified. "In this opinion," Corwin writes, "he . . . gives evidence, in their highest form, of his . . . notable qualities as a judicial stylist: his 'tiger instinct for the jugular vein'; his rigorous pursuit of logical consequences; his power of stating a case, wherein he is rivaled only by Mansfield; his scorn of the qualifying 'but's,' 'if's,' and 'though's'; the pith and balance of his phrasing, a reminiscence of his early days with Pope; the developing momentum of his argument; above all, his audacious use of the *obiter dictum*. Marshall's later opinion in *Gibbons* v. *Ogden* is, it is true, in some respects a greater intellectual performance, but it does not equal this earlier opinion in those qualities of form which attract the amateur and stir the admiration of posterity."† And in *McCulloch* v. *Maryland* all these stylistic qualities were utilized as nowhere else in a defense of his political philosophy here revealed in its full merits and defects.

Two separate issues of vast importance were decided in

---

*In the very year of the trial, its nominal protagonist, James W. McCulloch, cashier of the Bank of Maryland, was convicted of misappropriating $3,497,700.

†Corwin, *op. cit.*, p. 130.

McCulloch v. *Maryland*. The first concerned the right of
Congress to create such an instrument as the Bank under the
clause of Article III, Section 2, of the Constitution authorizing
it to pass all laws "necessary and proper" for the execution of
its enumerated powers. The attorneys for Maryland had
asserted that the Constitution was a compact between the
sovereign states; that the powers delegated to Congress must
be interpreted strictly; that since the establishment of a bank
was not listed among these powers and certainly was not
strictly necessary to the functioning of those that were listed,
it must be considered unconstitutional. Marshall insisted, in
the first place, that the Constitution was not a compact but an
outline of government created by the entire people, and that
"the government of the Union, though limited in its powers,
is supreme within its sphere of action." He then went on to
draw a distinction, recognized in the language of the Constitution itself, between "absolutely necessary" and the qualified
phrase "necessary and proper," holding that the latter was
equivalent to "needful," "requisite," "essential," or "conducive
to." "Let the end be legitimate," he said, "let it be within the
scope of the Constitution, and all means which are appropriate,
which are plainly adapted to that end, which are not prohibited,
but consist with the letter and spirit of the Constitution, are
constitutional." Congress had the admitted right "to lay and
collect taxes, to borrow money, to regulate commerce, to declare and conduct a war, and to raise and support armies and
navies"; it was admitted that a bank was an appropriate means
to those ends; the establishment of the Bank of the United
States was therefore constitutional.

Marshall's interpretation of the Constitution, which was in
line with the "loose construction" usually, though not always,
advocated by Hamilton and Webster, was of course violently
attacked by the defenders of state rights. Apart from the
specific question of the Bank, however, Marshall's position in
this instance was, in its implications, much more progressive
and liberal than that of the Jeffersonians. It was plainly more
adapted to the needs of an expanding country; and the wide
powers given by it to the federal government were capable of

being used for all kinds of social and ameliorative legislation.

Exactly the opposite can be said of the second part of Marshall's decision, in which his eagerness to strengthen the central government led him to a much more sweeping declaration of principles than was at all needful to cover the case in hand, a declaration, moreover, in which his devotion to logical dilemmas involved him in verbalism. Adopting Webster's statement that "the power to tax is the power to destroy," Marshall continued, "that the power to destroy may defeat and render useless the power to create; that there is a plain repugnance in conferring on one government a power to control the constitutional measures of another, which other, with respect to those very measures is declared to be supreme over that which exerts the control, are propositions not to be denied. . . . If the controlling power of the States be established; if their supremacy as to taxation be acknowledged; what is to restrain their exercising this control in any shape they may please to give it? . . . The question is, in truth, a question of supremacy; and if the right of the states to tax the means employed by the general government be conceded, the declaration that the constitution, and the laws made in pursuance thereof, shall be the supreme law of the land, is empty and unmeaning declamation."

It may be granted that a verbal dilemma was never more plausibly presented, but it remains verbal, nevertheless, resting upon the assumption that there is no alternative between destructive, confiscatory taxation and no taxation at all. As Corwin remarks, "The terms in which the Maryland statute was couched indicated clearly that it was directed specifically against the Bank, and it might easily have been set aside on that ground." The effect of Marshall's sweeping decision was to create a tax-free haven for investment which was gradually extended by the Court to include all government securities and even state and municipal bonds, reaching a climax in our own day when the Sixteenth Amendment specifically taxing income "from whatever source derived" was declared by the Supreme Court not to apply to income derived from governmental sources. According to President Franklin Roosevelt at least a

third of the wealth of large American fortunes is thus exempt from taxation; for this result, John Marshall by his decision in *McCulloch* v. *Maryland* was primarily responsible.

The decision was not accepted without resistance. The state of Ohio forcibly collected its tax from the Bank, for which act of insubordination the State Treasurer, in a suit initiated by the Bank, was tried in the Circuit Court and was sentenced to prison. His case was appealed to the Supreme Court in *Osborn* v. *Bank of the United States,* 9 Wheaton, 738, on the ground that he was protected by the Eleventh Amendment which asserted the non-suability of a state; but the Bank, again represented by Daniel Webster, once more gained the victory, the Court holding that though a state could not be sued its officials could be.

McCulloch v. *Maryland* and *Osborn* v. *Bank of the United States* were the most important cases in which the Bank was upheld by the Supreme Court but they were by no means the only ones. During 1816-1830 the Bank was involved in forty-four lawsuits, and Daniel Webster who spent a large part of his time in its service either in legal actions or in defending the Bank's interests on the floor of Congress—receiving retainers equally for each type of service—was informed by his employers that the Bank had never lost one of its cases before the Supreme Court. The Bank was unquestionably an agent of eastern and British capital eager to exploit the South and West; it spent huge sums in the corruption of public officials; it was repeatedly investigated by Congress and a mass of evidence was collected against it; but it seemed to be legally impregnable to attack.

Its nemesis did not come until 1832 when its recharter was vetoed by Jackson in a ringing message which denounced the Bank as a creature of special privilege and reasserted its unconstitutionality in despite of Marshall.

GIBBONS V. OGDEN

The last of Marshall's great decisions, delivered in 1824, was in the case of *Gibbons* v. *Ogden,* 9 Wheaton, 1, generally

known as the *Steamboat Case*. It overthrew the monopoly of steamboat transportation on the waters of New York state that had been granted by the state legislature twenty-five years before to Robert Livingston and Robert Fulton, that greatly over-rated individual popularly credited with the invention of the steamboat, actually the achievement of John Fitch. The monopoly was a hindrance to the commercial development of New York City and was a burden on the general public; hence the Supreme Court in abolishing it enjoyed the unprecedented experience of rendering a popular decision. Marshall held that it conflicted with the constitutional clause in Article III, Section 2, giving the United States Congress the right "to regulate commerce." Brushing aside the flimsy argument that "commerce" referred only to articles of trade and insisting that it also covered intercourse and navigation, the Chief Justice once more gave a wide latitude of authority to the national legislature. In attacking the theory of state rights he made the historically irrefutable point that the grant of specific powers to Congress did not, as the states perpetually contended, "convey power which might be beneficial to the grantor if retained by himself" but was instead "an investment of power for the general good"—which really, of course, had been granted by the states precisely because they had found themselves unable to exercise it in their separate capacities. Hence the powers of Congress, though specific, were supreme within their own field. The reasoning was similar to that in the first part of the McCulloch decision except that Marshall drew less from Hamilton and Webster than was his custom.

BROWN V. MARYLAND

Unfortunately, the second part of the McCulloch decision was also extended to a new field two years later in the case of *Brown* v. *Maryland,* 12 Wheaton, 19, in which the state was represented by the later Chief Justice, Roger B. Taney. Here Marshall maintained that articles of commerce imported into a state could not be taxed so long as they remained in the original package; to do so, would be in essence to use taxation

for the purpose of regulating interstate commerce, which the states had no power to do. The Chief Justice again resorted to his favorite dialectic of dilemmas. "Questions of power do not depend upon the degree to which it may be exercised; if it may be exercised at all, it may be exercised at the will of those in whose hands it is placed." Either absolute power or no power; a refusal to admit the basic fact that, in a pluralistic world, power is and must be always relative. According to Marshall's dictum, Congress, which has the admitted power to regulate commerce and to tax, might exercise these even to the point of confiscation—though, as it is hardly necessary to remark, the Supreme Court has never chosen to take his somewhat hasty utterance so literally. The chief effect of the decision has been to hamper the states in their attempts to keep out noxious articles of commerce, regulate labor conditions, or in any way restrain Big Business.

COHENS V. VIRGINIA

During these years, there were other decisions of the Court to irritate the states, especially those of the South. In *Cohens* v. *Virginia,* 6 Wheaton, 264, the question was whether under a Congressional law permitting a lottery in the District of Columbia the lottery tickets could be sold in Virginia where lotteries were forbidden. For doing so, the Cohens were tried and convicted in the Circuit Court, whence they carried the case to the Supreme Court on writ of error. Virginia pleaded non-suability under the Eleventh Amendment. Marshall put aside this plea on the ground that as the case was originally instituted by the state the appeal could not be regarded as a suit against the state, it being merely a later stage of the same case. Though the Court gave judgment against the Cohens, holding that the Congressional Act was not intended to authorize the sale of tickets outside of the District of Columbia, Marshall's strong insistence on the right of Congress to have done so, had it chosen, in spite of the Virginia law, exasperated the state fully as much as would have an unfavorable decision on the immediate question.

GREEN V. BIDDLE

To the ever-growing list of antagonists to the Court, Kentucky was added because of the decision in *Green* v. *Biddle,* 8 Wheaton, 1, which nullified the land laws by which the state had sought relief from absentee ownership through provisions that no claimant should be awarded possession without compensating the actual occupants for improvements made by them—laws held unconstitutional by the Court with regard to Virginia claimants on account of an agreement between the two states in 1791 that land claims should be regulated by the then existing laws of Virginia.   Though the manifest equity of the Kentucky laws induced the Court to grant a rehearing of the case, and though the state was represented by no less a person than Henry Clay, the influence of Marshall's insistence on the perpetual inviolability of any contract once entered into kept the Court in line.

ATTEMPTS TO LIMIT COURT'S POWER

Besides their other grievances, the Southern States were fearful lest the newly asserted power of the national government be exercised against slavery.   Seeing a confirmation of their fears in the Missouri Compromise of 1821, they began to agitate in Congress for action to limit the jurisdiction of the Supreme Court.   During the next decade most of the proposals that are being widely discussed today were presented in one form or another.   Of these, the most radical was that of ex-President Jefferson to limit the tenure of the justices to six years without reappointment save by agreement of both Houses of Congress.   Since, however, this would have required the tedious process of a constitutional amendment, more immediate measures were urged.   In 1821 Senator Richard M. Johnson of Kentucky introduced a resolution to give the Senate appellate jurisdiction in cases involving constitutional interpretation; in 1822 Congressman Andrew Stevenson of Virginia introduced a resolution to repeal the Twenty-Fifth Section of the Judiciary Act and thus deprive the Court of its

right of judicial review, a resolution that was again introduced in 1823; in 1824 Senator Johnson returned to the attack with a resolution requiring the concurrence of five out of seven justices in constitutional cases, and this was favorably reported by the Committee on Judiciary headed by Senator Van Buren; in 1825 an attempt to "pack" the Court was made in a bill to provide three new Western Circuits and three additional justices—a measure greatly needed by the Western States on other grounds.

None of these endeavors except the last came even distantly near to success—a result attributed by defenders of the Court to popular approbation of the institution. A more realistic view would see the cause in the failure of the different states and sections of the country to act together; the South dreaded the North, and the East feared the growing power of the West; Virginia did not support Kentucky on the land law question; and so it went. The Supreme Court was thus able to pick off the separate states one at a time. Furthermore, Congress naturally could not be brought to act against the Supreme Court at a time when the latter was so busily enlarging the powers of Congress. The only place where "the people" had any chance to express themselves directly was in the presidential vote, and they did so unmistakably in 1828 in the election of Andrew Jackson, who was, after Jefferson, the strongest opponent of the Supreme Court that American history has yet seen.

SLAVERY CASES

The fears of the South with regard to slavery were premature. Neither Congress nor the Supreme Court was at all eager to burn its fingers with that question. Marshall, himself a slaveholder, looked upon the institution with an indulgent eye; Story, though fond of denouncing it in theory, was ready to compromise with it in practice; only the Southerner, Justice Johnson, was bold enough to face the hostility of his own section. Virginia and South Carolina had passed laws prohibiting the entrance of free Negroes into those states,

laws in direct contravention of that Congressional regulation of commerce which had been repeatedly asserted in the strongest terms by Marshall.   When the South Carolina law was tested before Justice Johnson in the Circuit Court, he roundly declared it to be unconstitutional, thereby bringing upon himself a flood of abuse throughout the South.   The South Carolina officials continued to enforce the statute, regardless of the federal court's decision, for the next twenty-five years, and the judiciary took no further notice of it.   When one remembers what happened to those states which ventured to resist the judiciary in the matter of the Bank one is impressed by the difference.

Marshall wrote to Story in regard to his colleague's discomfiture: "Our brother Johnson, I perceive, has hung himself on a democratic snag in a hedge composed entirely of thorny State-Rights in South Carolina, and will find some difficulty, I fear, in getting off into smooth, open ground. . . You have, it is said, some laws in Massachusetts, not very unlike in principles to that which our brother has declared unconstitutional.   We have its twin brother in Virginia; a case has been brought before me in which I might have considered its constitutionality, had I chosen to do so; but it was not absolutely necessary, and as I am not fond of butting against a wall in sport, I escaped on the construction of the act."

More serious than the violation of the rights of the free Negroes was the continuance of the slave trade which had been outlawed by repeated Congressional enactments but which flourished like the bay tree nonetheless.   During the 'twenties a number of particularly brazen cases came before the federal courts.   At the outset it seemed as if the judiciary, under the influence of Story, would take a strong stand against the trade; the *Plattsburg,* a slave-ship seized while engaged in it, was confiscated in a judgment affirmed by Story, and in the case of *La Jeune Eugenie,* 2 Mason, 90, he went further and declared the trade to be outlawed by "the law of nations" as well as by the laws of the United States.   This doubtful interpretation of international law, as what it ought to have been rather than as what it was, was reversed by the Supreme Court in *The Antelope,* 10 Wheaton, 66, in the year 1825.

A much more questionable decision—from the layman's viewpoint—in favor of the slave trade was rendered by the Court the same year in the case of *United States* v. *Gooding,* 12 Wheaton, 460. John Gooding, a wealthy and notorious slave-trader of Baltimore, sent to Africa the ship *General Winder,* fitted out with chains and the other apparatus of the trade, and the *General Winder* brought back a cargo of two hundred and ninety Negro slaves. Indicted in Baltimore, he appealed to the Supreme Court to dismiss the indictment, Roger B. Taney acting as his attorney. The Court, speaking through Justice Story gave judgment for Gooding: the indictment, said Story, was "fatally defective" in that it did not state that the ship was fitted out within American jurisdiction—though the evidence showed this; furthermore, the law prohibited an owner from fitting out a ship *"with intent to employ"* it in the slave trade whereas the indictment said the *General Winder* had been equipped "with the intent that the said vessel *should be employed"* in the slave trade.

JUSTICE TRIMBLE

In 1826 the death of Justice Todd led to the appointment, by President John Quincy Adams, of Robert Trimble, 49 years old and for nine years United States District Court judge in Kentucky. In the latter capacity he had zealously supported the federal judiciary on the land law issue, which was probably the main reason for his appointment.

OGDEN V. SAUNDERS

In the following year the thrice postponed case of *Ogden* v. *Saunders,* 12 Wheaton, 213, involving the status of the bankruptcy laws, was at last settled by a four-to-three decision. It definitely marked the beginning of a new era, as in it, for the first time, John Marshall was defeated on a major issue. Though on the specific question before the Court as to whether a citizen of New York could be discharged by a New York law from his obligations to a citizen of another state, the decision was in the negative with Marshall of course in agree-

ment, on the larger question of the constitutionality of state bankruptcy laws in general Johnson, Washington, Thompson, and Trimble voted in the affirmative against Marshall, Story, and Duval. Each of the four concurring Justices delivered a separate opinion; of these the most notable was that of Justice Johnson. After showing by a technical and historical argument that state bankruptcy laws were not outlawed by the Constitution, he went on to discuss the social philosophy behind them in language which revealed that he was about a hundred years in advance of the narrowly legalistic ideas of the rest of the Court.

"It is among the duties of society," Justice Johnson said, "to enforce the rights of humanity; and both the debtor and the society have their interests in the administration of justice, and in the general good; interests which must not be swallowed up and lost sight of while yielding attention to the claim of the creditor. The debtor may plead the visitations of Providence, and the society has an interest in preserving every member of the community from despondency—in relieving him from a hopeless state of prostration, in which he would be useless to himself, his family, and the community. When that state of things has arrived in which the community has fairly and fully discharged its duties to the creditor, and in which, pursuing the debtor any longer would destroy the one, without benefiting the other, must always be a question to be determined by the common guardian of the rights of both; and in this originates the power exercised by governments in favor of insolvents. It grows out of the administration of justice, and is a necessary appendage to it."

This remarkable opinion, so extraordinarily modern in its conception of social psychology, indicates the heights to which Johnson might have risen as a jurist had he not at a relatively early age come under the restraining influence of Marshall.

JUSTICE MC LEAN

After two years of service on the Court, Justice Trimble died in September, 1828. Having vainly offered the position to

Charles Hammond of Ohio and Henry Clay, both of whom declined it, President Adams nominated John J. Crittenden, an able ex-senator from Kentucky, but the Senate, determined that the appointment should be made by the incoming President, Andrew Jackson, refused to act upon the nomination. Immediately after his inauguration, Jackson appointed John McLean of Ohio, a conservative Democrat, 43 years old, for six years a judge of the Ohio supreme court, and latterly United States Postmaster-General. Rumor had it that Jackson put McLean on the Court because he didn't want him in the Cabinet where the Postmaster-General's declared opposition to the Spoils System would have proved embarrassing.

JUSTICE BALDWIN

In 1830 another vacancy occurred in the Court through the death of Bushrod Washington, whose place was taken by Henry Baldwin, a fiery congressman from western Pennsylvania, of quite ungovernable temper and so eccentric that he was often considered insane. He owned the finest law library in the West and had the praiseworthy habit of working all night, while smoking innumerable black cigars, after which three or four hours of sleep seemed all that were necessary for his full recuperation.

On Jackson's recommendation in 1830, a renewed effort was made in the House of Representatives to repeal the Twenty-Fifth Section of the Judiciary Act, but it was defeated by a two-to-one vote. An attempt to limit the term of the judges met with the same reception.

CHEROKEE CASES

Meantime, the Supreme Court was once again embroiled with its old antagonist, the state of Georgia. One of the first treaties ever made by the United States had been that with the "Cherokee Nation" of Indians in Georgia, which was achieved through the efforts of George Washington in 1791. At that time, the white population of Georgia was small, Florida still belonged to Spain, and there was cause to dread an alliance be-

tween the Indians and the Spanish, wherefore the United States was willing enough to recognize the Cherokees as a nation. But in 1823 when the nature of the Indian title first came before the Supreme Court, the situation had changed: Georgia had grown strong, the Indians had become weak, and Spain was out of the picture. The Court decided that the title to the country had first belonged to the British by right of discovery and had passed to the United States at the time of the Revolution; as to the Indians, they possessed merely a "right of occupancy." When gold was discovered on the lands of the Cherokees in 1828, Georgia immediately passed laws abrogating all the ordinances of the Indians and dividing up their lands. An injunction against the state was then sought by the Cherokees. While this was pending in the Supreme Court, an Indian named Corn Tassel, who had killed another Indian, was seized and tried for murder in a white court contrary to the provisions of the treaty. Application was made to the Supreme Court for a writ of error.

In the Corn Tassel case, the Court granted the application, the writ was issued, Georgia ignored it, and Corn Tassel was executed. Georgia had won the first skirmish.

By the time the injunction case came up, Jackson had indicated his sympathy with the attitude of Georgia. Hampered by its own decision in 1823, and uneager for a conflict with both Georgia and the President, the Court decided that the Cherokee Nation was not a "foreign" nation; hence the Court could not take original jurisdiction. "If it be true," said Marshall, "that wrongs have been inflicted and that still greater are to be apprehended, this is not the tribunal which can redress the past or prevent the future." Thompson and Story dissented; the latter, deeply moved by the wrongs of the Indians, wrote to a friend, "Depend on it, there is a depth of degradation in our National conduct, which will irresistibly lead to better things. There will be, in God's Providence, a retribution for unholy deeds, first or last." Barring such an act of special Providence, Georgia seemed to have won a complete victory.

But meanwhile, in order to prevent the local agitation of

white sympathizers with the Cherokees, the state had passed a law requiring all white residents in the Cherokee country to obtain a license and to take an oath of allegiance to the state. Two missionaries, Samuel A. Worcester and Elizur Butler, who refused to obey the law, were tried in the Georgia state court, were convicted, and were sentenced to four years' imprisonment at hard labor. This time the Supreme Court felt able to assume jurisdiction without question by writ of error under the Ellsworth Act and gave judgment against Georgia on the ground that the state had no power to pass laws affecting the Cherokee territory. By this decision the Indians gained that legal status as wards of the United States Government which they have enjoyed ever since. It remained to be seen what Georgia would do in the matter. President Jackson is reported, on somewhat doubtful authority, to have remarked, "Well, John Marshall has made his decision, now let him enforce it." But things worked out to the satisfaction of everyone but the Cherokees. Georgia, after a show of resistance to the Supreme Court, released the missionaries; Andrew Jackson assisted the Cherokees to emigrate unwillingly across the Mississippi to Indian territory; the white settlers in Georgia kept the gold lands. Thus the problem was solved.

LAND FRAUDS

The 1834 term of the Court was mainly concerned with an enormous number of land claims in Florida and Louisiana arising out of the Spanish Treaty of 1819. The circumstances surrounding these claims are admirably presented by Charles Warren: "During the long period while this treaty was pending, awaiting final ratification, a vast number of grants had been hurriedly made by Spanish officials in Florida and elsewhere, many of them without authority, many by fraud of subordinate officers, many with conditions attached which were never performed or expected to be performed by the grantees. . . . Copies of Spanish documents, coupled with the flimsiest excuses for the non-production of original certificates from notoriously rascally Spanish officials, and papers

bearing every earmark of fraud and forgery, constituted the chief evidence for many of the claims presented."*

The rawest of these cases was that of the Arredondo claim,† brought by various eastern capitalists in the name of F. M. Arredondo and Son, to 289,645 acres in northeastern Florida. The claimants produced only the copy of a copy of an alleged original grant by the Spanish intendant of Cuba in 1817; the government denied both the genuineness of the document and the validity of the grant under it, the intendant of Cuba having had no authority to make it at a time when the country was under the jurisdiction of Great Britain, and the Arredondos having failed to perform the requirement in the grant that they settle two hundred Spanish families in the assigned territory within three years. Nevertheless, the Court, with Justice Thompson alone dissenting, gave judgment in favor of the claimants represented by Webster and other leading attorneys.

"In this case," writes Mr. Warren, a little surprisingly in view of his description of the circumstances, "the Court established the public land policy of the government on the basis of the most scrupulous respect for treaties, preferring to preserve the honor, rather than the property of the government."

Speaking of "honor," one is inclined to ask what of the treaty with the Cherokees that had been negotiated by George Washington? What of the treatment of the Seminoles in the *Mitchel Case*‡ about to be discussed?

In this latter, which was decided in 1835, the claim was to no less than 1,200,000 acres in western Florida alleged to have been granted by the Seminole Indians, under confirmation of the Spanish Governor in 1806, to Panton, Leslie and Company, a firm of Indian traders, from whom through a series of conveyances it had reached the usual destination of these claims— a group of eastern speculators—again, as usual, represented by Daniel Webster. As in the *Arredondo Case,* no original deed was presented but merely the copy of a copy of the alleged concession and even this was shown before the Superior Court of

---

*Warren, *op. cit.,* Vol. I, pp. 781-82.
†*United States* v. *Arredondo,* 6 Peters, 691.
‡*Mitchel et al.* v. *United States,* 9 Peters, 711.

Florida to be highly suspicious since the watermark of the paper purporting to have been certified by the Spanish officials in 1806 was apparently of much later date. Nonetheless, the claim was validated by the Supreme Court. In what Mr. Warren calls a "superb opinion" delivered by Judge Baldwin the Court lightly dismissed the question of forgery with the words, "It [the alleged forged paper] is only one of numerous undisputed documents tending to establish the grant, the validity of which is but little, if it could be in any degree, affected by the date of the permission."

As a matter of fact, the rights of Spain were not involved in any of these cases; the actual claimants were not Spanish citizens but American capitalists; under Spanish rule the alleged concessions would not have been validated, as, even if genuine, they were merely preliminary assignments needing, under Spanish law, the confirmation of a final deed to the property— and unlike the suspicious concessions, these original deeds were all to be found in the archives. The Supreme Court was governed much less by "scrupulous respect for treaties" than by the formalistic procedure already established in the *Yazoo* and *Holland Company Cases* whereby it refused to go behind a formal grant to consider the evidence of fraud behind it.

All the claims validated by the Supreme Court had previously been rejected, after exhaustive examination, by the United States Land Office or in the lower courts, and the Supreme Court's decisions were scathingly criticized by Assistant-Attorney-General Call in an elaborate report on the Florida land claims submitted in response to a resolution of the House of Representatives. The Court, however, held to its position, and during the next twenty years validated over ninety claims similar to those discussed and involving millions of acres of government land. Roger B. Taney, who as attorney-general represented the government in the *Arredondo Case* and so was thoroughly familiar with the facts, when he became chief justice of the Supreme Court followed exactly the line marked out by Marshall.*

---

*For a full discussion of all these Land cases, see Myers, *op. cit.*, pp. 331-53, 372-90, 403-39, 446-69.

JUSTICE WAYNE

The time for Taney and a full Jacksonian Court had almost arrived.   On August 4, 1834, Justice Johnson died, to be succeeded by James M. Wayne, 45 years old, once mayor of Savannah, for five years a judge of the supreme court of Georgia and latterly a Democratic congressman, noted for his strong support of Jackson.   Next, the deaf Justice Duval at last resigned, and Jackson nominated for the post his right-hand man, Roger B. Taney.   But Taney, who as secretary of the treasury had carried out Jackson's order, given in defiance of the Senate, to remove the government funds from the Bank of the United States, was rejected by the close vote of twenty-four to twenty-one.   Jackson, enraged, refused to make another appointment.   He could afford to wait.   For his greatest enemy, John Marshall, who had been in feeble health for the last five years, was now fatally ill.

DEATH OF MARSHALL

At 79 years of age, Marshall could look back upon two Courts, that of the Federalists over which he had assumed command so long ago and that of the Jeffersonians all of whom he had outlasted.   He had worthily fulfilled his conscious destiny as a second Hamilton.   Inferior to his great legal predecessor in brilliance and originality, he was his superior in steadiness and cool patient persistence.   Hamilton, after all, had swum with the current even while directing it; Marshall achieved the greater task of stemming the tide, holding back the advancing forces of democracy for over a generation.   Under the most unfavorable circumstances, he had succeeded in establishing the principles of a strong centralized capitalistic government in advance of the facts; when industry should become sufficiently developed to make full use of them it would find in those principles an adequate bulwark for most of its pretensions until that far distant time when a centralized government would turn against it.   When John Marshall died on July 6, 1835, he had won his place as one of the great makers of the America of the nineteenth century.

CHAPTER V

THE COURT UNDER CHIEF JUSTICE TANEY

1835-1864

ROGER BROOKE TANEY, JOSEPH STORY, SMITH THOMPSON, JOHN McLEAN, HENRY BALDWIN, JAMES MOORE WAYNE, PHILIP BARBOUR, JOHN CATRON, JOHN McKINLEY, PETER V. DANIEL, SAMUEL NELSON, LEVI WOODBURY, ROBERT GRIER, BENJAMIN R. CURTIS, JOHN ARCHIBALD CAMPBELL, NATHAN CLIFFORD, NOAH H. SWAYNE, SAMUEL F. MILLER, DAVID DAVIS, STEPHEN J. FIELD.

1. The Career of Chief Justice Taney

OWING to his unfortunate opinion in the *Dred Scott Case,* the reputation of Chief Justice Roger B. Taney fell under eclipse for over fifty years after his death. Only recently has it come to be recognized that the period of his régime represented an interlude of moderate liberalism between the preceding and following conservatisms.* But, as a pendulum always tends to swing to extremes, there is danger today that this contrast will be over-emphasized; just as it is easy to overstress the progressiveness of the White Court of 1910-1920 in comparison with the conservative Fuller Court and the reactionary Taft Court.

The case for Taney and his Court is presented in its strongest light and with marked ability by Charles Warren:

"Taney differed from Marshall in one respect very fundamentally, and this difference was clearly shown in the decisions of the Court. Marshall's interests were largely in the constitutional aspects of the cases before him; Taney's were largely economic and social. . . . Under Marshall, 'the leading doctrine of Constitutional law during the first generation of our Na-

---

*See Carl Brent Swisher, *Roger B. Taney* (1936); Charles W. Smith, *Roger B. Taney: Jacksonian Jurist* (1936); Boudin, *op. cit.,* Chaps. 15-21; Warren, *op. cit.,* Chaps. 21-27; also Felix Frankfurter in *Harvard Law Review,* June, 1935.

tional history was the doctrine of vested rights.' . . . Under Taney, however, there took place a rapid development of the doctrine of the police power, 'the right of the State Legislature to take such action as it saw fit, in the furtherance of the security, morality and general welfare of the community.' . . . It was this change of emphasis from vested, individual property rights to the personal rights and welfare of the general community which characterized Chief Justice Taney's Court."*

No objection to this can be taken as a general picture save that it neglects the shadows which were destined to darken and deepen until they obliterated most of its fair features. Taney and the ablest members of his Court were Southern agrarians; as agrarians they represented the broad interest of seven-tenths of the people as opposed to the three-tenths represented by Marshall; but more narrowly they were as willing to maintain vested interests in land as Marshall had been to maintain them in commerce—and also in land; and as Southerners they were interested in preserving slavery. The last named issue eventually came to absorb the attention of the Court; its attempt to postpone the inevitable conflict merely hastened it; and in the resulting débâcle and loss of influence the benefit of its earlier liberal decisions largely disappeared. The chief lesson to be drawn from Chief Justice Taney's régime is the incapacity of the Supreme Court to function effectively in times of economic and political crisis.

The man who was appointed by Andrew Jackson on December 28, 1835, to succeed John Marshall, and who after two and a half months' stormy debate in the Senate was at last confirmed by a vote of twenty-nine to fifteen, was unquestionably one of the best lawyers ever appointed to the Supreme Court. Born on March 17, 1777, and so nearly 59 years old at the time of his succession to office, he was descended from an indentured servant, one Michael Taney, who came to Maryland about 1660. Michael's son, Michael II, prospered, acquired a tobacco plantation, became sheriff of his county, and gained the status of "Gentleman." Three more Michaels, notable only for successfully marrying into the plantation aris-

*Warren, *op. cit.* Vol. II, pp. 34-35.

tocracy and for becoming, at some unknown date, Roman Catholics, inherited the family property until it passed to Roger B. Taney's elder brother, Michael VI. The future Chief Justice was the first member of the family to be in any way outstanding. He graduated from Dickinson College, studied law in the office of Judge Jeremiah Chase at Annapolis, was admitted to the bar in 1799, and in the same year was elected as a Federalist to the state legislature where in accordance with the attitude of his social class he opposed the introduction of the secret ballot and the enactment of a penalty for buying votes. But though he was twice later returned to the legislature, his position there was of little importance in comparison with his rapid rise in the legal profession.

Taney's success was not in the least due to personal charm or power of oratory, for he had nothing of either. His appearance was the reverse of attractive: he was tall but unusually stoop-shouldered and flat-chested; his mouth was too large, his prominent and irregular teeth were stained with tobacco juice; his gums showed when he smiled—which, perhaps fortunately, was seldom; his rather weak voice was hollow and husky. But all these disadvantages were forgotten soon after he rose to speak through the compelling logic of his arguments, the simplicity of his style, and, at least in his early days, the overwhelming impression of personal sincerity which he created.

TANEY'S ATTITUDE TOWARD SLAVERY

In the summer of 1818, Jacob Gruber, a Methodist minister from Pennsylvania, delivered a violent anti-slavery sermon at Hagerstown, Pennsylvania, and was in consequence indicted for an attempt to incite an insurrection among the slaves. Taney, though he belonged to a slaveholding family, was at this time hostile to the institution, and furthermore he was always keenly interested in free speech; he accordingly took Gruber's case and actually succeeded in gaining his acquittal before a plantation jury. And that without mincing words, for in his speech to the jury he declared:

"Any man has a right to publish his opinions on that subject

whenever he pleases. It is a subject of national concern, and may at all times be freely discussed. Mr. Gruber did quote the language of our great act of national independence, and insisted on the principles contained in that venerated instrument. He did rebuke those masters, who, in the exercise of power, are deaf to the calls of humanity; and he warned them of the evils they might bring upon themselves. He did speak with abhorrence of those reptiles, who live by trading in human flesh, and enrich themselves by tearing the husband from the wife—the infant from the bosom of the mother: and this I am instructed was the head and front of his offending. Shall I content myself with saying he had a right to say this? That there is no law to punish him? So far is he from being the object of punishment in any form of proceeding, that we are prepared to maintain the same principles, and to use, if necessary, the same language here in the temple of justice, and in the presence of those who are ministers of the law.

"A hard necessity, indeed, compels us to endure the evil of slavery for a time. It was imposed upon us by another nation, while we were yet in a state of colonial vassalage. It cannot be easily or suddenly removed. Yet while it continues it is a blot on our national character, and every real lover of freedom confidently hopes that it will be effectually, though it must be gradually, wiped away; and earnestly looks for the means, by which this necessary object may be best attained. And until it shall be accomplished: until the time shall come when we can point without a blush, to the language held in the Declaration of Independence, every friend of humanity will seek to lighten the galling chain of slavery, and better, to the utmost of his power, the wretched condition of the slave. Such was Mr. Gruber's object in that part of his sermon, of which I am now speaking. Those who have complained of him, and reproached him will not find it easy to answer him: unless complaints, reproaches and persecution shall be considered an answer."

By 1819 Taney's legal reputation had risen so high that he was engaged in an important case, in which Daniel Webster also appeared, before the Supreme Court. The Maryland branch

of the Bank of the United States on the defalcation of $3,497,700 by its cashier, Charles McCulloch, kept the matter concealed until the latter's security bonds had been endorsed by various merchants of Baltimore, from whom the Bank then sought to collect. One of these merchants, Solomon Etting, with Taney as his attorney, contested the suit on the ground that by continuing the cashier in office and thereby apparently vouching for his character the Bank had fraudulently procured the endorsement. Chief Justice Marshall took the same position as in other cases of alleged vitiation of contract by fraud. It must be assumed, he said, from the character and reputation of the officials of the Bank that they had not deliberately intended any legal or moral wrong. Taney's experience in this case was an important factor in his later hostility to the Bank and in his becoming a supporter of Andrew Jackson.

With prosperity and wealthy clients, his sympathy for the exploited classes of humanity underwent considerable modification. His defense of the notorious slave-trader, Gooding, has already been mentioned. At about the same time, having become a stockholder in the Union Bank of Maryland, a local rival to the Bank of the United States, and acting as its chief attorney, he was led through this connection to defend several of its directors in a surprisingly discreditable suit. In 1806 the ship *Warren,* owned by them, had sailed, ostensibly for China, but really under secret instructions to the supercargo, for the coast of Chile to engage in smuggling operations. On divulgence of the nature of the undertaking, the crew refused to take part in it, whereupon the supercargo, by connivance with the Spanish authorities, had them imprisoned for periods of from eight months to four years. The ship was confiscated, but eventually the owners in 1824 obtained from Spain $184,011.90 in compensation. The surviving members of the crew thereupon sued for their wages from the time of leaving Baltimore to the time of their return to the United States, and won their case, against Taney's arguments, in the Supreme Court. In giving judgment for the crew, Justice

Story said: "Few cases could be presented under circumstances of more aggravation, and in which the proofs were more clear, that the seamen were the victims of an illegal voyage, for which they never intended to contract, and in which they had no voluntary participation."*

Appointed attorney-general by Jackson in 1829, Taney was consulted by the Department of State as to the legal standing of the stringent South Carolina law forbidding the entrance of free Negroes, which had been declared unconstitutional by Justice Johnson. His reply shows that he had already formulated the illiberal opinions developed at greater length in his famous Dred Scott decision.

"The African race in the United States," he wrote, "even when free, are everywhere a degraded class, and exercise no political influence. The privileges they are allowed to enjoy, are accorded to them as a matter of kindness and benevolence rather than of right. They are the only class of persons who can be held as mere property, as slaves. And where they are nominally admitted by law to the privileges of citizenship, they have no effectual power to defend them, and are permitted to be citizens by the sufferance of the white population and hold whatever rights they enjoy at their mercy. They were never regarded as a constituent portion of the sovereignty of any state. But as a separate and degraded people to whom the sovereignty of each state might accord or withhold such privileges as they deemed proper. They were not looked upon as citizens by the contracting parties who formed the Constitution. They were evidently not supposed to be included by the term *citizens*. And were not intended to be embraced in any of the provisions of the Constitution but those which point to them in terms not to be mistaken."†

Evidently fearful that the law would be declared unconstitutional by the Supreme Court, Taney went on to add, "If the judgment pronounced by the court be conclusive it does not follow that the reasoning or principles which it announces in coming to its conclusions are equally binding and obligatory."

---

*See Myers, *op. cit.*, pp. 366-70.
†Quoted from original manuscript, by Carl Swisher, *op. cit.*, p. 154.

HIS ATTITUDE TOWARD THE SUPREME COURT

In 1832, as secretary of the treasury, in writing Jackson's veto of the Bank bill, Taney went much further. "The opinion of the judges," he said, "has no more authority over Congress than the opinion of Congress has over the judges and on that point the President is independent of both. . . . Each public official who takes an oath to support the Constitution swears that he will support it as he understands it, and not as it is understood by others."

In the whole United States there was no one, not even excepting Andrew Jackson, who was more disposed to limit the powers of the Supreme Court than was the man who was now appointed to head that Court. And at the same time with Taney's appointment, Jackson promoted to the vacant seat of Gabriel Duval a congressman who had introduced a bill to require the concurrence of five out of seven judges on any constitutional question, Philip Pendleton Barbour of Virginia, Speaker of the House in the Seventeenth Congress, the man unjustly characterized by J. Q. Adams as "a shallow-pated wild-cat, fit for nothing but to tear the Union to rags and tatters."

2. *The Progressive Phase of the Taney Court*

Five out of the seven members of the Taney Court had been appointed by Andrew Jackson; the conservative Story and the hesitant Thompson were the only relics of the old Marshall period. And in three important cases of its first term the new Jacksonian Court showed its claws. All of these cases had already been argued more than once before the Court, but no decision had been reached because the judges had been hopelessly divided; in each instance, Chief Justice Marshall is known to have been opposed to the solution now adopted by the triumphant Jacksonians.

The first case was that of *The Mayor of New York* v. *Miln,* 11 Peters, 102. It involved the right of the City of New York to take certain initial steps toward the prevention of pauper immigration. With Justice Story alone dissenting, the Court

held that such action was not in conflict with the commerce clause of the Constitution, as Justice Marshall had maintained, and that it legitimately came under the police powers of the state.

The next case, that of *Brisco* v. *Commonwealth Bank*, 11 Peters, 257, involved the validity of a Kentucky law authorizing a state bank to issue bank notes. In one of the last of Marshall's victories, in the case of *Craig* v. *Missouri*, 4 Peters, 410, a similar Missouri law authorizing state "loan certificates" had been held to violate the Constitutional provision against state bills of credit, but in the present case the Court, Story again dissenting, without directly reversing *Craig* v. *Missouri*, decided that "bank notes" were not bills of credit. Bank notes and loan certificates had a different name; the Supreme Court, while the same in name, was a different Court; hence, a different decision.

THE CHARLES RIVER BRIDGE CASE

The third and most important case, that of *The Charles River Bridge* v. *The Warren Bridge*, 11 Peters, 420, was much more complicated. In 1786 a bridge had been built over the Charles River between Boston and Charleston under a grant from the legislature of toll rights for a period of forty years. Before the expiration of its charter the bridge, proving extremely profitable, collected over thirty times the cost of investment, and its stock rose from one hundred dollars a share to two thousand dollars a share. And incidentally, it had obtained an extension of its charter for another thirty years. Public indignation rising against this expensive monopoly, a second bridge was chartered with toll rights for six years, after which it should revert to the state. The old bridge thereupon brought suit, alleging that the competition of its rival lowered the value of its own charter and was therefore an instance of "impairment of contract."

There could be no doubt as to how the Marshall Court would have decided such a case. But in the present instance the Court, with Story and Thompson dissenting, adjudged that a contract must be interpreted in the light of its own words and

where these did not contain any monopoly implications such could not be drawn from the mere fact of its being a contract. Though, as always, the Court professed to be guided by the law regardless of the economic consequences, Chief Justice Taney devoted a long paragraph of his opinion to these consequences and in its final sentence practically admitted that they were the controlling factors in the decision.

"And what would be the fruits of this doctrine of implied contracts on the part of the States, and of property in a line of travel by a corporation, if it should now be sanctioned by this Court? To what results would it lead us? If it is to be found in the charter to this bridge, the same process of reasoning must discover it in the various acts which have been passed within the last forty years, for turnpike companies. And what is to be the extent of the privileges of exclusion on the different sides of the road? The counsel who have so ably argued this case, have not attempted to define it by any certain boundaries. How far must the new improvement be distant from the old one? How near may you approach without invading its rights in the privileged line? If this Court should establish the principles now contended for, what is to become of the numerous railroads established on the same line of travel with turnpike companies; and which have rendered the franchises of the turnpike corporations of no value? Let it once be understood that such charters carry with them these implied contracts, and give this unknown and undefined property in a line of traveling, and you will soon find the old turnpike corporations awakening from their sleep, and calling upon this Court to put down the improvements which have taken their place. The millions of property which have been invested in railroads and canals, upon lines of travel which had been before occupied by turnpike corporations, will be put in jeopardy. We shall be thrown back to the improvements of the last century, and obliged to stand still until the claims of the old turnpike corporations shall be satisfied, and they shall consent to permit these States to avail themselves of the lights of modern science, and to partake of the benefits of those improvements which are now adding to the wealth and prosperity, and the convenience

and comfort, of every other part of the civilized world.   Nor is this all. This Court will find itself compelled to fix, by some arbitrary rule, the width of this new kind of property in a line of travel; for if such a right of property exists, we have no lights to guide us in marking out its extent, unless, indeed, we resort to the old feudal grants, and to the exclusive rights of ferries, by prescription, between towns; and we are prepared to decide that when a turnpike road from one town to another had been made, no railroad or canal, between these two points, could afterwards be established. *This Court is not prepared to sanction principles which must lead to such results."**

Taney's eyes were evidently upon the future. As evidently, those of Story, who wrote a dissenting opinion nearly twice as long as the Chief Justice's, were upon the past. Basing his arguments upon the British common law, with quotations from Blackstone, Lord Coke (Chief Justice under James the First), etc., etc., he said, "I stand upon the old law; upon law established *more than three centuries ago. . . .* I will not consent to shake their title-deeds by any speculative niceties or novelties." As Boudin remarks, "The *naïveté* with which Mr. Justice Story appeals to the authority of the remnants of the feudal law still lingering in the English Common Law as the proper constitutional rule for the government of the United States is indeed tragic. Again and again he pathetically reverts to the fact that he is placing himself squarely on a rule of law three centuries old—little realizing that the older the rule of law the less serviceable is it likely to be in our times."† A humorous side to the "tragedy" was furnished by Judge Baldwin's separate opinion of one hundred thousand words in which with an assiduity greater than Story's own he met the latter's contentions by citing, case for case, from the common law itself a still greater number of instances on the other side, the whole argument being reminiscent of that once popular amusement of proving anything whatsoever by some passage in the literature of a thousand years collected in the Bible.

Obviously enlightened and progressive as was Chief Justice Taney's opinion, obviously favorable to the general develop-

*Italics ours.
†Boudin, *op. cit.*, Vol. I, p. 390.

ment of business as was the decision of the Court, the Big Business interests of the time resented it as an obstruction to monopolistic opportunities. Their chief legal representative, Daniel Webster, had argued the case for the Old Bridge; Story wrote to Judge McLean, "I think I may say that a great majority of our ablest lawyers are against the decision of the Court; and those who think otherwise are not content with the opinion of the Chief Justice," adding despondently, "There will not, I fear, ever in our day, be any case in which a law of a State or of Congress will be declared unconstitutional." And Chancellor Kent wrote to Story: "I have re-perused the *Charles River Bridge Case,* and with increased disgust. It abandons, or overthrows, a great principle of constitutional morality, and I think goes to destroy the security and value of legislative franchises. It injures the *moral* sense of the community, and destroys the sanctity of contracts."

Before the next term of the Court, the long needed additional Circuits for the Western and Southwestern States were established, adding two new associate justices, the last Jackson appointee, John Catron, chief justice of the supreme court of Tennessee, 51 years old, and a Van Buren appointee, John McKinley, 57, a former United States senator from Alabama.

STATE RIGHTS

In 1838 a case came up, *Rhode Island* v. *Massachusetts,** which showed clearly that the question of state rights depended upon whose state was gored. It involved a matter of disputed territory, between the two states, and Massachusetts, represented by her Attorney-General, Austin, and by Daniel Webster, normally an extreme opponent of state rights, now acted exactly like Virginia and other Southern States in denying the jurisdiction of the Court, Austin going so far as to hint that an unfavorable judgment would be disobeyed by Massachusetts. Undeterred by this threat, the Court, with Taney dissenting, assumed jurisdiction, and eight years later, in the slow manner of the law, decided against Rhode Island.

*12 Peters, 657; 15 Peters, 233; 4 Howard, 591.

The next year three much more exciting cases* arose, all argued together and all turning upon the constitutionality of a Circuit Court decision of Judge McKinley holding that corporations had no power to do business outside of their home states. Here was an agrarian decision with a vengeance. Had it stood, the commercial development of the country would have been paralyzed, and the United States, for good or ill, would have remained an agricultural community. But the other Justices, agrarian though they were with the exception of Story and Thompson, lacked the courage to go to such extreme lengths; the decision, rendered by Taney, was a compromise, upholding the right of the states to prohibit the entrance of foreign corporations by specific enactments, but holding that in the absence of such enactments the corporations were free to enter. Naturally, the decision fully satisfied neither side.

SLAVERY CASES

The same may be said in regard to the adjudication of three slavery cases that came before the Court in 1841 and 1842. One of these, *United States* v. *Schooner Amistad,* 15 Peters, 518, attracted the attention of the public because of the sensational circumstances connected with it. The Spanish schooner, *L'Amistad,* transporting a cargo of slaves kidnaped from Africa, was captured by the slaves, who rose in revolt and killed the captain, and the ship was then brought into port by a United States brig. The Spanish owners demanded the return of their property, material and human. The case for the Negroes was argued by John Quincy Adams, 74 years old, and the Court, through Justice Story, rendered judgment in their favor on the ground that the slave trade was outlawed by Spain as well as by the United States. The slaves, now free, were ordered sent back to Africa.

But meanwhile in another case, *Groves* v. *Slaughter,* 15 Peters, 449, the slave-traders had had their innings. The Mississippi state constitution, adopted in 1832, prohibited the importation of slaves after May, 1833, but in 1835 one Groves

---

Bank of Augusta v. *Earle, Bank of the United States* v. *Primrose, New Orleans and Carrollton Railroad* v. *Earle,* 13 Peters, 519.

of Mississippi purchased on a promissory note a number of slaves from Slaughter, a slave-trader of Louisiana. Having obtained his slaves, Groves then refused to pay for them on the ground that the contract was void under the state constitution. The difficult question as to which of the two scoundrels should be upheld was wholly subordinate to much more important issues: if slaves were persons, did they not come under the protection of the state constitution? if they were property, did they not come under the protection of the federal government through the commerce clause? Undesirous of deciding either way, the Court gave judgment for Slaughter on the technicality that no enforcement law had been enacted in Mississippi to carry out the constitutional provision; therefore the contract, even though unconstitutional, was not illegal. The decision, according to Justice Thompson, did not raise the question of state or federal control over the slave trade, but in separate concurring opinions Justices Taney and McLean not only raised the question but answered it to the effect that the power of control lay in the states, McLean of the free state of Ohio having in mind especially the right to exclude slavery, and Taney of the slave state of Maryland thinking chiefly of the right to protect it.

The third case, that of *Prigg* v. *Pennsylvania,* 16 Peters, 539, brought before the Court for the first time the legality of a state fugitive slave law. Margaret Morgan, conceded to have been a slave of Margaret Ashmore of Maryland, escaped to Pennsylvania in 1832 and resided there in peace until 1837 when her whereabouts were discovered by Edward Prigg, an agent of her former owner. The Pennsylvania law provided that in such cases a preliminary warrant for arrest could be obtained from a magistrate, after which, proof of ownership must be established before a court. Prigg went through the preliminary proceeding but then encountering delay carried off the Negress and her children, one born in Pennsylvania, back to Maryland. His act was a plain violation of the Pennsylvania law, but the Supreme Court decided that the law was unconstitutional as interfering with the exclusive power of Congress to deal with fugitive slaves. This

left the extremely loose Federal Fugitive Slave Act of 1793, which did not require a court decision as to ownership, the only one in force. Justice Story who delivered the opinion of the Court was roundly abused for having gone over to the slaveholders; but there was a joker in his ruling. By prohibiting, as Story took care to do, *all* state laws on the subject, even those designed to support the federal law, he made it possible for the free states to refuse to co-operate in enforcing it, so that Massachusetts the very next year passed a law making it a penal offense for any state official to assist in any way in carrying the Fugitive Slave Law into effect. Shrewd enough to foresee this consequence, Taney, Thompson, and Peter V. Daniel of Virginia—a federal judge appointed associate justice on Barbour's untimely death in 1841—all dissented from Story's interpretation, but their dissent did not affect the law, determined as this was by the majority decision.

THE GIRARD WILL CASE

In 1844 a hilarious case came before the Court, *Vidal et al.* v. *Philadelphia,* 2 Howard, 127, popularly known as the *Girard Will Case.* A philanthropic millionaire, Stephen Girard, had left a bequest of several millions to the City of Philadelphia to found a college for poor white orphans, with the peculiar condition attached that no clergyman should ever be allowed on the campus. Daniel Webster and Walter Jones undertook to break the will. As Story wrote to his wife, "Mr. Girard excluded ministers of all sects from being admitted into his college as instructors or visitors; but he required the scholars to be taught the love of truth, morality, and benevolence to their fellow-men. Mr. Jones and Mr. Webster contended that these restrictions were anti-Christian, and illegal." Webster, with a fifty-thousand-dollar fee in the offing, worked himself up to the point of weeping as he declared that the will opposed "all that is in heaven and all on earth that is worth being on earth." It is recorded that Webster's pathos had moved the Marshall Court to tears in the *Dartmouth*

College Case, but the Taney Court was made of sterner stuff. Without sobbing or weeping, it upheld the will, regardless of the dire effects upon morality prophesied by Jones and Webster.

Meanwhile, important changes were occurring in the Court. Justice Thompson died in 1843, Justice Baldwin in 1844; and in 1845 Justice Story resigned. President Tyler appointed to the first vacancy Samuel Nelson of New York, 52 years old and for seven years chief justice of the state supreme court. To the second and third President Polk appointed Robert Cooper Grier, a Pennsylvania district judge, 52 years old, and Levi Woodbury of New Hampshire, 56 years old, former judge of the state supreme court, governor, senator, and member of Jackson's and Van Buren's Cabinets.

STATE POLICE POWERS

During the decade 1845-1855 a number of cases came up involving state police powers. The most important of these have generally been known as the *License Cases** and the *Passenger Cases,*† the former concerning the first prohibition laws by which Massachusetts attempted to control the traffic in liquor by requiring a license for its sale, the latter turning on Massachusetts and New York laws restricting immigration. Nominally the decisions were made under the commerce clause, the license laws being upheld and the passenger laws condemned, but actually each justice wrote a separate opinion with one eye on the slavery question so that eighteen different sets of reasons were given for or against the two decisions. Of these separate opinions by far the most notable was the one in which Chief Justice Taney attempted to define the vague term, "police powers."

"What are the police powers of a State?" he asked. "They are nothing more or less than the powers of government inherent in every sovereignty to the extent of its dominions. And whether a State passes a quarantine law, or a law to

---

*5 Howard, 554.
†7 Howard, 283.

punish offenses, or to establish courts of justice, or requiring certain instruments to be recorded, or to regulate commerce within its own limits, in every case it exercises the same power; that is to say, the power of sovereignty, the power to govern men and things within the limits of its dominion. It is by virtue of this power that it legislates; and its authority to make regulations of commerce is as absolute as its power to pass health laws, except in so far as it has been restricted by the Constitution of the United States."

In other words, the police powers of the states were as broad as the reserved powers of the states. Had this liberal and logical position been consistently upheld by the Taney Court and its successors, the condition of the United States today would be very different from what it is, and we should not see the Supreme Court constantly ruling on purely local questions of street-car franchises, power rates, etc.

In 1851 and 1852 two cases were decided nominally on Constitutional principles but palpably, in actuality, on the basis of economic considerations. The first, *Genesee Chief et al. v. Fitzhugh et al.*, 12 Howard, 443, raised the immediate problem of whether the admiralty jurisdiction of the federal government was limited to tide waters or extended to all navigable lakes and rivers used in interstate commerce, and also the larger problem whether such questions should be decided by the language of the Constitution or by the intent of its framers—the latter a problem which the Supreme Court has never finally determined, using one or the other method according to the particular decision it has wished to reach, but on the whole favoring the narrower interpretation, by which the intent of the Convention of 1787 must be perpetually carried out, in the absence of Constitutional amendments, regardless of changing conditions in the country. Obviously the determination of that intent is a historical and not a legal problem, a problem complicated moreover by the fact that the members of the Convention were divided, both at the time and later, as to what they really did intend. In the *Genesee Chief Case,* however, all the members of the Court admitted that the framers of the Constitution, influenced by

British precedent and unendowed with prophecy, had considered admiralty jurisdiction to be confined to tide waters. Nevertheless, Taney and the majority of the Court decided that as an extension of admiralty powers would not violate the language of the Constitution it must be granted, and the reason it must be granted was explicitly economic.

"It is evident," said Taney, "that a definition that would at this day limit public rivers in this country to tide-water rivers is utterly inadmissible. We have thousands of miles of public navigable water, including lakes and rivers in which there is no tide. And certainly there can be no reason for admiralty power over a public tide water, which does not apply with equal force to any other public water used for commercial purposes and foreign trade. The lakes and the waters connecting them are undoubtedly public waters; and we think are within the grant of admiralty and maritime jurisdiction in the Constitution of the United States."

A judgment that admittedly overruled not only the Founding Fathers but two decisions of the Court itself (in the less important cases of *The Thomas Jefferson,* 10 Wheaton, 428, and *Steamboat Orleans* v. *Phoebus,* 11 Peters, 175) was too much for the more legalistically minded Justice Daniel who caustically dissented from an opinion, which, he said, held "that the Constitution may, nay must be enlarged, not by amendment in the modes provided, but according to the opinions of the judiciary, entertained upon their views of expediency and necessity."

The "enlargement of the Constitution" in the *Genesee Chief Case* was unquestionably in the interest of economic progress, but in *Pennsylvania* v. *Wheeling and Belmont Bridge Company,* 13 Howard, 518, the majority of the Court were on the side of the past against the future. It involved the existence of a railroad bridge over the Ohio River in what was then still a part of Virginia. The bridge had been authorized by the state of Virginia, but the state of Pennsylvania brought a bill in equity against it as a public nuisance since it interfered with the passage of river steamboats with high funnels. That the bridge was a nuisance to the steamboat companies

was evident; whether the nuisance was also public depended upon whether steamboats or railroads were more useful to the community. On this question the Court divided, the majority supporting the older form of transportation. As Justice McLean said in the majority opinion, "If the obstructions which have been demonstrated to result from the Wheeling Bridge, are to be multiplied as these crossways are needed, our beautiful rivers will, in a great measure, be abandoned." (An almost unique recognition of the legal value of esthetic qualities!) . . . "What would the West now have been if steam had not been introduced upon our rivers, and their navigation had not remained free? Without an outlet for the products of a prolific soil and the instruments of mechanical ingenuity, the country could have made but little advance."

Taney, as usual on the side of progress, had no trouble in annihilating McLean's economic arguments, and he and Daniel united in denouncing the decision as an assumption of legislative authority. Daniel's opinion was as fiery as any criticism from outside the Court could have been:

"I ask upon what foundation the courts of the United States, limited and circumscribed as they are by the Constitution, and by the laws which have created them and defined their jurisdiction, can, upon any speculation of public policy, assume to themselves the authority and functions of the Legislative Department of the government, alone clothed with those functions by the Constitution and laws, and undertake of their mere will, to supply the omissions of that department? Is it either in the language or theory of the Constitution, that this court shall exercise such an auxiliary or rather guardian and paramount authority? Cannot the Legislative Department of the government be intrusted with the fulfillment of its peculiar duties? Such an act as this court has been called upon to perform; such an act as it has just announced as its own, is, in my opinion, virtually an act of legislation, or, in stricter propriety (I say it not in an offensive sense), an act of usurpation."

Heartened by the vigor of Justice Daniel's dissent, Congress for once found courage to overrule the Supreme Court and

within six months after the decision passed an act whereby
the Wheeling Bridge and another of like nature were "declared
to be lawful structures, in their present position and elevation,
and shall be so held and taken to be. . . ." And the Supreme
Court submitted. When the Act of Congress in due time came
before it in a second *Wheeling Bridge Case,* the Court held
that the Act was strictly constitutional.

3. The Reactionary Phase of the Taney Court

In 1851 and 1853 further changes in the personnel of the
Court occurred through the deaths of Justices Woodbury and
McKinley. The new appointments, one by President Fillmore,
the other by President Pierce, marked a break in what had
become the almost uniform custom of requiring earlier judicial experience as a prerequisite to membership in the Supreme Court. Benjamin Robbins Curtis, who succeeded
Woodbury, had studied under Story, was an intimate friend
of Daniel Webster, and could fairly be called a "corporation
lawyer" in the modern sense, having built up a lucrative practice as attorney for various railroads and large commercial
firms. As he was an avowed follower of the legalistic theories
of Marshall and Story, his coming represented an inroad from
the past—or future—into the contemporaneously minded
Taney Court.

John Archibald Campbell of Georgia, appointed to succeed
McKinley, was probably the leading lawyer of the South and
was certainly as devoted to the doctrine of state rights as
Curtis was to the opposite. He had appeared before the
Supreme Court in the pathetic case of Myra Clark Gaines, a
woman who devoted practically her entire life to proving her
legitimacy and who at last, after her cause was seven times
appealed to the Supreme Court, succeeded, largely through
Campbell's efforts, in establishing, shortly before her death,
the conditions of her birth. The owner of an inherited plantation, Campbell, at the time of his appointment, emancipated
all his slaves. He was the most scrupulous, and also, on the
whole, the most liberal-minded of the members of the Court.

LAND CASES

Following the Mexican War, there was a renewed orgy of land-grabbing, particularly in California, through the old method of producing fraudulent grants from the former government. In deciding the numerous cases of this kind that came before it, the Court usually validated the grants according to the principles laid down by John Marshall. In the particularly scandalous case of *Fremont* v. *United States,* 17 Howard, 542, in which General John Fremont claimed a "floating grant" from a Mexican governor of 44,386.33 acres, entitling him to that extent to any public land he might select in California, Chief Justice Taney, in the majority opinion upholding Fremont's claim—even though it had never been confirmed by the Mexican Departmental Assembly as required by Mexican law—cited Marshall's Arredondo decision as a ruling precedent. Justices Campbell and Catron (who would probably have been joined by Daniel had he sat in the case) vigorously dissented, stating that no California claim had been advanced more thoroughly "infected with fraud or forgery." In the similar Larkin-Misroon decision, from which Campbell and Daniel dissented, the latter said that the "avowed character" of the alleged grants "ought to consign them to the sternest reprobation."*

BANK CASES

In 1854 a still more important economic case came up, involving financial interests all over the United States. *Piqua Branch of the State Bank of Ohio* v. *Knoop,* 16 Howard, 369, concerned a bank organized under an Ohio law of 1845 which allowed banks a lower taxation rate than other corporations; this law was repealed by a substitute Act of 1851, but the bank, with the authority of Marshall's *Fletcher* v. *Peck* decision behind it, claimed the new law to be unconstitutional as constituting an impairment of contract. Chief Justice Taney,

---

*For full discussion of these and other Land cases under Taney, see Myers, *op. cit.*, pp. 409-39, 449-67.

who through the force of early association always had a weakness for state banks in striking contrast to his animosity toward a national bank, joined the majority, with certain qualifications, in giving judgment for the bank on the ground that it possessed an irrepealable contract. From this Marshall-like decision Justices Campbell, Daniel, and Catron dissented, Campbell taking occasion to express his opinion of the plaintiffs in pointed words. After referring to "the greedy appetites of adventurers for monopolies and immunities from the State right of Government," he continued, "We cannot close our eyes to their insidious efforts to ignore the fundamental laws and institutions of the States, and to subject the highest popular interests to their central boards of control and directors' management."

The Ohio supreme court, going back to the Jacksonian position of denying the constitutionality of the Judiciary Act of 1789, refused to accept the decision, and at about the same time California, smarting from the Court's validation of land frauds, took similar action on the same grounds in another case. Eventually, Ohio yielded to the extent of incorporating the repeal statute in an amendment to the state constitution which was then itself attacked as unconstitutional in the case of *Dodge* v. *Woolsey,* 18 Howard, 331. "Thus," in the words of Charles Warren, "confronted for the first time with the solemn question of its power to hold a Constitution of a sovereign State to be invalid, the Court did not flinch in its determination to hold a State to strict compliance with honesty in contracts."* "The moral obligations never die," the Court announced. "If broken by States and Nations, though the terms of reproach are not the same with which we are accustomed to designate the faithlessness of individuals, the violation of justice is not the less."

That such words as "honesty," "moral obligations," and "justice" have various applications was shown in the stinging reply of Justice Campbell, who was again joined in dissent by Justices Daniel and Catron. If, he asked, a state finds itself "the victim of vicious legislation, its property alienated,

---

*Warren, *op. cit.,* Vol. II, pp. 254-55.

its powers of taxation renounced in favor of chartered associations, what remedy have the people against the misgovernment? Under the doctrines of this court none is to be found in the Government, and none exists in the inherent powers of the people, if the wrong has taken the form of a contract. The most deliberate and solemn acts of the people would not serve to redress the injustice, and the over-reaching speculator upon the facility or corruption of their legislature would be protected by the powers of this court in the profits of his bargain."

It will be observed that the Supreme Court had now returned to type. The Taney Court, including Chief Justice Taney himself,. had become a Marshall Court, so far as the majority of its members was concerned. And, interestingly, political theory as always varying with economic needs, it was now the Northern States that were asserting the Jacksonian doctrine of state rights and the authority of the states to nullify the decisions of the Supreme Court.

THE DRED SCOTT CASE

The unpopularity of the federal judiciary throughout the North was enhanced by the consistent enforcement of the Fugitive Slave Law by the Circuit Courts in the steadily increasing instances of its violation by Northern citizens. Still, the Supreme Court skillfully avoided committing itself on the fundamental question of the existence of slavery until its fatal decision in the *Dred Scott Case* of 1856, a decision which precipitated the Civil War and incidentally deprived the Court of influence for over ten years.

The political background of the *Dred Scott Case*—and it was practically all political background—was an outgrowth of the Mexican War. After that event, the South, expecting to establish slave states in New Mexico, Arizona, and southern California, at first looked upon the Missouri Compromise, which would give it that right, as a veritable Magna Charta; but later, when it was recognized that the soil of the two former states precluded any extensive growth of cotton or to-

bacco, and when California had been admitted as a free state and the immense territory of the Northwest was being opened up for settlement, the South concentrated its efforts on getting rid of the Missouri Compromise, now denying the right of the federal government to exclude slavery from the territories.

The legal aspects of the case were much simpler. Dred Scott, a slave of one Doctor Emerson of Missouri, was taken by him to Rock Island in the free state of Illinois where the family resided for two years after which it moved to Fort Snelling then in the territory of Wisconsin (now in Minnesota) for another two years and then returned to Missouri. Dred Scott, an illiterate and shiftless old man, learned too late that he had been free for four years without knowing it, and instituted suit to recover that status. The lower state court gave judgment in his favor, but the decision was reversed by the state supreme court on the ground that on his return to the slave state of Missouri Scott became a slave whatever his status might have been in Illinois or Wisconsin—a decision strictly in harmony with that of the Supreme Court in the similar case of *Strader* v. *Graham,* 10 Howard, 82, in 1851, in which it had been decided by a unanimous Court that the temporary residence of a Kentucky slave in the free state of Ohio did not make him any the less a slave on his return to Kentucky.

Meanwhile Emerson died, and his widow married Dr. C. C. Chaffee, an abolitionist of Massachusetts who wanted to secure a new trial for Scott in the federal courts. For this purpose the ownership of the Negro was nominally transferred to Mrs. Chaffee's brother, John F. A. Sanford of New York (the name appearing incorrectly as Sandford in the Court report). Scott then brought suit as a citizen of Missouri unjustly held in slavery by a citizen of New York. In order to open up the whole question, Sanford submitted a "plea in abatement" denying the jurisdiction of the Court on the ground that even if Scott were a free Negro he could not be a citizen because he belonged to a degraded race which under the Constitution could never be entitled to citizenship. The Circuit Court of Missouri held that Scott was enough of a citizen to plead in court,

and the case was then argued "on its merits" resulting in a jury decision that Scott under the laws of Missouri was still a slave.   The next and final step was to carry the case to the Supreme Court on writ of error.

Dred Scott v. *Sandford,* 19 Howard, 393, was first argued before the Supreme Court early in 1856.   A majority agreement was easily reached, with Curtis and McLean dissenting, to affirm the decision reached in the Circuit Court that by Missouri law Scott was a slave—a judgment in accord with the state court's decision and with *Strader* v. *Graham.* Justice Nelson was commissioned to write the opinion, but owing to the fact that a presidential election would occur in the fall, it was agreed to withhold the decision until afterward.   Then the election of Buchanan, a Southern sympathizer, emboldened the Southern members of the Court to think that the time had come—in the interest of the whole country, as they viewed it— to settle the Missouri Compromise as well as Dred Scott, a thought which crystallized to a determination when it was learned that McLean, who had notorious presidential aspirations, was going to defend the Compromise in his minority opinion, in which he intended to give a history of slavery in the United States from the Free Soil point of view.   The four Southern justices, Wayne and Campbell of Georgia, Catron of Tennessee, and Daniel of Virginia, accordingly asked that the case be reheard, and, after this was done, they persuaded Taney that the judgment of the Circuit Court must be reversed, instead of affirmed, on the ground of lack of jurisdiction, to be proved by holding unconstitutional the Missouri Compromise, from which Scott's claim of citizenship in part derived.

In order to obtain the concurrence of a Northern judge, lest the decision appear as sectional as it really was, Justice Catron asked President-elect Buchanan to use his influence with Justice Grier; the influence was used successfully; and Buchanan was notified that the Missouri Compromise would be considered by the Court.   Thus it was with some knowledge of the nature of the approaching decision that Buchanan in his inaugural adjured the nation to accept it, "whatever it might be."

The remolding of the Court's opinion along the new lines was difficult, inasmuch as it was necessary at the same time to assert lack of jurisdiction to consider the case and yet to consider it; but Taney was equal to the emergency just as Marshall had been in the similar exigency of *Marbury* v. *Madison*. Omitting the legal technicalities with which his opinion bristled, his argument was beautifully simple, consisting of three logical steps: (1) The Court could not have jurisdiction because in general the Constitution prohibited the degraded race of Negroes from becoming citizens; (2) the Court could not have jurisdiction because, specifically, Scott's residence in Wisconsin had not affected his status, since the Missouri Compromise was unconstitutional; (3) the Court could not have jurisdiction because, again specifically, Scott's status in Illinois could not affect his status in Missouri. Hence, there was no jurisdiction, there was nothing to argue about, and Scott was still a slave. Granting that the logic was arranged to meet the situation, it must be admitted that it was arranged skillfully. The chief objection to the argument is that Taney failed to prove any of the three points.

His utterances on the first point were those which gave greatest offense. In violent contrast to his method in the case of *Genesee Chief,* he here sought to establish the intent of the framers of the Constitution by inference from the general sentiment of their time.

The beginning of his main argument ran as follows. "The question is simply this: Can a Negro, whose ancestors were imported into this country, and sold as slaves, become a member of the political community formed and brought into existence by the Constitution of the United States, and as such entitled to all the rights, and privileges, and immunities guarantied by that instrument to the citizen?

"It is difficult at this day," he went on, "to realize the state of public opinion in relation to that unfortunate race, which prevailed in the civilized and enlightened portions of the world at the time of the Declaration, and when the Constitution of the United States was framed and adopted. But the public history of every European nation displays it in a manner too plain to be mistaken.

"They had for more than a century before been regarded as beings of an inferior order, and altogether unfit to associate with the white race, either in social or political relations; and so far inferior, that they had no rights which the white man was bound to respect; and that the Negro might justly and lawfully be reduced to slavery for his benefit. He was bought and sold, and treated as an ordinary article of merchandise and traffic, whenever a profit could be made by it. This opinion was at that time fixed and universal in the civilized portion of the white race. It was regarded as an axiom in morals as well as in politics, which no one thought of disputing, or supposed to be open to dispute; and men in every grade and position in society daily and habitually acted upon it in their private pursuits, as well as in matters of public concern, without doubting for a moment the correctness of this opinion."

That these statements went far beyond the facts Justice Curtis in his dissenting opinion had no difficulty in showing. The individual opposition to slavery on the part of even many Southerners at the time of the Revolution, including such men as Washington, Jefferson, Madison, and Patrick Henry, and the collective opposition of the Quakers were of course well known by Justice Taney and, unfortunately for his opinion, were equally well known by many of his readers. The opinion, while ostensibly an objective historical account, in reality expressed his own views as they had been uttered many years before when he was attorney-general; without knowing this, the public rightly detected the subjective character of the opinion from the very gusto of its language.

Taney made short work of the Declaration of Independence by the simple method of denying that it meant what it said. "It is too clear for dispute," he asserted, "that the enslaved African race were not intended to be included, and formed no part of the people who framed and adopted this declaration [though some of them were counted good enough to be enrolled among the soldiers who fought for it]; for if the language, as understood in that day, would embrace them, the conduct of the distinguished men who framed the Declaration of Independence would have been utterly and flagrantly in-

consistent with the principles they asserted. . . ." Again the unwarranted assumption that the members of a group were all of one mind, coupled with the argument in John Marshall's style that "distinguished men" could not possibly have been inconsistent.

The malicious delight with which Taney went on to expose the hypocrisy in much of the Northern attitude was too plain to escape recognition. "It is very true," he said, "that in that portion of the Union where the labor of the Negro race was found to be unsuited to the climate and unprofitable to the master, but few slaves were held at the time of the Declaration of Independence; and when the Constitution was adopted, it had entirely worn out in one of them, and measures had been taken for its gradual abolition in several others. But this change had not been produced by any change of opinion in relation to this race; but because it was discovered, from experience, that slave labor was unsuited to the climate and productions of these States; for some of the States, where it had ceased or nearly ceased to exist, were actively engaged in the slave trade, procuring cargoes on the coast of Africa, and transporting them for sale to those parts of the Union where their labor was found to be profitable, and suited to the climate and productions. And this traffic was openly carried on, and fortunes accumulated by it, without reproach from the people of the States where they resided. And it can hardly be supposed that, in the States where it was then countenanced in its worst form—that is, in the seizure and transportation—the people could have regarded those who were emancipated as entitled to equal rights with themselves. . . .

"The first step taken by Connecticut upon this subject was as early as 1774, when it passed an act forbidding the further importation of slaves into the State. But the section containing the prohibition is introduced by the following preamble:

" 'And whereas the increase of slaves in this State is injurious to the poor, and inconvenient.'

"This recital would appear to have been carefully introduced, in order to prevent any misunderstanding of the mo-

tive which induced the Legislature to pass the law, and places it distinctly upon the interest and convenience of the white population—excluding the inference that it might have been intended in any degree for the benefit of the other. . . ."

The second part of Taney's opinion, invalidating the prohibition of slavery north of thirty-six degrees and thirty minutes north latitude, as enacted by the Missouri Compromise, was obliged at the outset to hurdle Article III, Section 4, of the Constitution giving Congress the power "to dispose of and make all needful rules and regulations respecting the territory or other property belonging to the United States." But after having silenced the Declaration of Independence, Taney was not to be daunted by a mere section of the Constitution; it, too, did not mean what it apparently said. "In the judgment of the Court," he stated, "that provision has no bearing on the present controversy, and the power there given, whatever it may be, is confined, and was intended to be confined, to the territory which at that time belonged to, or was claimed by, the United States, and was within their boundaries as settled by the treaty with Great Britain, and can have no influence upon a territory afterwards acquired from a foreign Government. It was a special provision for a known and particular territory, and to meet a present emergency, and nothing more."

But whatever the regulatory powers of Congress over the territories, Taney continued in what was to prove the one permanently influential part of his opinion, it certainly had no right to violate the Fifth Amendment and confiscate property without just compensation. The rights of property, he said, "are united with the rights of persons and placed on the same ground by the Fifth Amendment to the Constitution, which provides that no person shall be deprived of life, liberty and property without due process of law. And an act of Congress which deprived a citizen of the United States of his liberty or property merely because he came himself or brought his property into a particular territory of the United States, and who had committed no offense against the laws, could hardly be dignified with the name of due process of

law." As Corwin points out* Taney's argument here begged the question of the constitutionality of the Missouri Compromise—since if the Act was constitutional the slave-owner did commit an offense against the laws in bringing his slaves into free territory—unless the Chief Justice had in mind a recondite interpretation of "due process" which he did not elaborate and which would not be accepted by the Supreme Court until fifty years later. Furthermore, as Corwin also remarks,† the prohibition of the slave trade, the Embargo Act of Jefferson, and the recent prohibition laws all in effect confiscated property much more directly than did the Missouri Compromise.

Even the third main point in Taney's argument was not beyond criticism, since the Missouri laws to which he appealed so confidently were many, and the two state courts had not agreed in their interpretation of them. It all depended upon which laws one selected as the most authoritative.

Justices Curtis and McLean filed dissenting opinions, Curtis dealing with the historical aspects of the case and McLean attempting to refute Taney's use of the Fifth Amendment by making a distinction between property in persons and other kinds of property, a distinction actually recognized by more than half the Union—a contemporary point that Taney in happier days and on other issues might have been disposed to consider of importance—but certainly not a distinction openly recognized in the Constitution.

Justice Nelson filed his original opinion, concurrent in so far as it agreed with the disposition made of Scott but differing entirely from Taney's in its reasoning. The other justices filed brief opinions supporting the Chief Justice. But there was considerable delay between the filing of the minority and majority opinions, and a rumor went around that Taney was adding to his original statement in order to answer the arguments of Curtis (the latter always insisting privately that there were many pages in Taney's published opinion which he had never delivered orally). An acrimonious correspondence on

*Corwin, *op. cit.*, pp. 147-51.
†*Ibid.*, pp. 151-52.

this subject followed between Curtis and Taney until Curtis became so disgusted that he resigned from the Court. Buchanan nominated as his successor Nathan Clifford of Maine, a Northerner with Southern sympathies, 54 years old, formerly attorney-general in Polk's Cabinet. The Senate confirmed his appointment by the narrow margin of three votes.

Meanwhile the decision had created throughout the country a tempest the like of which had never before been seen. Seward in the Senate denounced it as the product of a deal between the President and the Supreme Court, and this charge of collusion was reiterated again and again by Lincoln in his debates with Douglas. Boldly, Lincoln took his stand upon the constitutional theory of Jefferson and Jackson: the decision however bad, must be accepted until reversed but there was nothing to prevent Congress from doing the reversing. As to the vaunted independence of the Court, "our judges," he said, "are as honest as other men and not more so. They have, with others, the same passions for party, for power, and the privilege of their corps. . . . Their power is the more dangerous as they are in office for life, and not responsible, as the other functionaries are, to the elective control."

But the power of the Supreme Court was no longer "dangerous" north of the Mason and Dixon line. The Dred Scott decision ended the Court's influence in the free states. When a peculiarly brazen violation of the Fugitive Slave Law, which had occurred in 1854 when a slave was openly rescued in Wisconsin by an abolitionist editor named Booth, came before the Court in 1859 in the case of *Ableman* v. *Booth,* and the Court upheld the law in one of Taney's most eloquent decisions, the state supreme court scornfully refused to obey the decision, and there the matter rested. And in 1860 the Dred Scott decision elected Lincoln president.*

---

*For detailed study of the *Dred Scott Case,* its background and its effects, see the following: Boudin, *op. cit.,* pp. 1-31; Hampton L. Carson, "Note on the Dred Scott Case," *American Law Review* (1902), Vol. 36; Corwin, *op. cit.,* pp. 129-57, also "The Dred Scott Case in the Light of Contemporary Legal Doctrine," *American Historical Review* (1911), Vol. 17; Elbert W. H. Ewing, *Legal and Historical Status of the Dred Scott Case* (1909); Timothy Farrar, "The Dred Scott Case," *North American Review* (Oct., 1857), Vol. 85; John Lowell and Horace Gray, "Legal Re-

4.   The Taney Court in the Civil War

In 1860 Justice Daniel died, in 1861 Justice McLean, and in the latter year Justice Campbell resigned in order to join the Confederacy.   Deprived of its four strongest associate justices—Campbell, Daniel, Curtis and McLean—the Court was in no condition to maintain its power against what Taney regarded as the usurpations of President Lincoln.   Within six months after the beginning of the Civil War, the conflict between the Chief Justice and the President came to a head in the Circuit Court of Maryland in the case of *Ex Parte Merryman*.* Had a popular vote been taken in Maryland that slave state would probably have joined the Confederacy; lying as it did between the national capital and the free states, its possession was essential to the North; under these circumstances Lincoln felt himself compelled to authorize the military to enforce the sternest measures of repression in all instances of suspected disloyalty.   One Merryman, accused of secretly raising rebel forces, was arrested by General Cadwallader and temporarily imprisoned in Fort McHenry awaiting military trial, whereupon Merryman applied to Taney for a writ of habeas corpus.   In spite of the fact that the writ had already been suspended by Lincoln under his vague "war-time powers" as Commander-in-Chief of the Army, Taney issued it and, when his action was disregarded by Cadwallader, issued a further order for the General's arrest for contempt of court. When this, too, was disregarded, Taney wrote out his "decision" and sent it to the President, in which he held that Congress alone had the legal right under the Constitution to suspend the writ of habeas corpus.   He went on to cite other instances of the suppression of civil liberties, and then said :

"These great and fundamental laws, which congress itself could not suspend, have been disregarded and suspended, like the writ of habeas corpus, by a military order supported by

---

view of the Dred Scott Case," *Law Reporter* (June, 1857) ; Myers, *op. cit.,* pp. 469-82; Smith, *op. cit.,* pp. 155-76; Swisher, *op. cit.,* pp. 476-523; Warren, *op. cit.,* Vol. II, pp. 279-320.   The full text of Taney's opinion is given in Doskow, *op. cit.*
*Federal Case 9, 487.

force of arms. Such is the case now before me, and I can only say that if the authority which the constitution has confided to the judiciary department and judicial officers, may thus, upon any pretext or under any circumstances, be usurped by the military power, at its discretion, the people of the United States are no longer living under a government of laws, but every citizen holds life, liberty and property at the will and pleasure of the army officer in whose military district he may happen to be found."

However liable to bias from group or sectional interests, Taney was never lacking in courage (a notable contrast to Marshall in this respect); in writing this opinion, he fully expected to be himself imprisoned in Fort McHenry as a result of it. Lincoln was far too wise and fundamentally tolerant to take such a false step, but he was determined to maintain his position. The old saying, "Necessity knows no law," would be truer if it read, "Necessity can always find a law." On submission of the problem to Attorney-General Edward Bates, the latter upheld Lincoln's stand, Congress did not object, the methods applied in Maryland were extended to the other Border States, and Lincoln, fortunately for the country a man of most undictatorial disposition, was allowed to exercise most of the powers of a military dictator.

With his unfavorable opinion of the judiciary, the President was slow to fill the three vacancies on the Supreme Court. But in 1862 the question of the legality of the Northern blockade of Southern ports was on the horizon, and Lincoln decided that the time had come to make appointments. His range of choice was limited by other considerations; he had political debts to pay, and the war could not be prosecuted to a successful conclusion without the support of Big Business. Accordingly, the first appointment, vigorously urged by Senators Sherman and Wade of Ohio, was that of Noah H. Swayne,* a prominent corporation lawyer of that state, 57 years old, entirely without judicial experience. Having thus paid his necessary obeisance to politics and industry, Lincoln

---

*The reader will find rather unsavory details of Swayne's legal career in Myers, *op. cit.*, pp. 497-98.

felt free to exercise his own judgment in two other appointments, which were admittedly among the best ever made. One went to Samuel F. Miller of Iowa, also without judicial experience but with a wide and varied legal practice and with a "judicial mind"—something not always produced by judicial experience; the other place was given to Lincoln's personal friend, David Davis, for fourteen years judge of the Eighth Judicial Circuit in Illinois; Miller was 46 years old, Davis 47.*

The question of the blockade did come before the Court in the *Prize Cases,* 2 Black, 635, which were decided in March, 1863. The argument against the government was that war had never been declared by Congress; therefore no war legally existed, even though one had been going on for two years; therefore the blockade of Southern ports was illegal. To be sure, Congress by its Act of July 13, 1861, had expressly authorized the President to declare the existence of an "insurrection," to forbid commerce between the rebels and the other states, and to seize and confiscate property engaged in such traffic. But going somewhat further, the United States was undoubtedly seizing Confederate property destined not for the other states but for foreign parts.

Without the blockade the national government could hardly have carried on the war successfully; thus the entire war as well as the blockade was on trial before the Court. And the government won its case by the narrowest possible margin, a five-to-four decision, Lincoln's three new justices joining with Wayne and Grier to defeat Taney, Nelson, Catron, and Clifford.

The majority decision, delivered by Grier, rested the case on what might be called "the logic of facts." The opposing argument, according to Grier, assumed "that where a civil war exists the party belligerent claiming to be sovereign, cannot, for some unknown reason, exercise the rights of belligerents. . . . The insurgent may be killed on the battle field or by the executioner; his property on land may be confiscated under the municipal law; but the commerce on the ocean, which

---

*Even Myers can find nothing to say against these two appointments, which is the best possible testimony to their merit.

supplies the rebels with means to support the war, cannot be made the subject of capture under the laws of war, because it is *'unconstitutional'!!!"**

Justice Nelson in reply admitted that "in one sense, no doubt this is war," but insisted that this was true only "in a material sense" and had "no relevancy or weight when the question is what constitutes war in a legal sense."   And a real, true, genuine, legal war required a declaration by Congress.   Had the majority of the Court agreed with Justice Nelson, the blockade, no doubt, would still have been continued "in a material sense," and some more or less legal means would have been found to get around the Court's decision.   In actual fact, as opposed to theory, it was less the existence of the Union that was at stake, as some writers have thought, than it was the existence of the Supreme Court.

On the same day as the decision in the *Prize Cases,* Lincoln made another appointment, as Congress by creating a new Circuit for Oregon and California had raised the number of the justices to ten.   His nominee was Stephen J. Field, 46 years old, son of a Connecticut clergyman, brother of Cyrus W. Field, inventor of the submarine cable, and of David Dudley Field, the wealthy New York corporation lawyer who later became the chief attorney for Jay Gould and James Fiske, Jr. Stephen J. Field's own ability was unquestionable; in California, to which he emigrated at the time of the gold rush, he acquired wealth through land speculations and rose to be chief justice of the state supreme court; his appointment was mainly owing to the insistence of Governor Leland Stanford of California, one of the four owners of the Central Pacific Railroad whose fraudulent methods were destined to furnish the chief scandal of the decade.   For thirty-six years after his appointment Field was to be a very Rock of Gibraltar in the defense of capitalism.

After their futile gesture in the *Prize Cases,* the Taney Justices practically accepted their defeat; interference with the government on the questions of military commissions and the issue of paper legal tender, raised respectively in *Ex Parte*

*Italics and triple exclamation points Justice Grier's.

Vallandigham, 1 Wallace, 243, and *Roosevelt* v. *Meyer,* 1 Wallace, 512, was avoided by the easy method of declining jurisdiction.   To all intents and purposes, the Supreme Court became a silent Court for the duration of the war.   Chief Justice Taney, over 85 years old and too feeble to attend the meetings of the Court, wrote out two opinions which he had no occasion to use, declaring unconstitutional both the Legal Tender Act and the Conscription Law, and he sent to Chase a disregarded protest against including the judiciary in a three per cent tax on the salaries of all officers of the government—his opinion, however, that the inclusion of the judiciary was unconstitutional, being sustained by the government nine years later and the amount of the tax refunded to the judges.*

Taney did not live long enough to benefit from this change of policy.   His last years, burdened with financial embarrassment and shadowed by the hatred and contempt of official Washington, came to an unreluctant end on October 12, 1864. History has belatedly done justice to his greatness.   Though his judicial career did not fulfill the bright promise of its beginning, it is only fair to remember that he was caught up in mighty issues over which he had no control and on which the best minds of his period were divided and confused.

---

*For Taney's opinions during the Civil War, see Swisher, *op. cit.,* pp. 540-72.

CHAPTER VI

THE COURT UNDER CHIEF JUSTICE CHASE

1864-1873

SALMON PORTLAND CHASE, JAMES MOORE WAYNE, JOHN CATRON, SAMUEL NELSON, ROBERT GRIER, NATHAN CLIFFORD, NOAH H. SWAYNE, SAMUEL F. MILLER, DAVID DAVIS, STEPHEN J. FIELD, WILLIAM STRONG, JOSEPH P. BRADLEY, WARD HUNT.

1. *The Choice of Taney's Successor*

THERE were many candidates for the position left vacant by Chief Justice Taney's death. Three Cabinet members wanted it: Salmon P. Chase, Secretary of the Treasury; Edwin M. Stanton, Secretary of War; Montgomery Blair, former Postmaster-General. Associate Justice Wayne had hopes of being promoted to it. Judge William Strong of Pennsylvania, later appointed on the Court, had his supporters, and so had the great New York attorney, William M. Evarts, the best lawyer of them all. Lincoln on the whole favored Chase, yet he hesitated; and he frankly confided to Congressman George S. Boutwell the grounds for his hesitation.

"There are three reasons in favor of his appointment," Lincoln said, "and one very strong reason against it. First, he occupies the largest place in the public mind in connection with the office; then we wish for a Chief Justice who will sustain what has been done in regard to emancipation and the legal tenders. We cannot ask a man what he will do, and if we should, and he should answer us, we should despise him for it. Therefore, we must take a man whose opinions are known. But there is one very strong reason against his appointment. He is a candidate for the Presidency and if he does not give up that idea, it will be very bad for him and very bad for me."

The appointment was made on December 6, 1864. The new

Chief Justice was 56 years old, well known as a former abolitionist senator from Ohio and secretary of the treasury under Lincoln. Less well known were his earlier banking connections when he had acted as attorney for the Bank of the United States and for the Lafayette Bank of Cincinnati of which he was also a director.* As secretary of the treasury, his main achievement was to aid in formulating and carrying out the important Legal Tender Acts of 1862 and 1863, war measures constituting a revolution in the government's fiscal policy which hitherto had steadfastly avoided the use of paper money. As evidenced by Lincoln's remarks to Boutwell, Chase's support of these Acts was one of the reasons for his elevation to the chief justiceship.

The first years of the Chase régime were largely consumed in an effort to recover the prestige which the Court had lost through the Dred Scott decision. This effort was on the whole rendered futile by the conflict that arose almost at the outset between the Court and Congress, in which Congress was finally victorious. Only after the issues involved had begun to disappear toward the end of Chase's short term of office, did the Court begin to reassert its authority successfully in the field of economics, as distinguished from politics.

2. The Court's Skirmish with Iowa

During the Civil War, as has been shown, the Supreme Court, after an initial struggle, had ended by resigning itself to a position of impotence so far as its relations to the other branches of the federal government were concerned. But even before the war was over, it began once more to interfere with state legislation, and that in a most extraordinary manner, in the case of *Gelpcke* v. *Dubuque,* 1 Wallace, 175. The constitution of the state of Iowa prohibited the legislature from "in any manner" creating debts or liabilities that should "singly or in the aggregate, exceed the sum of $100,000." Nevertheless, in 1857, at a time when the state indebtedness

---

*The fraudulent activities of which these banks were accused during the period of Chase's connection with them are recounted in Myers, *op. cit.,* pp. 489-93.

already exceeded the prescribed amount, the legislature authorized a two hundred and fifty thousand dollar bond issue by the city of Dubuque to aid in the construction of the Dubuque Western, and Dubuque, St. Peter's & St. Paul's Railroad Companies, with the further provision that the principal and interest of the bonds should be met if necessary by a special tax. When this law was first tested in the state supreme court it was upheld by a two-to-one decision; it was tried again as soon as the personnel of the court changed, but the new court, while substantially admitting that the first decision was wrong, held again by a divided vote, that it must abide by it according to the principle of *stare decisis* (the decision of the court must stand); finally a third court unanimously held the law to be in conflict with the state constitution.

Now in the case of *Leffingwell* v. *Warren*, 2 Black, 599, decided only one year before, the Supreme Court of the United States, speaking through Justice Swayne, had explicitly restated the principle upon which all such issues had hitherto been decided by it, namely, that "If the highest judicial tribunal of a State adopt new views as to the construction of . . . a statute and reverse its former decisions, this court will follow the latest settled adjudications." But in the *Gelpcke Case* the majority of the Supreme Court, speaking through the same Justice Swayne, averred that when a contract was valid, as determined by the state judiciary at the time it was made, the latter could not later reverse its decision. This ruling in favor of the railroads, Justice Swayne declared, rested "upon the plainest principles of justice"; "we shall never," he said, "immolate truth, justice, and the law, because a State tribunal has erected the altar and decreed the sacrifice."

Justice Miller strongly dissented from the right of the Supreme Court thus to prohibit state courts from reversing themselves, especially when the Supreme Court had to reverse its own self to do so, and he went on to point out the further absurd consequences that would follow:

"The majority of the court . . . have said to the Federal Court sitting in Iowa, 'You shall disregard this decision of

the highest court of the State on this question. Although you are sitting in the State of Iowa, and administering her laws, and construing her constitution, you shall not follow the latest though it be the soundest exposition of its Constitution by the Supreme Court of that State.' . . .

"Thus we are to have two courts, sitting within the same jurisdiction, deciding upon the same rights, arising out of the same statute, yet always arriving at opposite results. . . . For there is in this court no power to . . . compel a uniformity of construction, because it is not pretended that either the statute of Iowa, or its constitution, or the decision of its courts thereon, are in conflict with the Constitution of the United States. . . .

"Is it supposed for a moment that this treatment of its decision, accompanied by language as unsuited to the dispassionate dignity of this court, as it is disrespectful to another court of at least concurrent jurisdiction over the matter in question, will induce the Supreme Court of Iowa to conform its rulings to suit our dictation in a matter which the very frame and organization of our government places entirely under its control?"

Disregarding the warnings of Justice Miller, the Court proceeded to decide a second Iowa case, that of *Myers* v. *Muscatine,* 1 Wallace, 384, in favor of the railroad bondholders, thereby, according to Justice Miller's dissenting opinion, fastening upon other property owners, "who never assented to the contract," a debt of twenty million dollars. Finally, in the case of *United States* v. *Muscatine,* 8 Wallace, 575, the Supreme Court, with Justice Miller dissenting for the third time, issued a mandamus to the city of Muscatine ordering it, in spite of the state constitution, to levy a special tax to pay the railroads.

The outcome was exactly as Miller had prophesied—continued defiance by the state courts to the extent of their ability and a continuance of divided authority until at last, though much later, the Supreme Court again tacitly reversed itself and repudiated *Gelpcke* v. *Dubuque* in *New Orleans Water Works* v. *Louisiana Sugar Company,* 126 U. S., 18, and in *Merrill* v. *Monticello,* 138 U. S., 673.

3. The Court's Defeat by Congress

While still engaged in this skirmish with the state of Iowa, the Supreme Court started a more serious battle with the United States Congress. In 1866 the justices refused to sit on Circuit Courts in the South until, in the words of Chief Justice Chase, "all possibility of claim that the judicial is subordinate to the military power is removed, by express declaration of the President." This exposed the Chief Justice to criticism on the charge of inconsistency in refusing to hold Court in Virginia, and thereby preventing the trial of Jefferson Davis for treason, although he had not scrupled to serve in Maryland during the period when martial law was executed in that state with a high hand. But this incident was of little importance in comparison with the issues in the famous *Milligan Case*, decided on April 3, 1866, in which the Court once more challenged the authority of the executive and legislative.

Ex Parte Milligan, 4 Wallace, 2, concerned the legal status of the military tribunals created by President Lincoln during the war. One Milligan had been tried by a military commission in Indiana in 1864 on the charge of conspiracy against the government, had been found guilty, and had been sentenced to be hanged. Nine days before the date set for his execution, May 19, 1865, he applied to the Supreme Court for a writ of habeas corpus. The case was exactly similar to that of *Ex Parte Vallandigham*, 1 Wallace, 243, in 1864, in which the Court had declared that it had no power under the Judiciary Act to issue such a writ to a military commission. The case was the same, but the situation was different. In 1866 Lincoln was dead, the war was over, and the Court granted the writ.

Milligan, who was defended by David Dudley Field, James A. Garfield, and Jeremiah S. Black, won his cause, and the Court unanimously decided in his favor, declaring the military tribunals of Lincoln to have been unconstitutional, as having been erected by the Executive in areas where the civil courts were still open. The eloquent passage in Justice Davis's opinion, leading up to this conclusion, has been often quoted:

"The Constitution of the United States is a law for rulers and people, equally in war and in peace, and covers with the shield of its protection all classes of men, at all times, and under all circumstances. No doctrine, involving more pernicious consequences, was ever invented by the wit of man than that any of its provisions can be suspended during any of the great exigencies of government. Such a doctrine leads directly to anarchy or despotism, but the theory of necessity on which it is based is false; for the government, within the Constitution, has all the powers granted to it which are necessary to preserve its existence, as has been happily proved by the result of the great effort to throw off its just authority."*

Thus far the Court was in unanimous agreement in a harmless decision which applied only to the past and to the distant future; the sting of the judgment lay in the rest of the decision which applied to the immediate present, and there the Court divided. The majority, consisting of Davis, Field, Nelson, Clifford, and Grier, held that in the given circumstances military tribunals were illegal, whether created by the President or by Congress; the minority—Chief Justice Chase, and Justices Miller, Swayne, and Wayne—held that the prohibition extended only to the President. Had the minority been the majority, the conflict with Congress—then busily engaged in establishing just such military tribunals throughout the South—would have been avoided.

The answer of Congress to the Milligan decision was quick and decisive, so far as it went. Justice Catron having died, at the age of 79, in 1865, and President Johnson, already embroiled with the national legislature, nominating Attorney-General Stanberry as his successor, Congress disposed of this nomination and the likelihood of others from Johnson, by a law which reduced the number of the justices to seven as soon as two more should be removed by death. In thus expecting its difficulties to be settled by the laws of nature, Congress

---

*With regard to the concluding lines of this opinion, Boudin comments caustically: "Judge Davis' last sentence seems nonsensical in view of the fact that the very case before the Court showed that in fighting 'the effort to throw off its just authority' the Government went beyond what is permissible under the Constitution." *Op. cit.,* Vol. II, p. 48.

acted with some confidence since the three oldest members of the Court were Wayne, 75; Nelson, 74; and Grier, 72, and of these the last two belonged to the hostile majority, and Wayne, a Southerner, though he had voted with the minority in the *Milligan Case,* was likely to oppose the future acts of severity toward the South that were in contemplation. The reliance of Congress on the natural limits of mortality proved justified, since Wayne died in 1867, Grier resigned in 1870, and Nelson departed from the earthly scene in 1873.

Meanwhile, however, much water flowed under the congressional and judicial bridges. In 1867 in the cases of *Cummings* v. *Missouri,* 4 Wallace, 277, and *Ex Parte Garland,* 4 Wallace, 333, the Supreme Court, once more by five-to-four decisions, held unconstitutional, first, a state law requiring clergymen to take oath that they had not by act or word favored the cause of the Confederacy, and second, an Act of Congress requiring a similar oath from lawyers. But all these instances, including the *Milligan Case* itself, were merely preliminary skirmishes before the great battle that was expected between Congress and the Court over the constitutionality of the Reconstruction Acts passed in 1867. These laws establishing military rule over the South were vetoed as unconstitutional by President Johnson and were enacted over his veto; in the light of all the recent decisions of the Supreme Court, the opponents of these measures looked to the Court for a second and more authoritative veto.

But the Court failed them. It refused to come to the assistance of the hard-pressed President, and at the cost of its own consistency declined the combat with Congress. In order to test the constitutionality of the Reconstruction Acts, suits were instituted nominally against the President and the Secretary of War to prevent their enforcement of the Acts. The first of these cases, *Mississippi* v. *Johnson,* 4 Wallace, 475, involved the jurisdiction of the Court over the President, and was dismissed on the technical ground that the Court had "no jurisdiction of a bill to enjoin the President in the performance of his official duties . . ." The second case, *Georgia* v. *Stanton,* 6 Wallace, 50, was more difficult to handle, the suit being brought against Secretary of War Stanton and General

Grant; but an equally good technical reason for declining jurisdiction was found by holding that the case concerned purely
political matters, instead of personal or property rights.   Then
a third suit was brought in which a part of the Reconstruction legislation was cleverly turned against itself, namely, an
Act of 1867 designed to protect Federal officials in the South
but so carelessly drawn that it authorized habeas corpus proceedings in "all cases where any person may be restrained of
his or her liberty, in violation of the Constitution or of any
treaty or law of the United States."   Taking advantage of this
Act a Mississippi editor held for trial before a military commission petitioned the federal Circuit Court for a writ of
habeas corpus and on denial appealed to the Supreme Court.
This time the Court, with Congress apparently unable to object,
assumed jurisdiction, and the constitutionality of the Reconstruction Acts was at last about to be tested in the case of *Ex
Parte McCardle,* 6 Wallace, 318, with a negative verdict generally expected.

Confronted with an immediate emergency, the Radical Republicans in control of Congress rushed through a bill repeal-
ing the appellate jurisdiction of the Supreme Court under the
Act of 1867 and prohibiting it from proceeding on any appeals
already before it.   With all their haste, however, the arguments
in the *McCardle Case* had been finished while the bill was still
pending, and the Court, had it so chosen, could have rendered
its decision before Congress acted.   But it did not choose to
do so.   Instead, it waited until the bill was passed and then
postponed further consideration of the matter until the next
term.   Finally, at the next term, in a unanimous decision delivered by Chief Justice Chase, it said: "This court cannot
proceed to pronounce judgment . . . for it has no longer jurisdiction of the appeal; and judicial duty is not less fitly performed by declining ungranted jurisdiction than in exercising
firmly that which the Constitution and the laws confer."

The postponement and final decision greatly lowered the
prestige of the Court.   Its warmest defenders no longer defended it.   At the time of the postponement, Gideon Welles
in the Cabinet confided to his diary: "The Judges of the Supreme Court have caved in, fallen through, failed in the *Mc-*

Cardle Case," and former Justice Curtis wrote, "Congress, with the acquiescence of the country, has subdued the Supreme Court as well as the President." Writing today of the postponement, Charles Warren says, "While there was some justification for the view that the Court had not been firm in its stand . . . the intimations that its action was influenced by the political situation were clearly unfair, in view of its previous courageous action in sustaining its jurisdiction over the case."* In the absence of written evidence, whether the Court was influenced in withdrawing from the case by the fact that in January, 1868, the House by a vote of one hundred sixteen to thirty-nine had passed a bill favorably reported by its Judiciary Committee providing that two-thirds of the justices must concur to render invalid any act of Congress—a bill dropped in the Senate but liable at any time to be revived— this question must be left to the reader's ideas of human nature in general and of judicial nature in particular as to what was most probable under the circumstances.

In another case, *Texas* v. *White,* 7 Wallace, 700, which was decided on the same day as *Ex Parte McCardle,* the Court rendered a guarded opinion on the fundamental question which had divided the executive and legislative whether, as Lincoln and Johnson contended, the Confederate States had never really been outside of the Union but merely thought they were—and so after the war should be treated as an integral part of the Union, or whether, as Thaddeus Stevens and the Radical Republicans maintained, the Confederacy had in fact set itself up as a hostile nation and should be treated as such. The specific issue was whether notes issued by the state of Texas while a part of the Confederacy were still redeemable. The opinion delivered by Justice Chase skillfully boxed the compass on the major point. The case, he said, did not make it necessary to pronounce judgment upon the constitutionality of the "military authority or . . . the paramount authority of Congress"—on which, of course, the majority of the Court had already pronounced judgment, and that an unfavorable

---

*Warren, *op. cit.,* Vol. II, p. 484.

one, in the *Milligan Case;* he then asserted that the secession ordinance of Texas was a nullity, the state having always remained within the Union in spite of itself, and ended by declaring that this legal nullity had nevertheless changed the relation of Texas to the rest of the Union so that those of her laws which had been passed in support of the rebellion, such as the bond issue under discussion, were absolutely void. The general effect of the decision, and of the Court's careful avoidance of unnecessary conflict with Congress was to enhance further the authority of the latter.

A last attempt to obtain a definite ruling on the constitutionality of the Reconstruction Acts was made in the case of *Ex Parte Yerger,* 8 Wallace, 85, by another editor imprisoned under the military who appealed for a writ of habeas corpus, this time under the original Judiciary Act of 1789. Again the Court assumed jurisdiction, and its action was immediately answered by the introduction of a bill in the Senate explicitly prohibiting the Supreme Court from considering any case which involved the validity of the Reconstruction Acts, followed by another, still more radical, prohibiting the judicial review of any act of Congress. What promised to be a final combat between the Supreme Court and Congress, with the odds on Congress, was averted by a compromise outside of court whereby Yerger on being turned over to the civil authorities withdrew his petition.

More important for an abatement of the conflict between the two branches of the government were the failure of the Radical Republicans in the impeachment trial of President Johnson, the death of their leader, Thaddeus Stevens, and the passing of power in Congress to a more moderate group. With the gradual abandonment of the attempt to enforce the Reconstruction Acts, the interest of the country turned to economic problems. Like the national War of 1812, the second great war between the Supreme Court and Congress was terminated by the disappearance of the cause of conflict, and it ended like the struggle between Marshall and the Jeffersonians without any change in the legal or constitutional position of the Court.

4. *The Legal Tender Cases*

The first of the new problems was a fiscal one. It will be recalled that a main reason for the appointment of Chief Justice Chase had been Lincoln's belief that he would support the Legal Tender Acts. With the depreciation of the paper money issued under them, these Acts came to be more and more violently attacked by the banks, the holders of mortgages, and the creditor class in general;* on the other side was the whole debtor class, including in this instance the powerful group of the expanding railroads all over the country, constructed as they had been on borrowed capital.

An indication of what the Court's decision might be expected to be was furnished in two preliminary cases, *Bronson* v. *Rodes,* 7 Wallace, 229, and *Butler* v. *Horwitz,* 7 Wallace, 258, in which it was held that the Legal Tender Acts did not apply to contracts calling explicitly for payment in coin. A year later, in the fall of 1869, the question of the constitutionality of the Acts themselves came before the Court in the case of *Hepburn* v. *Griswold,* 8 Wallace, 603. In the first conference on the case the Court was divided four to four, Miller, Swayne, Davis, and Grier upholding the Acts, the other four opposing. An inconsistency in Grier's position being pointed out in the discussion, Grier, 76 years old and intellectually as well as physically feeble, switched his vote. The next week all the other Justices took the unprecedented action of sending a message by Justice Field to the half-senile member of the Court "that it was their unanimous opinion that he ought to resign."† This he accordingly did, and the decision adverse to the Acts was rendered, on February 7, 1870, by Chief Justice Chase, with Justices Nelson, Clifford, and Field concurring, and Justices Miller, Swayne, and Davis dissenting.

---

*To these Charles Warren adds all those who "opposed legalized cheating" (*op. cit.,* Vol. II, p. 499)—a rather harsh phrase from so great an admirer of the Supreme Court, considering that it ultimately validated this "legalized cheating."

†James Ford Rhodes, *History of the United States, 1850-1877,* Vol. 6, pp. 262-63.

The decision affected the Acts only in so far as they applied to prior contracts, but the opinion of Chief Justice Chase strongly implied that they were as a whole unconstitutional, since the authority of Congress to issue paper money was not among its delegated powers and its right to do so under the "necessary and proper" clause was denied by the Chief Justice on the ground that it was not "an appropriate and plainly adapted means for carrying on war" (though he had taken the opposite view at the time) and that no act could be necessary and proper which impaired the obligation of contracts. Justice Miller in his dissent stoutly maintained that the appropriateness and suitability of an act to carry out an admittedly constitutional purpose, *i. e.* the preservation of the nation, were questions for Congress and not the Court to decide.

The question was apparently settled that the United States would have no more paper money as legal tender. But on April 10, 1869, Congress, having in Grant a president to its taste, had increased the number of the Court—then at eight— to nine; Edwin M. Stanton had been appointed but had died before taking office; thus the resignation of Grier enabled Grant to appoint two new justices,* and at the very moment when the Legal Tender decision was being read, he sent in to the Senate the names of two exceedingly able lawyers connected with the railroad interests, as attorneys, stockholders, and directors. William Strong of Pennsylvania had been chief counsel for the Philadelphia and Reading Railroad before his elevation to the supreme court of Pennsylvania in 1857, a position which he resigned in 1868 to return to his railroad practice. Joseph P. Bradley was attorney for and a director of the United Railway Companies of New Jersey, a corporation with a particularly large bonded debt.

Four days after the confirmation of the new Justices, the government through Attorney-General Hoar moved to take up in the Supreme Court two Legal Tender cases, *Latham* v.

*Secretary of the Treasury Boutwell knew of the decision in advance; it is uncertain whether Grant did. See article by Sidney Ratner, "Was the Supreme Court Packed by General Grant?" *Political Science Quarterly,* September, 1935.

United States and *Deming* v. *United States,* 12 Wallace, 529, which did not involve the retroactive feature of *Hepburn* v. *Griswold.* They were accordingly argued, and during the discussion the point was made that the Court had already ordered that these cases be disposed of under the earlier decision. Attorney-General Hoar said that no such order had been given, Chase said he remembered that it had been, Miller said it hadn't been, Nelson's memory coincided with Chase's, Davis's agreed with Miller's, the Chief Justice reiterated his statement with a good deal of passion, and the dispute was ended by the Attorney-General's ironical remark that while one of course could not question the recollection of the Chief Justice it was unfortunate that there was no record of so important a decision. The incident occasioned considerable comment of a nature unfavorable to the Court,* but the more important matter of Legal Tender constitutionality was postponed through withdrawal of the plaintiffs' suits.

The matter soon came up again during a reargument of the case of *Knox* v. *Lee,* 12 Wallace, 457, and the Court on May 1, 1871, by a five-to-four vote—Strong, Bradley, Swayne, Miller, and Davis against the former majority, Chase, Nelson, Clifford, and Field—reversed *Hepburn* v. *Griswold* and held the Legal Tender Acts constitutional in regard to all contracts, whether made before or after the passage of the Acts.

The Court's reversal within fourteen months of its earlier decision was deplored by many as calculated to lower respect for the judiciary, and the same position is taken, in writing of these cases, by Charles Warren† and Charles Evans Hughes.‡   But, regardless of the possible bias of the new Justices in favor of the railroads, the constitutionality of the second decision has never been assailed nor is it denied that it

---

The Nation deplored "an unseemly squabble on the bench in open Court," and the *American Law Review* observed in its gentle way that there was evidently "a state of feeling in the Court by no means pleasant." Chase prepared a statement accusing the *Hepburn* v. *Griswold* minority of bad faith but withdrew it on learning that they were preparing a reply. Later the substances of both statements were published, and according to Charles Warren, *op. cit.,* Vol. II, p. 523 *n.,* Chase's allegation was completely disproved.

†Warren, *op. cit.,* Vol. II, pp. 522, 525.
‡Hughes, *op. cit.,* pp. 52-53.

established the currency on a workable basis, gave Congress a highly necessary power over it, and benefited the mass of American citizens.

Justice Strong in delivering the Court's opinion answered the Chief Justice's argument on the contract clause in language which was for its day and in view of the Marshall tradition, decidedly radical:

"The *obligation* of a contract to pay money is to pay that which the law shall recognize as money when the payment is made. . . . No one ever doubted that a debt of one thousand dollars, contracted before 1834, could be paid by one hundred eagles coined after that year, though they contained no more gold than ninety-four eagles such as were coined when the contract was made, and this, not because of the intrinsic value of the coin, but because of its legal value. The eagles coined after 1834 were not money until they were authorized by law, and had they been coined before, without a law fixing their legal value, they could no more have paid a debt than uncoined bullion, or cotton, or wheat. Every contract for the payment of money, simply, is necessarily subject to the constitutional power of the government over the currency, whatever that power may be, and the obligation of the parties is, therefore, assumed with reference to that power. . . . It cannot, therefore, be maintained that the legal tender acts impaired the obligation of contracts.

"Nor can it be truly asserted that Congress may not, by its action, indirectly impair the obligation of contracts, if by the expression be meant rendering contracts fruitless, or partially fruitless. Directly it may, confessedly, by passing a bankruptcy act, embracing past as well as future transactions. This is obliterating contracts entirely. So it may relieve parties from their apparent obligations indirectly in a multitude of ways. It may declare war, or, even in peace, pass non-intercourse acts, or direct an embargo. All such measures may, and must operate seriously upon existing contracts, and may not merely hinder, but relieve the parties to such contracts entirely from performance. It is then, clear that the powers of Congress may be exerted, though the effect of

such exertion may be in one case to annul, and in other cases to impair the obligation of contracts."

5. *The Slaughter-House Cases*

The most celebrated decision of the Supreme Court during the Chase régime, and the one of most enduring interest, was that given in the *Slaughter-House Cases,* 16 Wallace, 36, in 1873. The legal and social issues involved were possibly the most tangled and confused that ever confronted the Court. In 1869 the carpetbag legislature of Louisiana, almost certainly influenced by bribery, had passed "An Act to Protect the Health of the City of New Orleans, to Locate the Stock-landings and Slaughter-houses, and to Incorporate the Crescent City Livestock Landing and Slaughter-House Company." To this company, the Act further granted monopoly privileges over landing-places and slaughter-houses, which must, however, be located within certain prescribed areas. The territorial limitation was undoubtedly beneficial to the health of the city; on the other hand, the immediate effect of the law was to throw over a thousand people out of employment. The Act aroused great indignation among the citizens of New Orleans, and it was decided to make use of the hated Thirteenth and Fourteenth Amendments to protect their economic interests. The constitutionality of the law was accordingly attacked as creating a state of "involuntary servitude" forbidden by the Thirteenth Amendment (an obviously strained construction of the Amendment) and as abridging "the privileges and immunities of citizens of the United States," as denying to the plaintiffs "equal protection of the laws," and as depriving them of property "without due process of law," contrary to the Fourteenth Amendment.

Thus the first case to arise under the famous Fourteenth Amendment and, typical of many that were to follow it, did not directly involve the civil rights of the Negroes on whose behalf the Amendment had been passed but instead raised questions of the extent of the state police power and the granting or withholding of monopoly privilege. Nevertheless, in-

directly, as in so many police power laws before the Civil War, the status of the Negro was involved, since by upholding the Louisiana Act the Court would weaken the Fourteenth Amendment, while by invalidating the Act, it would weaken the police power of the states and would throw down the bars to that perversion of the Fourteenth Amendment into a defense of private property against the state which later actually occurred. Incidentally, the persistent question of the right of the Court to investigate instances of alleged bribery and to go behind a specific law to its motivation arose once more.*

By a five-to-four decision the Court validated the Louisiana law. The majority group of justices contained the usual alignment of Miller, Strong, and Davis, strengthened in this instance by the adherence of Clifford and that of Ward Hunt, a New York judge, 62 years old, who had been appointed on the recent resignation of Justice Nelson. In rendering the majority opinion, Justice Miller, the ablest and most progressive member of the Court, strove heroically to accomplish what he found an insuperable task: to uphold the original purpose of the Fourteenth Amendment—to prevent discrimination against the Negro—and also to uphold the state police powers against the economic attacks which, with rare clairvoyance, he foresaw. His initial account of the origin and intent of the Reconstruction Amendments was a masterpiece of condensed historical writing.

"The process of restoring to their proper relations with the Federal government and with the other states those which had sided with the rebellion, undertaken under the proclamation of President Johnson in 1865, and before the assembling of Congress, developed the fact that, notwithstanding the formal recognition by those States of the abolition of slavery, the condition of the slave race would, without further protection of the Federal government, be almost as bad as it was before. Among the first acts of legislation adopted by several of the States in the legislative bodies which claimed to be in

---

*A further interest attaches to the case because John Archibald Campbell, former Justice of the Supreme Court, who had lost all his property in the Civil War and then built up a new practice in Louisiana, was attorney for the defeated plaintiffs.

their normal relations with the Federal government, were laws which imposed upon the colored race onerous disabilities and burdens, and curtailed their rights in the pursuit of life, liberty, and property to such an extent that their freedom was of little value, while they had lost the protection which they had received from their former owners from motives both of interest and humanity.

"They were in some States forbidden to appear in the towns in any other character than menial servants. They were required to reside on and cultivate the soil without the right to purchase or own it. They were excluded from many occupations of gain, and were not permitted to give testimony in the courts in any case where a white man was a party. It was said that their lives were at the mercy of bad men, either because the laws for their protection were insufficient or were not enforced.

"These circumstances, whatever of falsehood or misconception may have been mingled with their presentation, forced upon the statesmen who had conducted the Federal government in safety through the crisis of the rebellion, and who supposed that by the thirteenth article of amendment they had secured the result of their labors, the conviction that something more was necessary in the way of constitutional protection to the unfortunate race who had suffered so much. They accordingly passed through Congress the proposition for the fourteenth amendment, and they declined to treat as restored to their full participation in the government of the Union the States which had been in insurrection, until they ratified that article by a formal vote of their legislative bodies.

"Before we proceed to examine more critically the provisions of this amendment, on which the plaintiffs in error rely, let us complete and dismiss the history of the recent amendments, as that history relates to the general purpose which pervades them all. A few years' experience satisfied the thoughtful men who had been the authors of the other two amendments that, notwithstanding the restraints of those articles on the States, and the laws passed under the additional powers granted to Congress, these were inadequate for the protection

of life, liberty, and property, without which freedom to the slave was no boon. They were in all those States denied the right of suffrage. The laws were administered by the white man alone. It was urged that a race of men distinctively marked as was the negro, living in the midst of another and dominant race, could never be fully secured in their person and their property without the right of suffrage.

"Hence the fifteenth amendment, which declares that 'the right of a citizen of the United States to vote shall not be denied or abridged by any State on account of race, color, or previous condition of servitude.' The negro having, by the fourteenth amendment, been declared to be a citizen of the United States, is thus made a voter in every State of the Union.

"We repeat, then, in the light of this recapitulation of events, almost too recent to be called history, but which are familiar to us all; and on the most casual examination of the language of these amendments, no one can fail to be impressed with the one pervading purpose found in them all, lying at the foundation of each, and without which none of them would have been even suggested; we mean the freedom of the slave race, the security and firm establishment of that freedom, and the protection of the newly-made freeman and citizen from the oppressions of those who had formerly exercised unlimited dominion over him. It is true that only the fifteenth amendment, in terms, mentions the negro by speaking of his color and his slavery. But it is just as true that each of the other articles was addressed to the grievances of that race, and designed to remedy them as the fifteenth.

"We do not say that no one else but the negro can share in this protection. Both the language and spirit of these articles are to have their fair and just weight in any question of construction. Undoubtedly while negro slavery alone was in the mind of the Congress which proposed the thirteenth article, it forbids any other kind of slavery, now or hereafter. If Mexican peonage or the Chinese coolie labor system shall develop slavery of the Mexican or Chinese race within our territory, this amendment may safely be trusted to make it

void. And so if other rights are assailed by the States which properly and necessarily fall within the protection of these articles, that protection will apply, though the party interested may not be of African descent. But what we do say, and what we wish to be understood is, that in any fair and just construction of any section or phrase of these amendments, it is necessary to look to the purpose which we have said was the pervading spirit of them all, the evil which they were designed to remedy, and the process of continued addition to the Constitution, until that purpose was supposed to be accomplished, as far as constitutional law can accomplish it."

Having thus admirably demonstrated the intended meaning of the Amendments, Justice Miller still had left the more difficult task of showing that the specific case in hand did not come within the language of the Fourteenth Amendment in prohibiting any abridgment of "the privileges and immunities of citizens of the United States." In doing so, he was led to make a fatal distinction between the civil rights of a citizen of the United States and those of a state citizen, arguing that all the fundamental civil rights were left by the Constitution in the hands of the states save for the enumerated additions, such as "the prohibition against ex post facto laws, bills of attainder, and laws impairing the obligation of contracts."

"With the exception of these and a few other restrictions, the entire domain of the privileges and immunities of citizens of the States . . . lay within the constitutional and legislative power of the States, and without that of the Federal government. Was it the purpose of the fourteenth amendment, by the simple declaration that no State should make or enforce any law which shall abridge the privileges and immunities of *citizens of the United States,* to transfer the security and protection of all the civil rights which we have mentioned, from the States to the Federal government? And where it is declared that Congress shall have the power to enforce that article, was it intended to bring within the power of Congress the entire domain of civil rights heretofore belonging exclusively to the States?

"All this and more must follow, if the proposition of the

plaintiffs in error be sound. For not only are these rights subject to the control of Congress whenever in its discretion any of them are supposed to be abridged by State legislation, but that body may also pass laws in advance, limiting and restricting the exercise of legislative power by the States, in their most ordinary and usual functions, as in its judgment it may think proper on all such subjects. And still further, such a construction followed by the reversal of the judgments of the Supreme Court of Louisiana in these cases, would constitute this court a perpetual censor upon all legislation of the States, on the civil rights of their own citizens, with authority to nullify such as it did not approve as consistent with those rights, as they existed at the time of the adoption of this amendment."

The dissenting Justices were quick to point out that the majority opinion practically nullified the privileges and immunities clause which was the very keystone of the Amendment. Under this interpretation, Justice Field said tellingly, the Amendment "was a vain and idle enactment, which accomplished nothing, and most unnecessarily excited Congress and the people on its passage. With privileges and immunities thus designated no State could ever have interfered by its laws, and no new constitutional provision was required to inhibit such interference." To the same effect, Justice Swayne said: "This Court has no authority to interpolate a limitation that is neither expressed nor implied. Our duty is to execute the law, not to make it. . . . The construction adopted by the majority of my brethren is, in my judgment, much too narrow. It defeats, by a limitation not anticipated, the intent of those by whom the instrument was framed and of those by whom it was adopted. To the extent of that limitation it turns, as it were, what was meant for bread into a stone." And Justice Bradley pointed out that the state police power might have been safeguarded without the sweeping generalizations of the majority opinion. "That portion of the Act," he said, "which requires all slaughter-houses to be located below the city and to be subject to inspection, etc., is clearly a police regulation. That portion which allows no one but the favored Company

to build, own, or have slaughter-houses is not a police regulation, and has not the faintest semblance of one."

Viewed in the light of Justice Miller's generous intentions and the reasoning power shown, his opinion doubtless deserves Charles Warren's eulogistic comment that it "has justly been regarded as one of the glorious landmarks of American law";* viewed in the light of its consequences, however, it was a "landmark" that was quickly washed away: the first part of it, designed† to protect the Negro against discrimination was negatived by the second part which was used to perpetuate that discrimination, while the second part failed in the long run to provide the intended bulwark against invasion of the state police power.

In striking contrast to the solemnity with which the rights of butchers were discussed in the *Slaughter-House Cases* was the levity which characterized a decision denying the right of women to practice law under the privileges and immunities clause of the Fourteenth Amendment. The case, *Bradwell* v. *The State,* 16 Wallace, 130, concerned a refusal of the supreme court of Illinois (acting on its construction of state law) to license women attorneys. The decision of the majority of the United States Supreme Court was rendered on the basis of the definition of United States citizenship given by Justice Miller in the *Slaughter-House Cases,* but Justice Bradley, with Swayne and Field concurring, insisted on a broader ground for their judgment, declaring that "in view of the peculiar characteristics, destiny and mission of women, it is within the province of the Legislature to ordain what offices, positions and callings shall be filled and discharged by men, and shall receive the benefit of those energies and responsibilities, and that decision and firmness which are pre-

---

*Warren, *op. cit.,* p. 546.
†Boudin, *op. cit.,* Vol. II, p. 106, in the course of an excellent chapter on "The Battle of the Slaughter-Houses," strongly implies that Justice Miller's opinion was deliberately intended to have precisely the effect of destroying the Negroes' civil rights that it ultimately did have. There is nothing in the character of the great Justice, who in 1850 preferred to move from his native state of Kentucky and begin life anew in Iowa rather than sacrifice his anti-slavery convictions, to justify such an imputation of hypocrisy.

sumed to predominate in the sterner sex." It is recorded that the Supreme Bench and the assembled lawyers evinced "no little amusement" during the delivery of Justice Bradley's opinion.

Three years later, the Court denied the right of women attorneys to appear before it in an opinion which, in its wording, is revelatory of the Court's psychology: "By the uniform practice of the Court, from its organization to the present time, and by the fair construction of its rules, none but men are admitted to practice before it as attorneys and counsellors. This is in accordance with immemorial usage in England, and the law and practice of all the States until within a recent period; and the Court does not feel called upon to make a change, until such a change is required by statute." The statutory requirement was quickly passed by Congress, and women, more fortunate than Negroes, found no further barrier to their civil rights in the Supreme Court.

Less than a month after the Slaughter-House decision, Chief Justice Chase died, after having been largely incapacitated for his last two years of office from a paralytic stroke suffered in 1871. Great as was his native ability, he had entirely failed to dominate a Court on which sat such legal giants as Miller,* Strong, Bradley, and Field, and unlike Jay, Marshall and Taney, he had delivered no outstanding opinions. In fact, the only major decision of the Supreme Court during his period which has stood the test of time was that in which the Chief Justice was reversed in the Legal Tender cases. Aside from that instance, the Chase Court was a dramatic episode, but none the less merely an episode, in the turbulent transition from war conditions to those of settled peace.

---

*Chief Justice Chase generously confessed that Miller was "beyond question the dominant personality . . . upon the bench." This is particularly interesting in view of the fact that Miller was a "self-made" man who spent twelve years in the practice of medicine before he took up law, which he learned by himself without attending any law school. As with Chief Justice Marshall, his actual "legal learning" was decidedly less than that of other members of the Court.

Chapter VII

THE COURT UNDER CHIEF JUSTICE WAITE

1874-1888

Morrison R. Waite, Nathan Clifford, Noah H. Swayne, Samuel F. Miller, David Davis, Stephen J. Field, William Strong, Joseph P. Bradley, Ward Hunt, John M. Harlan, William B. Woods, Stanley Matthews, Horace Gray, Samuel Blatchford, Lucius Quintus Cincinnatus Lamar.

1. *Personnel of the Waite Court*

President Grant was not particularly noted for the excellence of his appointments. There was plenty of legal talent in the country from which to select Chase's successor: among liberals, there were on the Court itself Justice Miller—whose advancement was strongly urged—and Justice Davis, while off the Court were such outstanding figures as Senator Allen Thurman and Secretary of the Treasury Benjamin Bristow; among conservatives, who would naturally have been more acceptable to the Administration, were William M. Evarts and Benjamin R. Curtis; on the border line with conservative leanings were Senators Lyman Trumbull and George F. Edmunds. Any one of these men could have been counted upon to add to the reputation of the Court.

Instead, the President followed his usual principle of appointing personal friends to any vacant office. His first nomination* was that of Attorney-General George H. Williams of Oregon, a mediocre lawyer who like most of the members of Grant's Cabinet was ultimately forced to resign under suspicions of corruption. Such an outcry went up from Congress and the press that Grant withdrew the nomination and followed

---

*Grant's original selection was the worst of all, that of the New York orator and machine politician, Roscoe B. Conkling, but luckily for the country, Conkling had the good sense to decline an office for which he was utterly unfit.

it with that of another personal friend, Caleb Cushing of Massachusetts, formerly an able lawyer but now 74 years old and furthermore suspected of having had Southern sympathies during the Civil War. Another public outcry and another withdrawal. After these two fiascos, Grant presented the name of Morrison R. Waite of Ohio, who had at least the negative virtue of being unknown. Fearing a worse appointment if they hesitated, the Senate gave its confirmation by a vote of sixty-three to six. Judge Rockwood Hoar, who had himself been prominently mentioned for the position and would unquestionably have been a better choice, remarked with some malice, "Waite is that luckiest of all individuals known to the law, an innocent third party without notice."

The new Chief Justice, now 57 years old, was a native of Connecticut, who after graduating from Yale had moved to the small town of Toledo, Ohio, where he had gradually built up a considerable practice as a railroad attorney.* Not usually reckoned among the first ten or twenty lawyers even of Ohio, he had nevertheless done efficient work in urging American claims as a member of the Geneva Arbitration Commission, and it was to this—and possibly also to his railroad connections—that he owed his appointment. Generally regarded at the time as the weakest of all those who had ever attained his exalted position as chief justice, he was to surprise the public by rising to the responsibilities of his new office much as President Chester A. Arthur would do a few years later.

One of the early activities of the Waite Court, or at least a majority of it, was in connection with the Electoral Commission appointed to decide the disputed presidential election of 1876. The Commission consisted of five Senators (three Republicans and two Democrats), five Congressmen (three Democrats and two Republicans) and five Justices of the Supreme Court (Clifford, Strong, Field, and Miller—evenly divided in their political affiliations—and Davis, an Independent). But Davis, knowing his fellow men, declined to be put in the probable position of final arbiter, and Bradley, a Re-

*For an account of his practice, some of it rather discreditable, see Myers, *op. cit.*, pp. 531-38.

publican, was appointed instead.   By that action, Hayes was made practically sure of election.   Although the Commission listened solemnly for over a month to legal arguments from both sides, on every one of the many questions involved its members voted strictly in accord with their political convictions.

Prominent among those who had secured the nomination of Hayes at the Republican National Convention had been John M. Harlan, head of the Kentucky delegation, which, after a gallant struggle on behalf of Bristow, switched to Hayes in order to defeat Blaine.   When Justice Davis resigned, on the inauguration of Hayes, his position was conferred on Harlan.   The appointment was unquestionably in payment of a political debt but at the same time it proved by accident* to be one of the best ever made.

Justice Harlan, 44 years old at the time of his appointment to the Supreme Court, was by temperament a "Southern gentleman," the son of a Kentucky attorney and politician of some ability; after a slender legal education at Transylvania College and service on the Union side in the Civil War, he had entered politics as a Democrat, then becoming a Radical Republican had been twice defeated for governor, and had finally ended as a law partner of Benjamin Bristow, one of the leaders of the Civil Service Reform movement.   There was perhaps much in this varied career of an unsuccessful politician to suggest a high degree of personal independence and a capacity to learn from experience, but there was certainly little to indicate stability of judgment.   Yet as a matter of fact, Harlan had achieved a synthesis of civil liberties, property rights, and state police powers which was beyond the ability of even Justice Miller, and though this synthesis was ultimately to break down it led before that to many great judicial opinons, nearly always on the minority side.   In his general philosophy, as well as in his reputation as "The Great Dissenter," Justice Harlan was to be the direct predecessor of Justice Oliver Wendell Holmes.

---

*The word "accident" is chosen deliberately in view of the character of Hayes's later appointments.

2. *Judicial Nullification of the Fourteenth and Fifteenth Amendments*

The legal status of the Negro, left in doubt by the Slaughter-House decision, was settled through a whole series of cases that came before the Supreme Court in the decade between 1875 and 1885. Congress had passed a number of Civil Rights Acts on behalf of the Negroes in 1866, 1870, 1871, and 1875; all but the first of these were essentially enforcement acts designed to carry into effect the provisions of the Fourteenth or Fifteenth Amendments. The result of the Court's decisions, as Charles Warren writes, "was to leave the Federal statutes almost wholly ineffective to protect the Negro, in view of the construction of the Amendments adopted by the court";* in other words, the Court not only nullified the Acts of Congress but nullified the intent of the Amendments themselves, adopted not only by Congress but by the supposedly sovereign people of the United States.

Justice Miller, hamstrung by his own opinion in the *Slaughter-House Cases,* did nothing to support the rights of the Negro which he had in the first part of that opinion so eloquently expounded; Justices Field and Bradley who had protested against the second part of Miller's opinion because it limited the rights of white citizens were now eager to support it as limiting the rights of Negroes; the majority of the Court was willing to avail itself of the most strained legal technicalities in order to get around the plain intent of the Amendments and the Acts of Congress. The only consistent supporter of Negro rights was that Southern gentleman and one-time slaveowner, Justice Harlan.

The first case to be decided, that of *United States* v. *Reese,* 92 U. S., 214, concerned an Act passed to enforce the Fifteenth Amendment by penalizing all state officers who deprived anyone of the right to vote on account of race or color. That such deprivation had occurred in the case before the Court involving an electoral inspector was admitted. But the major-

---

*Warren, *op. cit.,* Vol. II, p. 604.

ity of the Court declared the law was inoperative because, although its second clause, applying to all state officers used the phrase "on account of race and color," the third clause, applying specifically to electoral inspectors, did not repeat that phrase but used the words "as aforesaid." Therefore, the Court held, Congress had failed to provide "appropriate legislation." Aside from the verbal hair-splitting, the Court in this decision achieved the remarkable logical feat of affirming that "some state officers" are not included under "all state officers." Justice Ward Hunt, though he cared little about the civil rights of Negroes, was so outraged by the nature of the technicalities invoked that he filed a vigorous dissenting opinion.

The second case, that of *United States* v. *Cruikshank,* 92 U. S., 542, was decided in a similar manner. Here, the issue involved the First as well as the Fourteenth Amendment since the indictment charged, and the fact was admitted, that certain "persons of African descent and persons of color" had been deprived among other rights of that of "peaceable assembly" guaranteed by the First Amendment. On this point the Court's decision was illuminating: "The right of the people peaceably to assemble for lawful purposes existed long before the adoption of the Constitution of the United States. . . . It is found wherever civilization exists" (except in the case immediately before the Court). "It was not, therefore, a right granted to the people by the Constitution."

But the main ground of the Court's decision was that the indictments had failed to charge that the acts against the "persons of African descent" were committed *because* of the African descent. "We may suspect," said the Court with unconscious humor, "that race was the cause of the hostility, but it is not so averred."

The next case, that of *United States* v. *Harris,* 106 U. S., 629, involved the constitutionality of the Congressional law directed against the outrages of the Ku Klux Klan. The heart of this law was its second section making it a crime for two or more persons to conspire to deprive another of the rights guaranteed by the recent Amendments; this section was declared unconstitutional by the Court on the ground that Con-

gress did not have the authority to enforce the Amendments against private persons but solely against state laws.

After it had been decided that the Fourteenth Amendment provided no protection to Negroes even against mob violence, the fate of Senator Sumner's famous Civil Rights Act prescribing equal treatment for them in hotels, restaurants, public conveyances, and theatres, was easily foreseen. In the *Civil Rights Cases,* 109 U. S., 3, these provisions were held unconstitutional according to the principle asserted in the *Harris Case.* In delivering the Court's decision, Justice Bradley, in an opinion directly contradicting his position in the *Slaughter-House Cases,* practically admitted the nullification of the Fourteenth Amendment. "If it is supposable," he said, "that the States may deprive persons of life, liberty and property without due process of law, *and the Amendment itself does suppose this,** why should not Congress proceed at once to prescribe due process of law for the protection of every one of these fundamental rights, in every possible case, as well as to prescribe equal privileges in inns, public conveyances, and theatres?"

It was in this case that Justice Harlan delivered the greatest of all of his three hundred and sixteen dissenting judgments. It is, of course, much too long to quote in full or even major part, but the most significant portions of it may be given.

"The opinion in these cases proceeds, it seems to me, upon grounds entirely too narrow and artificial. I cannot resist the conclusion that the substance and spirit of the recent Amendments of the Constitution have been sacrificed by a subtle and ingenious verbal criticism. . . . Constitutional provisions, adopted in the interest of liberty, and for the purpose of securing, through national legislation, if need be, rights inhering in a state of freedom, and belonging to American citizenship, have been so construed as to defeat the ends the people desired to accomplish, which they attempted to accomplish, and which they supposed they had accomplished by changes in their fundamental law. . . .

"If . . . exemption from discrimination, in respect of civil rights, is a new constitutional right, secured by the grant of

---

*Italics ours.

state citizenship to colored citizens of the United States—and I do not see how this can now be questioned—why may not the Nation, by means of its own legislation of a primary direct character, guard, protect and enforce that right? It is a right and privilege which the nation conferred. It did not come from the States in which those colored citizens reside. It has been the established doctrine of this court during all its history, accepted as essential to the national supremacy, that Congress, in the absence of a positive delegation of power to the state legislatures, may, by its own legislation, enforce and protect any right derived from or created by the National Constitution.

"... *It is for Congress, not the judiciary, to say what legislation is appropriate; that is, best adapted to the end to be attained.* The judiciary may not, with safety to our institutions, enter the domain of legislative discretion, and dictate the means which Congress shall employ in the exercise of its granted powers. That would be sheer usurpation of the functions of a co-ordinate department, which, if often repeated, and permanently acquiesced in, *would work a radical change in our system of government.*"*

"In view of the circumstances under which the recent Amendments were incorporated into the Constitution, and especially in view of the peculiar character of the new rights they created and secured, it ought not to be presumed that the General Government has abdicated its authority, by national legislation direct and primary in its character, to guard and protect privileges and immunities created by that instrument. Such an interpretation of the Constitution ought not to be accepted if it be possible to avoid it. Its acceptance would lead to this anomalous result: that whereas, prior to the Amendments, Congress with the sanction of this court, passed the most stringent laws—operating directly and primarily upon States and their officers and agents, as well as upon individuals—in vindication of slavery and the right of the master, it may not now, by legislation of a like primary and direct charac-

---

*Italics ours. The change foreseen by Justice Harlan actually occurred. In fact, the rest of this book is largely concerned with tracing its development.

ter, guard, protect and secure the freedom established, and the most essential right of the citizenship granted, by the constitutional amendments. With all respect for the opinion of others, I insist that the National Legislature may, without transcending the limits of the Constitution, do for human liberty and the fundamental rights of American citizenship, what it did, with the sanction of this court, for the protection of slavery and the rights of the masters of fugitive slaves.

". . . If it be adjudged that the obligation to protect the fundamental privileges and immunities granted by the Fourteenth Amendment to citizens residing in the several States, rest primarily, not on the Nation, but on the States, . . . then . . . *we shall enter upon an era of constitutional law, when the rights of freedom and American citizenship cannot receive from the Nation that efficient protection which heretofore was unhesitatingly accorded to slavery and the rights of the master."**

Justice Harlan took up in turn the specific rights guaranteed to the Negro by Senator Sumner's Act. Here the necessary quotations are relatively short, owing to the succinctness with which he stated his position.

". . . It would seem that the right of a colored person to use an improved public highway,† upon the terms accorded to freemen of other races, is as fundamental in the state of freedom established in this country, as are any of the rights which my brethren concede to be so far fundamental as to be deemed the essence of civil liberty.

". . . A keeper of an inn is in the exercise of a *quasi* public employment. The law gives him special privileges and he is charged with certain duties and responsibilities to the public. The public nature of his employment forbids him from discriminating against any person asking admission as a guest, on account of the race or color of that person.

---

*Again Justice Harlan proved a good prophet. In the course of limiting the civil rights of Negroes, the Court so denatured not only the Fourteenth and Fifteenth Amendments but also the Bill of Rights that when these were called upon during the World War and the Prohibition struggle to protect the civil rights of whites, this part of the Constitution was found to be practically a dead letter.

†The importance of this conception of a railroad as "an improved public highway" with relation to the police powers will be immediately recognized.

"A license from the public, to establish a place of public amusement, imports a law, equality of right, at such places, among all the members of that public. This must be so, unless it be—which I deny—that the common municipal government of all the people may, in the exertion of its powers, conferred for the benefit of all, discriminate or authorize discrimination against a particular race, solely because of its former condition of servitude."

It is obvious that if the central principle of Justice Harlan's opinion—that of giving to the individual what is by nature individual and giving to the public what is by nature public—had been accepted, it would both have protected civil liberties and at the same time without inconsistency would have extended the state police power and even established a national police power—all within the limits of the Constitution.

His powerful arguments were never refuted in later decisions by the majority of the Court; the majority took the more prudent course of simply ignoring them. In the cases of *Plessy* v. *Ferguson,* 163 U. S., 537, and *Berea College* v. *Commonwealth of Kentucky,* 211 U. S., 45, it was decided, with Harlan, of course, dissenting, that "Jim Crow" laws did not in any way violate the letter or the spirit of the Fourteenth Amendment. Hitherto, the Court had held that the Amendment could not be enforced against individuals, but only against the states; now it turned out that it could not be enforced against the states either. In other words, it could not be enforced.

With the Fourteenth Amendment disposed of, to render the Fifteenth ineffective was easy. Laws preventing the Negroes from voting, through various devices of affixing educational requirements, property qualifications, or the poll tax, were upheld; since they did not openly discriminate against the Negro, the Court maintained that the Negro was not discriminated against. Of all the many rights supposed to have been secured for the Negro by the Fourteenth and Fifteenth Amendments at the time of their passage, the only one upheld by the Court was the right of the Negro to sit upon juries—provided he could get there. The barrenness of this privilege is shown by

the fact that the question of even attempting to apply the Court's decision did not come up until fifty years later in the *Scottsboro Case.*

It is not necessary to suppose that the Court, in its decisions on the Amendments, was animated by vulgar prejudice or by any latent hostility against the Negro. Certainly this was not true of Justice Miller, and it may not have been true of the others. The majority of the Court may have felt with perfect sincerity that in the turbulent condition of the South the best interests of the Negroes as well as of the whites would be ultimately served by dropping the question of civil rights. But if we give the Court the benefit of the doubt in this way, that means that it rendered its decisions on grounds of expediency instead of law; and the Supreme Court has always asserted that no one, itself least of all, has the authority to nullify the Constitution of the United States on grounds of mere expediency.

The *coup de grace* to the Amendments, so far as civil liberties were concerned, was given in cases not against the Negroes but against the Chinese, *Barbier* v. *Connolly,* 113 U. S., 27, and *Soon Hing* v. *Crowley,* 113 U. S., 703, in which ordinances prohibiting laundry work at night (thus nominally not discriminative but actually aimed solely at the Chinese) were upheld in opinions delivered by Justice Field. The latter's course in all these Fourteenth Amendment cases was exceedingly tortuous; it will be recalled that he had dissented from the Slaughter-House decision as vitiating the Amendment; in the anti-Negro and anti-Chinese cases, he switched to the other side; in the important case of *Munn* v. *Illinois* to be described presently he switched back again.* The key to his apparent vacillation may be found in his *Barbier* v. *Connolly* opinion in which he maintained that the police power justified legislation "to increase the industries of the State, develop its resources and add to its wealth and prosperity." If these ends

*Cf. E. S. Corwin's remark in his admirable sketch of Justice Field in the *Dictionary of American Biography,* that Field's "positive manner of expression was very likely to lead him into a statement of principles which conflicted with other principles which he accepted with equal fervor."

could be promoted by the Fourteenth Amendment he was for the Amendment; and more and more he came to see in it a most potent weapon for the protection of private industry. Slowly, with changes in the Court, it, too, would gain that insight.

3. Perversion of the Fourteenth Amendment

Until almost the end of the Waite period, the influence of Justice Miller was strong enough to prevent the perversion of the Amendment into a defense of private property after the Amendment had been nullified in its original intent of protecting civil liberties. In this regard, he remained true to the principles set forth by him in the Slaughter-House decision. So definitely was the judgment of the Court in that instance supposed to have settled the question, that in the first case of the kind later brought under the due-process clause of the Amendment this clause was not mentioned. The case, that of *Loan Association* v. *Topeka,* 20 Wallace, 655, involved the validity of a state law authorizing taxation to pay city bonds issued to aid a bridge factory corporation—a case somewhat similar to that of *United States* v. *Muscatine,* previously mentioned, in which the Court, with Justice Miller dissenting, had ordered such taxation. Now, however, Miller carried the Court with him, and delivered an opinion in which he made what Charles Warren calls the "classic observation" that "to lay with one hand, the power of the government on the property of the citizen and with the other to bestow it upon favored individuals to aid private enterprises and build up private fortunes is none the less a robbery because it is done under the forms of law and is called taxation."

The first appeal to the due-process clause of the Fourteenth Amendment as a protection of private enterprises and private fortunes against state action was made in 1876 in *Davidson* v. *New Orleans,* 96 U. S., 97, in which the decision was again delivered by Justice Miller. Denying the relevance of the clause, he called attention to the lack of definition of the phrase

"due process" and went on to say, "If it were possible to define what it is for a State to deprive a person of life, liberty and property without due process of law, in terms which would cover every exercise of power thus forbidden to the State, and exclude those which are not, no more useful construction could be furnished by this or any other Court to any part of the fundamental law." Had Justice Miller foreseen that after fifty years the Court would still be without a definition of what turned out to be the most important phrase in the whole Constitution,* he might have been tempted to supply the omission. As it was, he contented himself with pointing out that in any case a plaintiff had certainly enjoyed "due process of law" if he had received "a fair trial in a court of justice, according to the mode of proceeding applicable to such a case." Justice Miller's understanding of "due process of law" was evidently exactly that which the ordinary layman would have, namely, that it meant a fair legal trial.

Justice Miller was sometimes irascible. The year before the *Davidson Case* he had permitted himself a remark generally true but subject to distinct exceptions: "It is in vain to contend with judges who have been, at the bar, the advocates of railroad companies, and all the forms of associated capital, when they are called upon to decide cases where such interests are in contest. All their training, all their feelings are from the start in favor of those who need no such influence."

Had there been no exceptions, the case of the country against the railroads would have been hopeless, since a majority of the members of the Court—Swayne, Strong, Bradley, Field, and Waite—had been railroad attorneys. But though there were certain cases,† scandalous to the lay mind, in which railroad claims involving proved bribery were upheld by the Court on the old principles laid down by John Marshall, the more important cases raising constitutional problems were decided against the railroads.

Thus the police powers of the states were upheld, not only

---

*Between 1888 and 1918 some 725 cases were decided under the Fourteenth Amendment usually turning on the due-process clause.

†For an account of these cases, see Myers, *op. cit.*, pp. 542-52.

with regard to the Prohibition laws of Iowa and Kansas* and a Pennsylvania statute suppressing the manufacture of oleo-margarine† but also in cases involving state regulation of railroad operations.‡ Finally, and most important of all, the right of the states to fix maximum charges for grain storage and for passenger rates was fully sustained in the famous Granger cases** of 1877.

In delivering the opinion of the Court upholding price fixing for grain storage in the most notable of the Granger cases, that of *Munn* v. *Illinois,* Chief Justice Waite took over from the common law a phrase, "affected with a public interest," which had been used by Lord Chief Justice Hale over two hundred years before. "Property does become clothed with a public interest when used in a manner to make it of public consequence, and affect the community at large. When, therefore, one devotes his property to a use in which the public has an interest, he, in effect, grants to the public an interest in that use, and must submit to be controlled by the public for the common good, to the extent of the interest he has thus created." Though the phraseology of this opinion, based on old aristocratic usage, already represented a retreat from Justice Harlan's words in the *Civil Rights Cases* in that it derived the authority of the police powers from an assumed "grant" to the public by the original private owner whereas Harlan more philosophically implied that it concerned what was essentially public property that had become semi-private by the permission of society, nevertheless, Chief Justice Waite went on to assert the authority of the police powers in language calculated to satisfy its warmest supporters at the time his opinion was delivered.

"In their exercise," he said, "it has been customary . . . in this country from its first colonization, to regulate ferries, com-

---

Bartemeyer v. *Iowa,* 18 Wallace, 129; *Mugler* v. *Kansas,* 123 U. S., 123.
†*Powell* v. *Pennsylvania,* 127 U. S., 678.
‡*Railroad Company* v. *Richmond,* 96 U. S., 521; *Missouri Pacific Railway Company* v. *Humes,* 115 U. S., 512.
**Munn* v. *Illinois,* 94 U. S., 113; *Chicago, Burlington & Quincy Railroad* v. *Iowa,* 94 U. S., 155; *Peik* v. *Chicago & Northwestern Railroad,* 94 U. S., 164; *Chicago, Milwaukee & St. Paul* v. *Ackly,* 94 U. S., 179; *Winona & St. Peter Railroad* v. *Blake,* 94 U. S., 180.

mon carriers, hackmen, bakers, millers, wharfingers, innkeepers, etc. and in so doing to fix a maximum of charge to be made for services rendered, accommodations furnished, and articles sold."

Justice Field alone dissented. By this time once more an enthusiastic admirer of the Fourteenth Amendment, he asserted, "By the term 'liberty' as used in the provision, something more is meant than mere freedom from physical restraint or the bounds of a prison. It means freedom to go where one may choose, and to act in such manner, not inconsistent with the equal rights of others, as his judgment may dictate for the promotion of his happiness; that is, to pursue such callings and avocations as may be most suitable to develop his capacities, and give to them their highest enjoyment."

The railroads were naturally greatly perturbed by the majority decision. Agreeing with Justice Miller in his derogatory opinion of railroad attorneys as justices, except that it was not deemed derogatory, they set themselves to bring every possible pressure to bear as soon as vacancies occurred on the Court. In this they were aided by the laws of mortality. In 1880 Justice Strong resigned at the age of 72; in 1881 Justice Clifford died at the age of 77, and Justice Swayne resigned at 76;* in 1882 Justice Hunt resigned at the age of 71. Their places were taken by: William B. Woods, 56 years old, a carpetbag politician and judge from Georgia appointed by President Hayes; Stanley Matthews, of Ohio, 56 years old, Jay Gould's chief attorney in the Middle West and a director in the Knoxville & Ohio Railroad, who was nominated by Hayes, resisted by the Senate because of the public outcry, renominated by Garfield, and confirmed by a vote of twenty-four to twenty-three; Horace Gray, 53 years old, an extremely wealthy judge of the supreme judicial court of Massachusetts; and Samuel Blatchford, 62 years old, a railroad lawyer and federal judge in the New York Circuit Court, admittedly the most conservative in the country, who was appointed after Roscoe Conkling had a second time declined a position on the Supreme Court.

---

*As Warren remarks, op. cit., Vol. II, p. 622, "at the comparatively youthful age of 76."

The influence of the new Justices began to make itself felt even while Waite was still alive.   In 1886 in the case of *Santa Clara County* v. *Southern Pacific Railroad,* 118 U. S., 394, the resuscitation of the Fourteenth Amendment in its new rôle as defender of private property rights was definitely begun.   The people of California after a desperate struggle against the arrogant autocracy of the Southern Pacific, had won a temporary victory and adopted a very liberal constitution under which a law was passed imposing a higher rate of taxation upon corporations than upon individuals.   The law was successfully opposed before the Supreme Court by George F. Edmunds, William M. Evarts, and Roscoe Conkling, and the Court, adopting their arguments, held that a corporation was also a person.   All that was needed now was a reinterpretation of the term "due process," and the civil rights of persons under the Fourteenth Amendment would be transmogrified into the property rights of corporations under a new amendment bearing the same name but passed not by the people but by the Supreme Court.

This development, however, was not to come in the time of Chief Justice Waite.   He died at the age of 71 on March 23, 1888, after a much better record than had been expected at the time of his appointment.

CHAPTER VIII

THE COURT UNDER CHIEF JUSTICE FULLER

1888-1910

MELVILLE W. FULLER, SAMUEL F. MILLER, STEPHEN J. FIELD,
JOSEPH P. BRADLEY, JOHN M. HARLAN, STANLEY MATTHEWS,
HORACE GRAY, SAMUEL BLATCHFORD, LUCIUS QUINTUS CINCIN-
NATUS LAMAR, DAVID J. BREWER, HENRY B. BROWN, GEORGE
SHIRAS, HOWELL E. JACKSON, EDWARD D. WHITE, RUFUS WHEELER
PECKHAM, JOSEPH MCKENNA, OLIVER WENDELL HOLMES, WILLIAM
R. DAY, WILLIAM H. MOODY, HORACE H. LURTON,
CHARLES EVANS HUGHES.

1. *Changing Personnel of the Court*

FOLLOWING the precedent established by Grant, President
Cleveland appointed as Chief Justice Waite's successor another
nationally unknown figure. Melville W. Fuller, 55 years old,
a native of Maine but citizen of Illinois, was primarily a very
clever corporation lawyer in Chicago. He was attorney for
the Chicago, Burlington & Quincy Railroad, one of the defeated plaintiffs in the Granger cases, and had among his
clients such prominent capitalists as Marshall Field, Jesse Hoyt,
and Philip D. Armour.* Owing to his prominent corporation
connections, there was considerable resistance to his appointment in the Senate, but it was eventually confirmed by a vote
of forty-one to twenty.

His long term of office, third longest in the history of the
Court, was a period of unprecedented continuous change in
personnel; whereas during Marshall's thirty-four years there
were only seven changes and in Taney's twenty-nine but eleven,
there were eleven in Fuller's twenty-two, or on an average one
in every two years. And during the first decade of his régime
nearly all of the changes were for the worse in point of mental caliber.

---

*For an account of Fuller's career as attorney, see Myers, *op. cit.*, pp.
582-89.

This could not be said of an appointment made shortly before Fuller's own, when Justice Woods was succeeded by Lucius Quintus Cincinnatus Lamar of Mississippi, a man 62 years old with a varied experience behind him as a law professor, United States congressman, Confederate soldier, and United States senator, in which capacity he had acted as chairman of the committee on Pacific railroads. His personal character and ability were recognized by the Senate, but his Confederate antecedents and his undoubted tendency to give the railroads what they wanted, as being necessary to the development of the country, caused his confirmation to be by the close vote of thirty-two to twenty-eight.

In 1889 Stanley Matthews died and was succeeded by David J. Brewer, 52 years old, a nephew of David Dudley and Stephen J. Field. He had studied law in the office of one uncle and was deeply influenced by the judicial opinions of the other, so that his appointment by President Harrison was almost equivalent to giving Justice Field two votes on the Court. Large, genial, and in private a famous story-teller, in public he delivered many lectures on the duties of citizenship, the beauty of philanthropy, and the claims of foreign missions. As circuit judge in Kansas, he had refused to be bound by the Supreme Court decision in *Munn* v. *Illinois,* and probably owed his appointment largely to his attitude on that issue. On the Supreme Court he established what was up to that time a high-water record of holding forty-one per cent of the police power laws that came before him unconstitutional—though this achievement was later to be equaled and possibly surpassed by Justices Peckham and McReynolds.

In 1890 Justice Miller died.* His place was taken by Henry B. Brown of Michigan, 54 years old, a former railroad attorney who had been appointed a federal district judge by Grant.

Justice Bradley died in 1892, to be succeeded by George Shiras of Pennsylvania, 60 years old, after strong opposition in the Senate on the ground that he had no particular repu-

---

*Curiously, or perhaps not curiously, Justices Miller and Field, who differed in all their political and economic convictions, were the closest of personal friends, each serving as a whetstone to the other's opinions. After Miller's death, Field, lacking the stimulus of this opposition, became a somewhat less notable figure on the Court.

tation except as a shrewd and successful railroad lawyer, his main practice having been that of an attorney for the Baltimore & Ohio.

Justice Lamar died in 1893 and was followed by Howell E. Jackson of Tennessee, 60 years old, another railroad lawyer who had later become a federal judge.

In 1894 Justice Blatchford died, and after two of Cleveland's nominees, William B. Hornblower and Wheeler H. Peckham, had been rejected by the Senate on the ground of their notorious capitalistic sympathies, Edward D. White of Louisiana was appointed. His selection was at least a variation in the unbroken sequence of railroad attorneys. Owner of a large sugar-beet plantation, White had gone into state politics, had been for three years a judge of the Louisiana supreme court and for another three years, after a considerable interval, had been United States senator* and was still only 48 years old when appointed to the Supreme Court. His continuance in the Senate for nearly a month after this appointment, in order to defend the sugar bounty, gave rise to considerable unfavorable comment, and even the Democratic New York *World* of March 6, 1894, excitedly declared that he was unfit for the Supreme Court, an opinion of course echoed by the Republican press. Once on the Court, however, Justice White, like Justice Waite, defeated expectations by rising to meet his new responsibilities to a very considerable extent.

Of all the appointments to the Court during this period probably the most important, after that of Brewer, was that of Rufus Wheeler Peckham, a brother of the Peckham recently rejected by the Senate. Justice Peckham was 57 years old and had been for sixteen years a judge in the New York circuit court of appeals, where, like Brewer in Kansas, he had denied the authority of the Supreme Court's decision in the *Munn Case.*

All of these changes, after the death of Justice Miller, were really no changes. One railroad attorney was succeeded by another railroad attorney, one corporation judge was followed

---

*The charge that White was elected senator through the corrupt influence of the Louisiana Lottery is discussed, with evidence *pro* and *con*, by Myers, *op. cit.,* pp. 704-708.

by another corporation judge. Taken as a whole, and allowing for individual exceptions, the Court was at its lowest ebb in respect to both ability and character. And yet within the brief space of ten years, the relatively mediocre Justice Fuller and his relatively mediocre colleagues secured for the Court powers beyond the dreams of the great John Marshall in his palmiest days—because now at last the Court with the support of presidents and congresses was floating on the high tide of capitalistic industry.

2. *Anti-Chinese Cases*

The new Triple Alliance of Executive, Legislative, and Judiciary first showed itself in a case where for once the interests of labor and capital seemed momentarily to coincide. The Chinese, who during the period of great railroad construction had been welcomed for their cheap labor, at the close of that period became a form of cheap industry—or in the contemporary phrase of today, "chiseling"—through their ability to undersell "legitimate" American business. In their first phase they were inimical to American labor, in their second they were inimical to American industry. Hence the Chinese Exclusion Act of October 1, 1888, prohibiting the entry of Chinese coolies and, as Charles Warren tersely but correctly states, "in violation of the Treaty with China," which was upheld, in spite of the treaty violation, by the Supreme Court in the case of *Chae Chan Ping* v. *United States,* 130 U. S., 581. Whatever the merits of the decision on the score of expediency, it was in striking contrast to the oft repeated utterances of the Supreme Court regarding the "sacredness of treaties" in cases where they confirmed the claims of American capitalists, although, it is true, these cases had always merely involved state laws, not acts of Congress.

Another anti-Chinese decision, delivered four years later in the case of *Fong Yue Ting* v. *United States,* 149 U. S., 698, was erroneously regarded at the time as a victory for American labor; by it, the national government was held to have an

absolute right to admit or deport foreigners at its pleasure; the right to determine admission had been already asserted in the previous decision, and the unlimited right of deportation (exercised by the Bureau of Immigration through secret trials without juries) was defended on the specious technical ground that deportation was not a form of "punishment." The majority opinion delivered by Justice Gray was reminiscent of the long discredited Alien Act of 1798, and Field, Brewer, and Fuller filed a vigorous dissent; but Field, at least, after helping to deprive American citizens of civil liberties in the Reconstruction cases, was hardly justified in attacking the Court for refusing to extend these liberties to aliens.

3.   Railroad Cases

Of more immediate importance was a series of railroad cases decided uniformly in favor of private capital.   The regulatory authority of the states supposed to have been guaranteed by the outcome of the Granger cases began to be whittled away as early as 1890 by the decision in *Chicago, Milwaukee, & St. Paul Railroad* v. *Minnesota,* 134 U. S., 418, in which for the first time the doctrine was set forth that rates must be "reasonable" (as determined by the Supreme Court) in order to conform to the due-process clause.

By what magical development had the meaning of "due process" become transformed in four short years from Justice Miller's understanding of it, set forth as the Court's opinion in the *Davidson Case* of 1886, in which "due process" was declared to refer primarily to "a fair trial in a court of justice" into this entirely new meaning of "legislation which is reasonable in the eyes of the Supreme Court"; changed in other words from a procedural limitation upon the courts into a substantive limitation upon the legislature?   No assistance can be derived from the Supreme Court on this question because in its usual manner of overruling previous opinions tacitly instead of explicitly it merely announced the new interpretation of "due process" as *the* interpretation, taking care not to admit that it was new.   So one is forced to turn to

the legal historians, who have accumulated a mass of information on the history of the term, much of it unfortunately irrelevant, since it was not known to the Supreme Court at the time of its decisions.

The clause, "Nor shall any State deprive any person of life, liberty, or property, without due process of law" in the Fourteenth Amendment merely extended to the states the limitation placed on Congress by the Fifth Amendment in its provision that "No person shall be . . . deprived of life, liberty, or property, without due process of law." The context in the Fifth Amendment shows that the words "due process" there referred to the necessity of a fair trial, the immediately preceding provisions being concerned with similar questions of procedure; the requirement of grand jury indictments, the prohibition of double jeopardy, and the provision that no person may be compelled to be a witness against himself in criminal cases. This much is clear and simple, but it does not carry us beyond Justice Miller's interpretation of the words.

Legal research has traced the origin of the phrase "due process" of the Fifth Amendment to a famous section of Magna Charta: "No free man shall be taken and imprisoned or disseized or exiled or in any way destroyed, nor will we go upon him nor send upon him, except by the lawful judgment of his peers and by the law of the land"; the origin of the phrase "law of the land" has been traced further back to "law of the Emperor" in an edict of Conrad II, May 8, 1039. The words "due process" apparently were first used in a statute of Edward III, and were, according to the definition of Lord Coke in the seventeenth century, equivalent to "law of the land."

But what did "law of the land" mean? Unfortunately, these words too were obscure, and Lord Coke did not greatly clarify the situation by saying that one vague phrase was equivalent to another vague phrase. In a general sense, "law of the land" undoubtedly referred to the unwritten British constitution, and was similarly used, with more precision, in Article VI, Section 2, of the American Constitution which states that "This Constitution, and the laws of the United

States which shall be made in pursuance thereof; and all treaties . . . shall be the supreme law of the land." If then, accepting Lord Coke as an adequate authority on American usage
a century later—as American jurists are fond of doing—we
should be able to substitute "law of the land" for "due process"
in the Fifth Amendment, reaching the statement that "No
person shall be deprived of life, liberty, or property except in
accordance with the Constitution and the laws of the United
States," which still gives no basis for nullifying laws of
Congress.

"Due process" and "law of the land," sometimes used in the
same vague general sense in America, though obviously not in
the Fifth Amendment were vaguely identified, contrary to the
Constitution, with that "natural right" to life, liberty, and
property so popular in the eighteenth century. The notion of
natural right to property slumbered on in a state of "suspended
animation" during the earlier part of the nineteenth century
as evidenced by the fact that no court had officially dismissed
the idea of vested rights, while the New York courts had always insisted that legislative powers were inherently limited
and the Massachusetts supreme court had consistently held
that state police powers must be "reasonable." Shortly before the *Dred Scott Case,* the New York court of appeals
had ruled in the *Wynehamer Case,** that "when a law annihi-
lates the value of property . . . the owner is deprived of it . . .
within the constitutional provision intended expressly to shield
personal rights from the exercise of arbitrary power," and
Chief Justice Taney, looking about for any ground on which
to declare the Missouri Compromise unconstitutional, was
probably inspired by the New York decision to use the words
"due process" in this sense.

The phrase was put into the Fourteenth Amendment by
the corporation congressmen, Roscoe Conkling and John A.
Bingham, without any revelation of sinister intentions, but in
a case before the Supreme Court in 1882 Conkling showed
that he had known perfectly what he was doing. "At the time
the Fourteenth Amendment was ratified," he said, "individuals
and joint stock companies were appealing for congressional

*Wynehamer v. New York, 13 N. Y., 378.

and administrative protection against invidious and discriminating state and local taxes. . . . Those who devised the
Fourteenth Amendment . . . planted in the Constitution a
monumental truth to stand foursquare to whatever wind might
blow. That truth is but the Golden Rule, so intrenched as to
curb the many who would do to the few as they would not
have the few do to them."

It may be doubted whether the Justices of the Supreme
Court were very familiar with the statutes of Edward III or
the edicts of Conrad II, but they were certainly acquainted
with the Dred Scott decision and with the Gospel according to
Conkling. To this ignoble origin may be directly traced the
new interpretation of the Fourteenth Amendment sanctioned
by the Court in the *Chicago, Milwaukee & St. Paul Case*. The
majority opinion, set forth by Justice Blatchford, so clearly
involved the assumption of legislative powers by the judiciary
that it was too much for even Justice Bradley.

"I cannot agree to the decision of the court in this case," he
said. "It practically overrules *Munn* v. *Illinois,* 94 U. S., 113,
and the several railroad cases that were decided at the same
time. The governing principle of those cases was that the
regulation and settlement of the fares of railroads and other
public accommodations is a legislative prerogative and not a
judicial one. This is a principle which I regard as of great
importance. . . . All human institutions are imperfect—courts
as well as commissions and legislatures. . . . The important
question always is, what is the lawful tribunal for the particular case. In my judgment, in the present case, the proper tribunal was the legislature, or the board of commissioners which
it created for that purpose."

In *Reagan* v. *Farmers' Loan and Trust Company,* 154 U. S.,
362, in which it was decided in 1894 that the rates fixed by
the Texas State Commission were unreasonable, Justice
Brewer, speaking for the majority, attempted to answer Bradley, who by that time was safely dead, with the following ingenious bit of quibbling:

"The courts are not authorized to revise or change the body
of rates imposed by a legislature or a commission," he admit-

ted; "they do not determine whether one rate is preferable to another, or what under all circumstances would be fair and reasonable as between the carriers and the shippers; they do not engage in any mere administrative work; but still there can be no doubt of their power and duty to inquire whether a body of rates prescribed by a legislature or a commission is unjust and unreasonable, and such as to work a practical destruction to rights of property, and if found so to be, to restrain its operation." In other words, though the Court had no authority to decide between rates, it nevertheless could so decide, and Justice Bradley's doubts of judicial power were refuted by the statement that there could be no doubt of such power.

Less significant from the point of constitutional law were a number of decisions in the early 'nineties confirming railroad grants, originally obtained through bribery, to extensive timber lands and other valuable property; in these cases, the majority opinion, usually delivered by Brewer or Shiras, with Harlan and occasionally Brown dissenting, followed the precedents laid down by John Marshall that an official grant, however secured, must be validated by the Court. "It is enough," said Justice Brewer, that the claimant "has the legal title; and, if so owning, he must be paid the actual cash value of the property." On the other hand, still following Marshall, the Court held that an official annulment of grants did not have the same authority. As Justice Brewer said, in the case of *Camou* v. *United States,* 171 U. S., 277, concerning a decree of President Santa Anna of Mexico, "It is going too far to hold that the mere declaration of law made by a temporary dictator . . . against an individual grantee . . . is to be regarded as operative and determinative of the latter's rights."*

Thus far, in all these cases decided in favor of the railroads the issue concerned the rights of a private corporation as against the rights of the general public. The further question of employers versus employees was not directly involved. In fact, the reader will have been struck with the singular absence

---

*For a detailed account of these cases, see Myers, *op cit.,* pp. 598-611.

of labor cases in the history of the Supreme Court hitherto,* although there had been plenty of labor problems in the United States from the beginning. The explanation is fairly simple: problems do not give rise to lawsuits unless there are laws to cover them, and they do not give rise to significant suits, unless the parties involved are sufficiently well matched to engage in a real conflict. For the first seventy-five years of national life, labor was too poorly organized to invoke the law on its behalf or to tempt employers to invoke the law very earnestly against them. But beginning with the 'seventies the situation changed owing to the enormous increase of the working class through immigration, the growth of labor unions, and the augmenting number of strikes. By the 'nineties it had become so serious that the employers were more and more resorting to injunctions against the unions as the most effective method of strike-breaking.

A test case, *In re Debs,* 158 U. S., 564, arose in 1895. During the Pullman strike of the previous year in Chicago (eventually broken by the totally unnecessary† sending of federal troops over Governor Altgeld's protest), Federal Judge Peter S. Grosscup of Chicago issued what was popularly known as his "Gatling Gun Injunction," addressed to Eugene V. Debs, leader of the railway union involved in the strike. This decree read, in the section which gave it its name:

"You are hereby restrained, commanded, and enjoined absolutely to desist and refrain from in any way or manner interfering with, hindering, obstructing, or stopping any of the business of any of the following named railroads: (22 named) . . . and from compelling or *inducing,* by threats, or attempting to compel or *induce,* by threats, intimidation, *persuasion,* force or violence any of the employees of the said railroads to refuse to perform any of their duties . . . or to leave the service of such railroads. . . ."‡

---

*Of course, there had been many minor cases, but they were of little importance in comparison with those major ones which alone merit consideration in a work of such limited scope as the present volume. And, again of course, from the economic viewpoint the slavery question was a labor problem, but it was not so considered at the time, or in the courts.

†See Allan Nevins, *Grover Cleveland* (1933), pp. 611-28.

‡Italics ours.

These words, enjoining not merely force and violence (which, contrary to the popular impression, had not been used) but also persuasion, might as well have been an injunction against striking at all, and Debs applied to the Supreme Court for a writ of habeas corpus. Although he was represented by one of the ablest lawyers in the country, Lyman Trumbull, his petition was denied, Justice Brewer in announcing the opinion of the Court asserting that the only issue was whether "the relations of the general government to interstate commerce" were such as to justify its intervention through a local court "to prevent a forcible obstruction thereof."

4. The Income Tax Case

Two other very important decisions made 1895 the banner year of conservatism. One of these, in *Pollock* v. *Farmers' Loan and Trust Company,* 157 U. S., 429, 158 U. S., 601, nullified* the income tax of 1894 which the Bryan Democrats had succeeded in forcing upon an unwilling Congress as the price for their acceptance of the high rates in the Wilson-Gorman Tariff.

The law imposed a flat tax of two per cent on all incomes above four thousand dollars. The argument against it of Attorney Joseph Choate was considered in many quarters at the time a masterpiece.

"If you approve this law," he said, "with this iniquitous exemption of $4000, and this communistic march goes on and five years hence a statute comes to you with an exemption of $20,000 and a tax of 20% upon all having incomes in excess of that amount, how can you meet it in view of the decision

---

*The propriety of this word in connection with Supreme Court declarations of unconstitutionality is sometimes denied, but it is difficult to see what word could be more distinctly appropriate for decisions that certain laws are "null and void." Similarly, when the practical effect of such decisions is to nullify the constitutional source of the laws, as in the earlier cases under the Fourteenth Amendment, the broader popular meaning of the word seems to the author justified. Legally, of course, the Reconstruction Amendments have never been nullified in the South; practically, they have been with regard to the Negro, as everyone admits. The author uses the word occasionally in either its broad or narrow sense where the context makes plain which meaning is intended.

which my opponents ask you now to render? *There is protection now or never.* . . .

"One of the fundamental objects of all civilized government—we are informed—was the preservation of the rights
of private property. I have thought that it was the very keystone of the arch upon which all civilized government rests,
and that this once abandoned, everything was at stake and in
danger. I was brought up at the feet of Gamaliel. That is
what Mr. Webster said in 1820, at Plymouth, and I supposed
that all educated men believed in that. According to the doctrines that have been propounded here this morning, even that
great fundamental principle has been scattered to the winds.

"One thing is certain, absolutely certain, that although the
power was given Congress to tax, no power was given it to
confiscate, and that, the learned Attorney General and his associates all admit. If this is *a confiscation under the forms of
law,* there is no power given to Congress in the Constitution
that could by any possibility enable it to validly enact such
a law."*

But the Court was not prepared openly to accept Choate's
contention that a two-per-cent tax was confiscatory. Instead,
it chose to reverse its own decisions both in cases which had
come up concerning the income taxes of the Civil War and
in a number of other cases which had involved the meaning
of "direct tax." That meaning had not been defined in the
Constitution further than by the provision in Article I, Section
9, that "No capitation or other direct tax shall be laid unless
in proportion to the census or enumeration hereinbefore directed to be taken," but in the *Hylton Case* in 1796 the Supreme Court had decided that the phrase "direct tax" applied
only to poll taxes and land taxes, and this interpretation had
always been accepted down to 1895. Now by a five-to-four
vote, the Court elected to change the meaning of the Constitution as it had been understood for the past ninety-nine years.

This revolutionary action was not accomplished without
difficulty. After a first argument, the Court held, by a six-to-
two vote with Justice Jackson absent and Justices White and

*Italics ours.

Harlan dissenting, that a tax on land included the income from land, in the form of rent,—a sufficiently novel decision in itself,—but on the further points involved, the Court was evenly divided, four to four, and a reargument was ordered. In its second still more startling decision, the Court declared that the income from personal property was also a direct tax; hence the law was unconstitutional throughout.

In this second instance Justice Jackson was present and voted with the minority, which would have made it a majority had not one of the former dissenters, believed to be Justice Shiras, changed his mind in the interval between the two decisions.

To add to the confused manner in which a changing majority of the Court ruled that an income tax was *clearly* unconstitutional, Justice Field filed a separate concurring opinion wherein he refused to abide within the discreet technicalities of his colleagues and very bluntly stated the real ground of his decision.

*"The present assault upon capital is but the beginning,"** he said. "It will be but the stepping-stone to others, larger and more sweeping, till our political contests will become a war of the poor against the rich. . . . If the purely arbitrary limitation of $4000 in the present law can be sustained . . . the limitation of future Congresses may be fixed at a much larger sum . . . or the limitation may be designated at such an amount as a board of 'walking delegates' may designate."

Both the legal and class implications of this momentous case† were ably pointed out by the dissenting Justices.

Said Justice White: "At the very birth of the government a contention arose as to the meaning of the word 'direct.' That controversy was determined by the legislative and executive

---

*Italics ours.

†Of course, the decision of the Court was overruled by the ratification of the Sixteenth Amendment in February, 1913. But during the intervening eighteen years most of the economic evils foreseen by the dissenting Justices had actually occurred. According to the estimate of Chief Justice Walter Clark of the North Carolina supreme court, the decision cost the government and saved the wealthier classes approximately eighteen billion dollars. Furthermore, after the passage of the Amendment, the judges' salaries and stock dividends were exempted from its operation by the Supreme Court.

departments of the government. Their action came to this court for review, and it was approved. . . . And now, after a hundred years, after long-continued action by other departments of the government, and after repeated adjudications of this court, this interpretation is overthrown, and the Congress is declared not to have a power of taxation which may at some time, as it has in the past, prove necessary to the very existence of the government. . . .

"Since the Hylton case was decided the Constitution has been repeatedly amended. The construction which confined the word 'direct' to capitation and land taxes was not changed by these amendments, and it should not now be reversed by what seems to me to be *a judicial amendment of the Constitution.**

"Let it be felt that on great constitutional questions this court is to depart from the settled conclusions of its predecessors, and to determine them all according to the mere opinion of those who temporarily fill its bench, and *our Constitution will, in my judgment, be bereft of value and become a most dangerous instrument to the rights and liberties of the people.*"†

The other dissenting members of the Court went as far as judicial propriety admitted toward asserting that the decision had been rendered because of class interest rather than regard for the law.

Justice Harlan declared: "The decree now passed dislocates—*principally, for reasons of an economic nature*‡—a sovereign power expressly granted to the general government. . . . The practical effect of the decision today is to give to certain kinds of property a position of favoritism and advantage inconsistent with the fundamental principles of our social organization, and to invest them with power and influence that may be perilous to that portion of the American people upon whom rests the larger part of the burdens of the government, and who ought not to be subjected to the dominion of aggregate wealth any more than the property of the country should be at the mercy of the lawless."

---

*Italics ours.
†Italics ours.
‡Italics ours.

Justice Jackson reiterated the position of Justice Harlan:

"The practical operation of the decision is not only to disregard the great principles of equality in taxation, but the further principle that in the imposition of taxes for the benefit of
the government the burdens thereof should be imposed upon
those having most ability to bear them. This decision, in effect
works out a directly opposite result, in relieving the citizens
having the greater ability, while the burdens of taxation are
made to fall most heavily and oppressively upon those having
the least ability. . . . *This decision is, in my judgment, the
most disastrous blow ever struck at the constitutional power*
of Congress."*

Most outspoken of all was Justice Brown. *"The decision,"*
he said, *"involves nothing less than a surrender of the taxing
power to the moneyed class.* By resuscitating an argument that
was exploded in the *Hylton Case,* and has lain practically dor-
mant for a hundred years, it is made to do duty in nullifying,
not this law alone, but every similar law that is not based upon
an impossible theory of apportionment. Even the spectre of
socialism is conjured up to frighten Congress from laying taxes
upon the people in proportion to their ability to pay them. It
is certainly a strange commentary upon the Constitution of
the United States and upon the democratic government that
Congress has no power to lay a tax which is one of the main
sources of revenue of nearly every civilized state."

5.   The High Point of Laissez Faire

The other great capitalist victory of 1895 was won in the
triumph of the Sugar Trust over the Sherman Anti-Trust Law
of 1890, declared by Congress to be "An Act to protect trade
and commerce against unlawful restraints and monopolies."
In *United States* v. *E. C. Knight Company,* 156 U. S., 1, the
Supreme Court, speaking through Chief Justice Fuller, virtually admitted the fact of monopoly. "By the purchase of
the stock of . . . four Philadelphia refineries, with shares of
its own stock," said the Chief Justice, "the American Sugar

*Italics ours.

Refining Company acquired nearly complete control of the manufacture of refined sugar within the United States." But a monopoly of manufacture, he continued, did not necessarily imply a monopoly of commerce. Besides, "the contracts and acts of the defendants related exclusively to the acquisition of the Philadelphia refineries and the business of sugar refining in Pennsylvania, and bore no direct relation to commerce between the States or with foreign nations."

The result of the decision was effectually to discourage for a period of nearly ten years any serious attempt to use the Act for its original purpose of outlawing monopolies. It is true that in 1897, in *United States* v. *Trans-Missouri Freight Association,* 166 U. S., 290, the Court rejected Justice White's contention that the "rule of reason" recently discovered in the Fourteenth Amendment should be applied to the Sherman Act, but there was yet little need for its application to protect the interests of capital; when the need should arise, as it did later, the "rule of reason" would be duly incorporated in the Act as it had been in the Amendment.

In a second case involving the Sugar Trust, in 1896, the Court overleaped limitations upon its action that it had always previously respected. In *United States* v. *Realty Company,* 163 U. S., 274, a suit was brought by the government to test the constitutionality of the Sugar Bounty Act of 1890 and if possible recover the sums paid out by the government under it. The Court, this time speaking through Justice Peckham, declared that regardless of the constitutionality of the Act the beneficiaries were entitled to the bounty.

"We regard the question of the unconstitutionality of the bounty provisions of the Act of 1890 as entirely immaterial to the discussion here," said Justice Peckham. *"These parties did not at the time (when manufacturing under its provisions) know that it was unconstitutional. . . .* The Nation, speaking broadly, owes a 'debt' to an individual, when his claim grows out of general principles of right and justice; when, in other words, it is based upon considerations of a moral or merely honorary nature, such as are binding on the conscience or the

honor of an individual, *although the debt could obtain no recognition in a Court of law.*"*

Also in 1896 another of the government's endeavors to regulate industry, through the establishment of the Interstate Commerce Commission in 1887, was rendered ineffective by the decision of the Fuller Court (really now the Brewer-Peckham Court) in what is known as the *Maximum Freight Rate Case,* 167 U. S., 479. The Interstate Commerce Commission had been created to carry out the general provisions of the Interstate Commerce Act which included one that "all charges . . . shall be reasonable and just; and every unjust and unreasonable charge for such service is prohibited and declared to be unlawful"; but the Commission had not been specifically authorized to enforce this specific provision; therefore, reasoned Justice Brewer, speaking for the Court, the rates were "to be made at the will of the carrier."

In 1897 the final touch to the transformation of the Fourteenth Amendment was given in the case of *Allgeyer* v. *Louisiana,* 165 U. S., 578, in which the Court held that a state law regulating insurance companies was in violation of the due-process clause of the Amendment. "The liberty mentioned in that amendment means," said Justice Peckham for the Court, "not only the right of the citizen to be free from the mere physical restraint of his person, as by incarceration, but the term is deemed to embrace the right of the citizen to be free in the enjoyment of all his faculties; to be free to use them in all lawful ways; to live and work where he will; to earn his livelihood by any lawful calling; to pursue any livelihood or avocation, and for that purpose to enter into all contracts which may be proper, necessary, and essential to his carrying out to a successful conclusion the purposes above mentioned."

This conception of liberty was not only foreign to the framers of the Fourteenth Amendment but had been rejected as a novelty by the Supreme Court itself only eleven years before; for what was now the majority opinion of Justice Peck-

---

*Italics ours.

ham was nothing but a restatement of the dissenting opinion of Justice Field in *Munn* v. *Illinois.*

Allgeyer v. *Louisiana* marked the high point, the utmost limit, of the onward march of industrial capitalism. With the power to regulate industry practically denied by the Supreme Court to both state and national government, *laissez faire* economics seemed to be secure. But it was so only momentarily. In the ensuing year the pendulum began to swing slowly the other way, as on the whole it has continued, with many a temporary setback, to do ever since. Since 1897 capitalism has been fighting to retain the powers it then possessed, and though the Supreme Court has continued to augment its own authority its decisions have not effected the same result for private industry.*

6. *Field into McKenna*

An outward symbol that the turning point had been reached was furnished in 1897 by the resignation of Justice Field at the age of 81. In his condition of approaching senility, the rest of the Court took the same action of requesting his resignation which they had formerly taken with regard to Justice Grier. Commissioned to convey to Field the message that Field had once carried to Grier, Justice Harlan tried to soften the blow by recalling Field's action on the earlier occasion, but the only response was an angry growl, "Yes, and it was the dirtiest deed of my whole life." A good fighting organism to the last, even after the mind had weakened, Justice Field resigned but made it clear that he did so only under protest.

His successor, appointed by McKinley, was Joseph Mc-Kenna, 54 years old, a small-town lawyer of California who had thrice secured election to Congress as a representative of the Southern Pacific, had been for five years a federal Circuit Court judge, and for a few months had been United States attorney-general. There was loud protest from the New York *World,* which declared, in an editorial of December 17, 1897,

---

*With the possible exception of very recent decisions—*if* they are allowed to stand.

that McKenna "has been the tool of corporations and the pet of plutocrats. His advancement has been due entirely to the favor of Stanford, Huntington and other multimillionaires of his section." Former Attorney-General George H. Williams of Oregon, whose own nomination to the Supreme Court had once raised a similar outcry, joined with other prominent lawyers of his state in sending in a lengthy protest to the Senate. But on investigation it turned out that most of McKenna's critics were simply working on behalf of the Northern Pacific against the Southern Pacific, and since it seemed to be a matter of having some kind of a railroad attorney anyway, the Senate decided that McKenna was as good as others. As a matter of fact, he turned out to be much better than most of the others; if there was nothing in his past career to justify his appointment there would be considerable in the future to vindicate it.

7.   The First Labor Victories

For the next five years the attention of the nation and of the Court was focused upon the Spanish-American War and the legislative problems arising out of it. But at the beginning and the end of that period, in two cases little noticed at the time, labor won its first victories in the Supreme Court, very minor victories, to be sure, because of the exceptional character of the employments covered, but none the less definite victories.

The first hours-of-labor case was that of *Holden* v. *Hardy,* 169 U. S., 366, decided in 1898. A Utah eight-hour law for laborers engaged in underground mining and in smelting was upheld as necessary to the health of the employees. In delivering the opinion of the Court, Justice Brown pointed out that "the proprietors of these establishments and their operatives do not stand upon an equality, and . . . their interests are, to a certain extent, conflicting. . . . The proprietors lay down the rules and the laborers are practically constrained to obey them. In such cases self-interest is often an unsafe guide, and the legislature may properly interpose its authority." The employers having contended that the law infringed the right of the

employees to work, Justice Brown continued: "The argument would certainly come with better grace and greater cogency from the latter class. . . . The fact that both parties are of full age and competent to contract does not necessarily deprive the State of the power to interfere where the parties do .not stand upon an equality, or where the public health demands that one party to the contract shall be protected against itself." The position of Justice Brown was overruled in the *Lochner Case* in 1905, but in *Holden* v. *Hardy* only Justices Brewer and Peckham dissented without offering an opinion.

In 1903, in the case of *Atkin* v. *Kansas,* 191 U. S., 207, the Court upheld a Kansas eight-hour law for state employees, the ground for the decision, rendered by Justice Harlan, being the right of the state to prescribe conditions for work undertaken by it. "Whether a similar statute," Justice Harlan said, "applied to laborers or employees in purely private work, would be constitutional, is a question of very large import, which we have no occasion now to determine or even to consider." Brewer and Peckham again dissented without opinion, and in this instance they were joined by Chief Justice Fuller.

8.   The Spanish-American War

The Insular cases that aroused a deal of sound and fury immediately after the Spanish-American War, may be dismissed very briefly since though of vast importance in the history of the United States they were of little significance in the history of the Supreme Court. They involved the status of Porto Rico and the Philippines after their cession by Spain to the United States; were these islands still foreign conquered territory or were they now domestic territory, an integral part of the United States, entitled to enjoy the blessings of the Constitution? In the phrase of the hour, did "the Constitution follow the flag" or didn't it? A much divided Court decided that it did and it didn't; the islands were not quite foreign and yet not quite domestic.

The two most important of these cases, *De Lima* v. *Bidwell,* 182 U. S., 1, and *Downes* v. *Bidwell,* 182 U. S., 244, turned

on the application to Porto Rico of the Dingley Tariff Act, passed before the war, and the Foraker Act passed subsequently with special reference to the island. Importers of Porto Rican goods maintained that these did not come under the provisions of either Act: not under the general tariff schedule on foreign goods of the Dingley Act, because the island was no longer foreign territory; and not under the special schedule of the Foraker Act, because as a part of the United States the island was entitled to ship its goods free of duty to any other part. In the two cases, the first contention was affirmed by the Court and the second was denied, both decisions being rendered by five-to-four votes, the majority in the first case, with one exception, being the minority in the second. The final outcome of these and other cases was the establishment of the "incorporative theory" of Justice White that territory could be held by the United States without being incorporated in it unless by special Act of Congress. Following this, it was easy for the Court to hold in subsequent cases that trial by jury and other Constitutional rights did not extend to the Philippines, Porto Rico, Hawaii, or Alaska, the net result of all these decisions being to transform the United States from a republic composed of equal states into an imperial power ruling over subject peoples. Against this mounting tendency of the decisions, that old Jeffersonian, Justice Harlan, was the only member of the Court to maintain a consistent opposition.

9.   The Theodore Roosevelt Period

Theodore Roosevelt had the opportunity to appoint three justices on the Supreme Bench in 1902, 1903, and 1906, through the successive resignations of Gray, Shiras, and Brown. The first vacancy went to Oliver Wendell Holmes, 61 years old, the foremost jurist of the state of Massachusetts. Son of the poet and essayist of the same name, Holmes had been a professor in the Harvard Law School before he became an associate justice of the Massachusetts supreme court in 1882 and its chief justice in 1889. In cul-

tural background, philosophic temperament, legal knowledge, and stylistic ability, he was far superior to any other member of the Court.

Roosevelt's other two appointments were less fortunate. William R. Day of Ohio, 53 years old, had been a successful railroad attorney of the old familiar type,* had had judicial experience on the federal Circuit Court, and had held the office of secretary of state, conferred upon him through the personal friendship of President McKinley. Roosevelt's last appointee, William H. Moody of Massachusetts, 52 years old, was a man of more ability who had been congressman, secretary of the navy, and attorney-general, but was supposed to owe his nomination chiefly to the influence of the reactionary senator, Henry Cabot Lodge.

The effect of Roosevelt's popular "trust-busting" campaign was seen in the 1904 decision of the Supreme Court delivered by Justice Harlan in *Northern Securities Company* v. *United States,* 193 U. S., 197, whereby the moribund Sherman Anti-Trust Law was temporarily resuscitated in the dissolution of a holding company formed to combine the interests of the supposedly competing Northern Pacific and Great Northern Railroads. But the resuscitation was only partial. Although the Sherman Act specifically stated that any person guilty of its violation should be "punished by fine not exceeding five thousand dollars, or by imprisonment not exceeding one year, or by both said punishments," the Court held on a technicality that the case before it, involving "persons" of such magnitude as J. P. Morgan and James J. Hill, was a civil and not a criminal suit. Thus while Charles Warren is undeniably correct in saying that the *Northern Securities Case* "for the first time showed that this law had teeth,"† the teeth were drawn at the very moment they were indicated.

The violation of the law's intent by the Supreme Court was pointed out by Justice Holmes in vigorous language: "It is vain to insist that this is not a criminal proceeding. . . . I am no friend of artificial interpretations. . . . So I say we must

---

*For Day's legal career, see Myers, *op. cit.,* pp. 650-57.
†Warren, *op. cit.,* Vol. II, p. 711.

read the words before us as if the question were whether two small exporting grocers should go to jail."

The words, of course, were never so read. The precedent established in the *Northern Securities Case* of merely enjoining corporations found guilty of criminal conspiracy from continuing their crimes in the future was consistently followed by the Court. It is therefore unnecessary to follow in detail the prolonged and tedious farce of the government's attempt to enforce the Sherman Act. Many "trusts" were nominally dissolved, but fear of the law, as emasculated by the Supreme Court, was so slight that all the time many more trusts of precisely the same nature were being formed. The nearest approach to an exercise of the law's teeth came in a different sort of case when in 1908 the Court announced in *Loewe* v. *Lawlor,* 208 U. S., 274, that labor unions were monopolies in restraint of trade if they attempted to boycott the goods of any firm engaged in interstate commerce. Although the nominal victory of the government in the *Standard Oil* and *American Tobacco Cases,* 221 U. S., 1, 106, was welcomed by the thoughtless as an extension of the government's power over industry, the Court actually restricted it by incorporating in its decisions Justice White's previously rejected contention that the Sherman Act did not mean what it said but was designed only to restrict "unreasonable" restraint of trade. This extension of the "rule of reason" to the Sherman Act was denounced by Justice Harlan as a judicial amendment of the Act. But Justice White's interpretation prevailed, and when in 1920 the dissolution of the United States Steel Corporation was denied the Court merely buried a law that it had kept on the edge of the grave from the beginning. By its decisions from 1895 to 1920 it established the principle that governmental control of monopolies could not be brought about with its consent.

During the last decade of the Fuller Court, its attitude toward the police powers of the states was much more ambiguous. On the whole, judged simply by the number of cases decided in favor of the states, the Court might have been considered friendly. Laws were sustained prohibiting the sale

of cigarettes without license,* outlawing the practice of contracting for options to buy or sell grain in the future,† prescribing that railroad companies on the discharge of an employee should pay all his back wages,‡ requiring the redemption in cash of store orders or other evidences of indebtedness issued in payment of wages,** forbidding the payment of sailors in advance and thereby reducing them to a condition of peonage,†† and prohibiting the screening of coal before it was weighed and credited to the employee.‡‡ In all these cases, the Fuller Court showed itself sensitive to the growing trend of progressive social opinion.

On the other hand, it continued to show particular favor to the railroads in enjoining the states of Nebraska and Minnesota from enforcing their rate legislation against the Union Pacific and the Northern Pacific, in enjoining the state of Indiana from enforcing its tax legislation against the American Express Company, in enjoining the state of North Carolina from enforcing orders regarding private sidings, and in enjoining the state of Mississippi from enforcing an order requiring mail trains to stop at county seats. And finally by a series of illiberal decisions against labor during 1905-1908, the Court once more placed itself definitely on the side of capital with regard to fundamental issues.

10. Great Labor Defeats

The first of these anti-labor decisions, in the celebrated case of *Lochner* v. *New York*,*** 198 U. S., 45, held a ten-hour law for bakers to be unconstitutional, primarily because it interfered with the freedom of bakers to work as long as they pleased, and because of its evil tendencies. Justice Peckham in the majority opinion cited statistics to prove that the trade of

*Grundling v. Chicago, 177 U. S., 183.
†Booth v. Illinois, 184 U. S., 425.
‡St. Louis, Iron Mountain Etc. Railway v. Paul, 173 U. S., 404.
**Knoxville Iron Company v. Harbison, 183 U. S., 13.
††Patterson v. Bark Eudora, 190 U. S., 169.
‡‡McLean v. Arkansas, 211 U. S., 539.
***An excellent bibliography of legal articles on the *Lochner Case* will be found in Warren, *op. cit.*, Vol. II, p. 713.

a baker was not a particularly unhealthy one, and then continued:

"It is unfortunately true that labor, even in any department, may possibly carry with it the seeds of unhealthiness. But are we all, on that account, at the mercy of legislative majorities? A printer, a tinsmith, a locksmith, a carpenter, a cabinetmaker, a dry goods clerk, a bank's, a lawyer's or a physician's clerk, or a clerk in almost any kind of business, would all come under the power of the legislature, on this assumption. No trade, no occupation, no mode of earning one's living, could escape this all-pervading power, and the acts of the legislature in limiting the hours of labor in all employments would be valid, although such limitation might seriously cripple the ability of the laborer to support himself and his family. In our large cities there are many buildings into which the sun penetrates for but a short time in each day, and these buildings are occupied by people carrying on the business of bankers, brokers, lawyers, real estate, and many other kinds of business, aided by many clerks, messengers, and other employés. Upon the assumption of the validity of this act under review, it is not possible to say that an act, prohibiting lawyers' or bank clerks, or others, from contracting to labor for their employers more than eight hours a day, would be invalid. It might be said that it is unhealthy to work more than that number of hours in an apartment lighted by artificial light during the working hours of the day; that the occupation of the bank clerk, the lawyer's clerk, the real estate clerk, or the broker's clerk in such offices is therefore unhealthy, and the legislature in its paternal wisdom must, therefore, have the right to legislate on the subject of and to limit the hours for such labor, and if it exercises that power and its validity be questioned, it is sufficient to say, it has reference to the public health; it has reference to the health of the employés condemned to labor day after day in buildings where the sun never shines; it is a health law, and therefore it is valid, and cannot be questioned by the courts.

"It is impossible for us to shut our eyes to the fact that many of the laws of this character, while passed under what is claimed to be the police power for the purpose of protecting

the public health or welfare, are, in reality, passed from other motives.* We are justified in saying so when, from the character of the law and the subject upon which it legislates, it is apparent that the public health or welfare bears but the most remote relation to the law. The purpose of a statute must be determined from the natural and legal effect of the language employed; and whether it is or is not repugnant to the Constitution of the United States must be determined from the natural effect of such statutes when put into operation, and not from their proclaimed purpose."

The decision against the bakers—or for the bakers, according to Peckham—was by a five-to-four vote, Justices Holmes, Harlan, White, and Day dissenting. Justice Holmes went to the root of the matter in his caustic words: "This case is decided upon an economic theory which a large part of the country does not entertain. If it were a question whether I agreed with that theory, I should desire to study it further and long before making up my mind. But I do not conceive that to be my duty, because I strongly believe that my agreement or disagreement has nothing to do with *the right of a majority to embody their opinions in law.* . . . The Fourteenth Amendment does not enact Mr. Herbert Spencer's Social Statics. . . . The accident of our finding certain opinions natural and familiar or novel and even shocking ought not to conclude our judgment upon the question whether statutes embodying them conflict with the Constitution of the United States."

The other dissenting Justices, following the lead of Justice Harlan, based their disagreement with the majority on the fact that the law in question was not a clear violation of the Constitution and therefore should have been given the benefit of the doubt that certainly existed. In the words of Justice Harlan: "The rule is universal that a legislative enactment,

---

*The reader will notice the departure from the traditional contention of the Court that it never examines the motives behind legislation. Such examination, overt or implied, has as a matter of fact become more and more frequent of recent years in the rejection of laws whose proclaimed purpose is held to be different from the obvious effects. Notable instances are the child labor and A.A.A. decisions. Whether this tendency of the Court is beneficial or the reverse may be matter of argument, but it evidently constitutes a further limitation upon the legislature.

†Italics ours.

Federal or state, is never to be disregarded or held invalid unless it be, beyond question, plainly and palpably in excess of legislative power. . . .

"It is plain that this statute was enacted in order to protect the physical well-being of those who work in bakery and confectionery establishments. It may be that the statute had its origin, in part, in the belief that employers and employees in such establishments were not upon an equal footing, and that the necessities of the latter often compelled them to submit to such exactions as unduly taxed their strength. Be this as it may, the statute must be taken as expressing the belief of the people of New York that, as a general rule, and in the case of the average man, labor in excess of sixty hours during a week in such establishments may endanger the health of those who thus labor. Whether or not this be wise legislation it is not the province of the court to inquire. . . . It is enough for the determination of this case, and it is enough for this court to know, that the question is one about which there is room for debate and for an honest difference of opinion."

Justice Harlan's opinion was in line with the consistent pretensions of the Court that it never considered the wisdom of legislation but solely the Constitutional power of the legislature to enact it, and that it never questioned this power except when it was indisputably abused. But the plain implications of his opinion were such as Justice Harlan himself might have been unwilling to accept. For since the dissent of even a single justice is conclusive proof that the alleged unconstitutionality is not indisputable, it would follow that judgments of unconstitutionality ought not to be made except by a unanimous court; furthermore, since the very existence of the law would seem to be proof that there must be at least some "room for debate and for an honest difference of opinion" about its constitutionality, there would be no occasion for judicial review at all.

The second of the great anti-labor decisions of this period, concerning the constitutionality of the Federal Employers' Liability Act of 1906* came as a surprise to everyone because in a

---

*First Employers' Liability Case, 207 U. S., 463.

long series of precedents the Fuller Court had upheld state laws providing compensation for injuries due to an employer's negligence.*   The principle involved seemed to have become one of the most settled parts of American jurisprudence when in 1908 the Supreme Court by another five-to-four decision overthrew the federal law, applicable to employees of interstate carriers, on the technical ground that it did not come under the power of Congress to regulate interstate commerce since it did not exclude from its provisions employees who were engaged in intrastate commerce at the time of accident.   Justices Holmes, Harlan, Moody, and McKenna vigorously dissented.   And in 1912 the second Federal Employers' Liability Act, modified by Congress to conform to the earlier decision, was sustained by the Court. †

It might be interesting to know how many thousands were killed or maimed without any compensation for the support of their families during the four years' interval.

Labor had hardly recovered from the First Employers' Liability decision when in the case of *Adair* v. *United States,* 291 U. S., 293, the Supreme Court legalized "yellow dog" contracts which had been outlawed ten years before by Section 10 of the Erdman Act, making it a misdemeanor for any employer or his officers or agents to "discriminate against any employee because of his membership in . . . a labor corporation, association, or organization."   Adair, an agent of the Louisville and Nashville Railroad, who had discharged an employee, O. B. Coppage, for belonging to the Order of Locomotive Firemen, had been convicted under the Erdman Act and had been fined one hundred dollars.   The conviction was set

---

Missouri Railway Company v. *Mackey,* 127 U. S., 205; *Minnesota & St. Louis Railroad Company* v. *Herrick,* 127 U. S., 210; *Kansas and Western Railway Company* v. *Pontius,* 157 U. S., 209; *Tullis* v. *Lake Erie & Western Railroad Company,* 175 U. S., 348; *Minnesota Iron Company* v. *Kline,* 199 U. S., 593; *Martin* v. *Pittsburgh & Lake Erie Railroad Company,* 203 U. S., 284; *Wilmington Mining Company* v. *Fulton,* 205 U. S., 60; *Louisville & Nashville Railroad Company* v. *Melton,* 218 U. S., 36; *Mobile, Jackson & Kansas City Railroad Company* v. *Turnipseed,* 219 U. S., 35.   For discussion of the principle involved in these cases, see John J. O'Connor, *The Supreme Court and Labor* (1932), Ch. IV.
†*Second Employers' Liability Cases,* 223 U. S., 1.

aside by the Supreme Court on the ground that Section 10 of that Act was unconstitutional because it did not come under the commerce clause and furthermore because it violated the personal liberty guaranteed by the Fifth Amendment. On the latter point, Justice Harlan, whose Jeffersonianism at last proved inadequate to meet modern conditions, declared:

"It is not within the functions of government—at least in the absence of contract between the parties—to compel any person in the course of his business and against his will to accept or retain the personal services of another, or to compel any person, against his will, to perform personal service for another. The right of a person to sell his labor upon such terms as he deems proper is, in its essence, the same as the right of the purchaser of labor to prescribe the conditions upon which he will accept such labor from the person offering to sell it. So the right of the employee to quit the service of the employer, for whatever reason, is the same as the right of the employer, for whatever reason, to dispense with the services of such employee. It was the legal right of the defendant Adair—however unwise such a course might have been—to discharge Coppage because of his being a member of a labor organization, as it was the legal right of Coppage, if he saw fit to do so—however unwise such a course on his part might have been—to quit the service in which he was engaged, because the defendant employed some persons who were not members of a labor organization. In all such particulars the employer and the employee have equality of right, and any legislation that disturbs that equality is an arbitrary interference with the liberty of contract which no government can legally justify in a free land."

This opinion, though written by one of the most enlightened judges on the Court, was one of the most reactionary ever uttered by the Court in its assertion of an abstract "equality of right" between employers and employees, neglecting the actual inequality recognized by the Court a decade earlier and at least implied in Justice Harlan's own dissenting opinion in the *Lochner Case*. The decision was fairly riddled to pieces

by Justices McKenna and Holmes. Justice McKenna pointed out that "the liberty which is attempted to be vindicated as the Constitutional right of the carriers" was one of "mere whim or caprice"—for what else was the meaning of the words that the employer could discharge an employee "for whatever reason" seemed good to him? Justice Holmes remarked ironically that the connection of labor unions with interstate commerce was at least as intimate and important as was that of "safety couplers," recently admitted by the Court to be within the jurisdiction of Congress.

"It cannot be doubted," Justice Holmes continued, "that to prevent strikes and, so far as possible, to foster its scheme of arbitration, might be deemed by Congress an important point of policy, and I think it impossible to say that Congress might not reasonably think that the provision in question would help a good deal to carry its policy along. But suppose the only effect really were to tend to bring about the complete unionizing of such railroad laborers as Congress can deal with, I think that object alone would justify the Act. . . .

"I quite agree that the question what and how much good labor unions do is one on which intelligent people may differ,— I think that laboring men sometimes attribute to them advantages, as many attribute to combinations of capital disadvantages, that are really due to economic conditions of a far wider and deeper kind—but I could not pronounce it unwarranted if Congress should decide that to foster a strong union was for the best interest, not only of the men, but of the railroads and the country at large."

However cogent the argument of the dissenting judges, it was the opinion of the majority which established precedent. On the authority of the Adair decision a Kansas "anti-yellow-dog" law was declared unconstitutional in 1915 in the case of *Coppage* v. *Kansas,* 236 U. S., 1, (the Coppage in this case being one T. B. Coppage, a superintendent of the St. Louis and San Francisco Railway who discharged a switchman, Hedges, for belonging to the Switchman's Union.) Justices Holmes, Day, and Hughes dissented, in separate opinions, but these added little to what had already been said in the *Adair Case*.

Still another blow at labor came when the Court to all intents and purposes upheld the kidnaping of John Moyer and G. A. Pettibone, officers of the Western Federation of Miners, in 1906. The public excitement over the killing of an anti-labor governor of Idaho in 1905 had been seized upon as furnishing an opportunity to break the power of the union, and the two union leaders, both of whom were out of the state, Moyer not having been in it for over ten years, were secretly kidnaped by Idaho officials on a rather flimsy murder charge. The Supreme Court, on a technicality, denied them a writ of habeas corpus, saying: "Even if the arrest and deportation of one alleged to be a fugitive from justice may have been effected by fraud and connivance arranged between the executive authorities of the demanding and surrendering States so as to deprive him of any opportunity to apply before deportation to a court in the surrendering State for his discharge, and, even if, on application to any court, State or Federal . . . he would have been discharged, he cannot, so far as the Constitution or the law of the United States are concerned, when actually in the demanding State, in the custody of its authorities for trial and subject to the jurisdiction thereof . . . be discharged on habeas corpus by the Federal court."

Justice McKenna earnestly dissented: "In the case at bar, the States, through their officers, are the offenders. They by an illegal exertion of power deprived the accused of a constitutional right. . . . And constitutional rights the accused certainly did have. The foundation of extradition between the States is, that the accused should be a fugitive from justice from the demanding State, and he may challenge the fact by habeas corpus immediately upon arrest. If he refute the facts, he cannot be removed. . . . No individual could have accomplished what the power of the two States accomplished . . . could have made two arrests of prominent citizens by invading their homes; could have commanded the resources of jails, armed guards, and special trains; could have successfully timed all acts to prevent inquiry and judicial interference."

The cause of labor seemed utterly defeated, so far as the Supreme Court could defeat it, when, still in 1908, an astound-

ing thing happened in the case of *Muller* v. *Oregon*, 208 U. S., 412.

11. *An Unforeseen Labor Victory*

Louis D. Brandeis, in defending the constitutionality of the state police law—an Oregon statute limiting the labor of women in factories or mechanical establishments to ten hours a day—presented a mass of contemporary legislative and statistical material on the condition of women in industry, so that the Court was definitely prevented from deciding the question in terms of formal law alone and was forced to consider the actual meaning of its legal terms in the full light of contemporary economic facts. The Court's lesson in economics impressed it so greatly that it upheld the Oregon statute, but it was careful to indicate that it did so only because the law applied to women and not to men.

Justice Brewer announced that "The legislation and opinions referred to [in the brief of Mr. Brandeis] . . . may not be, technically speaking, authorities . . . yet they are significant of a wide-spread belief that woman's physical structure, and the functions she performs in consequence thereof, justify special legislation restricting or qualifying the conditions under which she may be permitted to toil. . . . We take judicial cognizance of all matters of general knowledge." The inequality of women in the struggle for subsistence was aggravated "when the burdens of motherhood are upon her. Even when they are not, by abundant testimony of the medical fraternity continuance for a long time on her feet at work, repeating this from day to day, tends to injurious effects upon the body, and as healthy mothers are essential to vigorous offspring, the physical well-being of woman becomes an object of public interest and care in order to preserve the strength and vigor of the race." Of course the argument of inequality could be, and indeed had been by Justice Brown, equally well advanced on behalf of labor in its struggle with capital, and if the physical well-being of woman so that she can produce strong and vigorous men is an object of public interest, the physical

well-being of these men would also seem to be a matter of public concern. But Justice Brewer made it plain that he did not think so. "Without questioning in any respect the decision in *Lochner* v. *New York*," he said, "we are of opinion that it cannot be adjudged that the act in question is in conflict with the Federal Constitution, so far as it respects the work of a female in a laundry [the particular issue involved in the suit before the Court]."

12. *The Passing of the Fuller Court*

Just as the death of Field had been symbolic, so was that of Peckham on October 24, 1909. Its significance was not immediately apparent as his successor, Horace Harmon Lurton of Tennessee, appointed by President Taft, was a man of much the same ilk as Peckham. As railroad attorney, and later as a state and federal judge,* he was generally considered to be one of the strongest upholders of corporate interests. But he was 65 years old at the time of his appointment and death removed him from the scene five years later, giving him little time in which to influence the policies of the Court.

Justice Peckham's death was followed on March 28, 1910, by that of his juristic twin brother, Justice Brewer. President Taft then made a second appointment, far better than his first, in the person of Charles Evans Hughes, 48 years old, a corporation attorney who had nevertheless come into well-earned public esteem through his excellent work as state counsel in unearthing gas and insurance frauds, had defeated William Randolph Hearst for the state governorship, and had received the endorsement of the people by being re-elected for a second term. His selection as associate justice was generally welcomed as the first liberal appointment to the Supreme Court since that of Justice Holmes eight years before. While it is easy to overemphasize his influence on the Court, it remains true that his term of office, from 1910 to 1916, exactly coincided with the progressive phase of the White Court.

Not long after these changes, Chief Justice Fuller himself

---

*For Lurton's record on the Bench see Myers, *op. cit.*, pp. 718-38.

died at the age of 77, on July 4, 1910.   He had been almost the least important member of his own Court, rarely leading and only occasionally dissenting; in the course of twenty-two years in office he succeeded in delivering but one opinion—his not overly brilliant performance in the *Knight Case*—of sufficient importance to go down in history.   During its latter years he had seen the Court abandon its earlier uncompromising capitalistic stand and begin to compromise, and he had hardly known whether to approve or disapprove.   His departure left the Court in the hands of men a few years younger in age and on the whole considerably younger in ideas.

CHAPTER IX

THE COURT UNDER CHIEF JUSTICE WHITE

1910-1921

EDWARD DOUGLASS WHITE, JOHN M. HARLAN, JOSEPH MCKENNA,
OLIVER WENDELL HOLMES, WILLIAM R. DAY, HORACE H. LURTON,
CHARLES EVANS HUGHES, WILLIS VAN DEVANTER, JOSEPH R. LA-
MAR, MAHLON PITNEY, JAMES CLARK MCREYNOLDS, LOUIS D.
BRANDEIS, JOHN H. CLARKE.

1. The New White Court

THE people of the United States were by now so accustomed
to seeing the ablest justices on the Supreme Court in an inferior position that little emotion was aroused when Taft, depart-
ing from the usual custom of going outside of the Court for
its chief justice, appointed to that office Justice White instead
of Justice Oliver Wendell Holmes. In fact, a mild degree of
satisfaction was evinced that Taft had not done worse, as he
might easily have done.

More surprise and decidedly less enthusiasm was evoked by
the appointment of Willis Van Devanter of Wyoming to take
the place of Justice Moody. Van Devanter, 51 years old and
with a long life still before him, had been a railroad attorney,
an assistant United States attorney-general, and a federal circuit judge. His legal knowledge was not in doubt, but he was
violently accused by William Jennings Bryan in a speech at
Lincoln, Nebraska, on November 5, 1911, of having been
unduly partial as a judge toward his former clients on the
Union Pacific Railroad.*

To take the place left vacant by the promotion of Justice
White, Taft appointed another railroad attorney, Joseph R.
Lamar of Georgia, 53 years old, who had had judicial experi-

*For details of Van Devanter's legal career, see Myers, op. cit., pp.
767-74.

ence as a member of the state supreme court. The death of Justice Harlan, at the age of 78, on October 14, 1911, gave Taft the opportunity to make a fifth appointment to the Court. It went to Mahlon Pitney of New Jersey, 54 years old, who had been twice elected to the federal Congress, and had been a state senator, a member of the state supreme court, and state chancellor. Because of his drastic rulings against peaceful picketing, his appointment was bitterly opposed by labor organizations, but the Senate, after three days' discussion, confirmed it by a vote of fifty to twenty-six.

The majority of the Court were now Taft appointees, but its conservative Republican aspect was not destined to be of long continuance. On the death of Justice Lurton in 1912, President Wilson appointed his Attorney-General, James Clark McReynolds. The new Justice, 52 years old, had been originally a small-town lawyer of Tennessee, who had been taken by Philander C. Knox into the Attorney-General's department to assist in the prosecution of the trusts. At the time of his appointment to the Supreme Court he was regarded as a rather fiery radical because during the *American Tobacco Company Case* he had said threateningly: "There are some of us who have hoped for a peaceful solution of this great question under the law as declared by the courts. But if in the light of the facts here presented this court shall decide that this defendant has not violated the law, then our hopes are a dream."* Radical, in a sense, he was to prove, but it was as a radical conservative.

The death of Justice Lamar in 1916 led to a second Wilson appointment, that of Louis D. Brandeis, the epoch-making attorney of *Muller* v. *Oregon.* A native of Kentucky who had received his legal training at the Harvard Law School and then practiced in Boston, Brandeis, now 59 years old, had spent the preceding decade as counsel for the people in defending various progressive laws of the states of Oregon, Illinois, Ohio, and California, and as special counsel for the government in certain other cases. He had also published two influential volumes in 1914, *Other People's Money* and *Business a Profession,*

---

*Quoted in *Harper's Weekly,* February 5, 1914.

both highly critical of the methods of modern business. He was the first justice ever to come to the Supreme Court by the strange route of acting as counsel for the people, and the Senate was so perturbed by the novelty of this proceeding that it was only after prolonged and acrimonious discussion that his appointment was confirmed by a vote of forty-seven to twenty-two.

A third Wilson appointment was made possible, also in 1916, by the resignation of Justice Hughes on acceptance of the Republican nomination for president. This time the selection was sufficiently conventional, the appointee being a faintly progressive Ohio lawyer, John H. Clarke, 58 years old, who had had the much valued "judicial experience"—which had long since come back into favor—as a federal district judge.

Thus, during all its early years the White Court kept changing, not merely in personnel as had the Fuller Court, but in the political and social views represented by its members. To these facts may in large part be ascribed the responsiveness of the White Court to public sentiment in the beginning.

2. *Its Progressive Phase*

Between 1903 and 1916, under the influence of Theodore Roosevelt and Woodrow Wilson, and their popular support, Congress passed an enormous amount of what was in essence federal police power legislation, such as the Pure Food Act of 1906, the Hours of Service Acts of 1907 and 1916, the Narcotics Acts of 1909 and 1914, the White Slave Traffic Act of 1910, the Boiler Inspection Acts of 1911 and 1915, the Adamson Act of 1916, and the Child Labor Act of 1916. All of these, except the last, were sustained by the Supreme Court under the commerce clause.

In 1914-1915 various state laws limiting the hours of labor of women were upheld by the Court in harmony with its decision in *Muller* v. *Oregon:* a Massachusetts law providing that no women or children should be employed in manufacturing or mechanical establishments for more than ten hours a day;* a

Riley v. *Massachusetts,* 232 U. S., 671. Opinion delivered by Justice McKenna.

California law limiting such employment, with certain exceptions, to eight hours a day;* an extension of the last mentioned law to public lodging houses, apartment houses, hospitals, and places of amusement.†

At last in 1917, in the important case of *Bunting* v. *Oregon,* 243 U. S., 426, an hours-of-labor law for men as well as women was sustained by the Court. *Lochner* v. *New York* seemed, though legal appearances have a way of being deceptive, to be definitely overruled. The Oregon statute read: "No person shall be employed in any mill, factory or manufacturing establishment in this State more than ten hours in any one day, except watchmen and employees when engaged in making necessary repairs, or in case of urgency, where life or property is in imminent danger; provided, however, employees may work overtime, not to exceed three hours in any one day, conditioned that payment be made for said overtime at a rate of time and one-half of the regular wage." Because of this last clause the law was attacked as being a wage law instead of an hours-of-service law. On the face of it, the law was plainly both, but the Court, careful not to extend the power of the state to regulate wages, chose to consider it as purely an hours-of-service enactment. Somewhat tenuous reasoning was necessary to justify this position, as will be seen from the majority opinion rendered by Justice McKenna. "There is a certain verbal plausibility," Justice McKenna admitted, "in the contention that it was intended to permit 13 hours' work if there be 15 ½ hours' pay, but the plausibility disappears upon reflection. The provision for overtime is permissive, in the same sense that any penalty may be said to be permissive. Its purpose was to deter by its burden and its adequacy for this was a matter of legislative judgment under the particular circumstances." Chief Justice White and Justices Van Devanter and McReynolds dissented without opinion.

Fully as important but for its emergency character would have been a slightly earlier decision of the Court upholding in

Miller v. *Wilson,* 236 U. S., 373. Opinion delivered by Mr. Justice Hughes.
†*Bosley* v. *McLaughlin,* 236 U. S., 385. Opinion delivered by Mr. Justice Hughes.

the case of *Wilson* v. *New,* 243 U. S., 332, the famous Adamson law of Congress. This Act was passed in 1916, at a time when American entrance into the World War seemed imminent, to avert a threatened railroad strike; ready, under the circumstances, to make whatever concessions were necessary, Congress, at the request of President Wilson, enacted an eight-hour regulation for railroad employees, subject to the approval of a special commission, with the further proviso that, pending the report of the commission and for thirty days thereafter, the employees should work only eight hours and that without diminution of wages. Chief Justice White, speaking for the majority of the Court, sustained the law but did so on the conservative ground that it was a phase of compulsory arbitration. "The Act which was before us," he said, "was clearly within the legislative power of Congress to adopt, and . . . amounted to an exertion of its authority under the circumstances disclosed to compulsorily arbitrate the dispute between the parties by establishing as to the subject matter of that dispute a legislative standard of wages operative and binding as a matter of law upon the parties."

Loath to commit himself to this doctrine of compulsory arbitration, Justice McKenna concurred in the decision on the different ground that the statute was an hours-of-service act and not a wage law. Justice Day dissented on the ground that it was a wage law and not an hours-of-service act. Justices Pitney and Van Devanter dissented on the ground that it did not come under the commerce clause. Mr. Justice McReynolds dissented for virtually the same reason as Justice Day, but he took occasion, in addition, to strengthen the conservative implications of the majority decision in the words: "Considering the doctrine now affirmed by a majority of the court as established, it follows as of course that Congress has power to fix a maximum as well as a minimum wage for trainmen; to require compulsory arbitration of labor disputes which may seriously and directly jeopardize the movement of interstate traffic; and to take measures effectively to protect the free flow of such commerce against any combination, whether of operatives, owners, or strangers."

Under the reformist impulse of the Wilsonian era, employers' liability acts and workmen's compensation laws had begun to multiply throughout the Union,* the technical difference between these two types of remedial legislation being that the former gave protection only against the negligence of an employer while the latter offered compensation for injuries sustained in hazardous occupations, irrespective of the employer's carefulness. Both types of law were sustained by the White Court, although in 1917 in the case of an act passed by the state of Washington,† requiring periodical contributions from employers to a general compensation fund, the law was validated only by a five-to-four decision against the opposition of Justices White, McKenna, Van Devanter, and McReynolds.

The Court was similarly divided in 1919 in cases arising under the liberal Employers' Liability Law as prescribed by the constitution of Arizona.‡ Here, in the dissenting opinion of Mr. Justice McReynolds a certain emotionalism might be detected. Finding his support not in the language of the federal Constitution but in certain principles supposed to have inspired it, he boldly said:

"In the last analysis it is for us to determine what is arbitrary or oppressive upon consideration of the natural and inherent principles of practical justice which lie at the base of our traditional jurisprudence and inspirit our Constitution. A legislative declaration of reasonableness is not conclusive; no more so is popular approval—otherwise constitutional inhibitions would be futile. And plainly, I think the individual's fundamental rights are not proper subjects for experimentation; they ought not to be sacrificed to questionable theorization.

"Until now I had supposed that a man's liberty and property—with their essential incidents—were under the protection of our charter and not subordinate to whims or caprices or

---

*Chicago, Burlington & Quincy Railroad Company v. McQuire, 219 U. S., 549; Aluminum Company of America v. Ramsey, 222 U. S., 251; Missouri Pacific v. Castle, 224 U. S., 541; Easterling Lumber Company v. Pierce, 235 U. S., 380; Bowersock v. Smith, 243 U. S., 29; Chicago, Rock Island & Pacific Railway Company v. Cole, 251 U. S., 54. For discussion see O'Connor, op. cit., Chap. IV.
†Mountain Timber Company v. Washington, 243 U. S., 219.
‡250 U. S., 400.

fanciful ideas of those who happen for the day to constitute the legislative majority. The contrary doctrine is revolutionary and leads straight toward destruction of our well-tried and successful system of government."

Mr. Justice McReynolds need not have been so unjudicially excited. His hour was at hand. The liberalism of the White Court in its progressive phase had always been subject to not infrequent lapses. At the very beginning it had accepted Justice White's amendment of the Sherman Act and in 1914 had reaffirmed the Fuller Court's anti-boycott decision in *Loewe* v. *Lawlor,* which it once more reaffirmed in 1917; the "yellow dog" Adair decision was reaffirmed in *Coppage* v. *Kansas,* 236 U. S., 1;* although the Food and Drug Act was upheld, it was decided on technical grounds that the Act was not violated when labels on patent medicine bottles misrepresented the curative properties of the so-called medicines. The Court's later stand on civil liberties was already foreshadowed in 1914, when in *Frank* v. *Mangum,* 237 U. S., 309, it refused, on a technicality, to issue a writ of habeas corpus to Leo Frank, an almost certainly innocent man convicted of murder in Atlanta, Georgia, by a jury under the influence of anti-Semitic prejudice and terrorized by a howling mob outside the court house.† The White Court at best was a weak-kneed well-meaning sort of Court which responded to liberal pressure but as soon as that pressure was removed by the entrance of the United States into the World War immediately reverted to type—the traditional conservative type of the Supreme Court.

3. The Child Labor Case

In 1918 the question of child labor came before the Court in one of the most famous of all its cases, that of *Hammer* v. *Dagenhart,* 247 U. S., 251, involving the constitutionality of the Act of 1916 which prohibited the transportation in interstate commerce of articles manufactured in a factory in which child labor was employed. The law was invalidated on the ground that the admitted right of Congress to regulate com-

*Justice Holmes dissented.
†Justice Holmes wrote a powerful dissenting opinion with which Mr. Justice Hughes concurred.

merce was here being used to effect indirectly a different ulterior purpose. Laws of this type had very recently been sustained—the Narcotics Acts and the White Slave Act—and a few years later the Court would uphold a law prohibiting the transportation of stolen automobiles—all on the theory that Congress had the right to use its power over commerce to prevent crime, immorality, or the spread of evils disastrous to the whole nation. But the Supreme Court could not see that the health of the nation's youth was in any way a subject of national concern. It was purely a local matter.

The wider significance of the decision was that it revived the method used in the *Knight Case,* wherein, it will be recalled, the Court had managed to construe the Sugar Trust as a local industry unaffected by the Sherman Act. The prevention of all regulation of commerce could be accomplished through the use of a two-edged sword by the Court, first, to invalidate national regulation as an interference with the states, and then to invalidate state regulation as an interference with the nation. This two-edged sword would henceforth be brandished more and more frequently to retain the principles of *laissez faire* that were by this time abandoned by nearly all progressive economists and sociologists.

That the broader commercial implications of the decision were the controlling factors was practically admitted by Justice Day in the majority opinion: "The far reaching result of upholding the Act cannot be more plainly indicated than by pointing out that if Congress can thus regulate matters entrusted to local authority by prohibition of the movement of commodities in interstate commerce, all freedom of commerce will be at an end."

Hammer v. *Dagenhart* was another five-to-four decision. Justice Holmes wrote a pungent dissenting opinion in which Justices McKenna, Brandeis, and Clarke concurred. Its main argument ran as follows:

"If an act is within the powers specifically conferred upon Congress, it seems to me that it is not made any less constitutional because of the indirect effects that it may have. . . . The statute confines itself to prohibiting the carriage of certain

goods in interstate or foreign commerce. Congress is given power to regulate such commerce in unqualified terms. It would not be argued today that the power to regulate does not include the power to prohibit. Regulation means the prohibition of something, and when interstate commerce is the matter to be regulated I cannot doubt that the regulation may prohibit any part of such commerce that Congress sees fit to forbid. . . .

"The Act does not meddle with anything belonging to the States. They may regulate their internal affairs and their domestic commerce as they like. But when they seek to send their products across the state line they are no longer within their rights. If there were no Constitution and no Congress their power to cross the line would depend upon their neighbors. Under the Constitution such commerce belongs not to the States but to Congress to regulate. It may carry out its views of public policy whatever indirect effect they may have upon the activities of the States. Instead of being encountered by a prohibitive tariff at her boundaries the State encounters the public policy of the United States which it is for Congress to express. The public policy of the United States is shaped with a view to the benefit of the nation as a whole. If, as has been the case within the memory of men still living, a State should take a different view of the propriety of sustaining a lottery from that which generally prevails, I cannot believe that the fact would require a different decision from that reached in *Champion* v. *Ames*.* Yet in that case it would be said with quite as much force as in this that Congress was attempting to intermeddle with the State's domestic affairs. The national welfare as understood by Congress may require a different attitude within its sphere from that of some self-seeking State. It seems to me entirely constitutional for Congress to enforce its understanding by all the means at its command."

Meekly accepting its defeat, Congress sought to attain its

---

*The reference is to the once celebrated *Lottery Case,* 188 U. S., 321, wherein the Court in 1903 sustained a Congressional law prohibiting the Louisiana Lottery.

end by the subsequent passage of a law which laid a tax on the products of child labor; but this too was later invalidated by the Court.* Finally, the desired result seemed to have been attained through the exercise of the N.R.A. in 1933-1935 until the N.R.A. itself was nullified by the Court. Eventually, child labor, the most outstanding blot on American civilization, will presumably be done away with by one means or another, but as in the case of the Income Tax, and Employers' Liability laws, the Supreme Court must be held responsible for blocking a most important piece of legislation over a period of years.

4. Nullification of the First Amendment

The World War, like other wars, brought the question of civil liberties into renewed importance. Shortly after American entrance into the war, Congress passed the Selective Service Act (conscription under a prettier name) which the Supreme Court validated as a "necessary and proper" means to carry out the Constitutional power of Congress "to raise and support armies." Little justifiable criticism could be made of this decision (however repugnant to democratic principles it may seem to force men to die for a cause in which they may not believe and on which they have had no opportunity to be heard); the Court stood on the plain language of the Constitution, and the fault, if fault there was—which is, of course, debatable—lay not with the Supreme Court but with Congress or the Constitution.

The same can hardly be said of its decisions under the Espionage Act, passed on June 15, 1917, and amended on May 16, 1918, which in its final form read in part as follows:

"Whoever, when the United States is at war, shall wilfully utter, print, write, or publish any disloyal, profane, scurrilous, or abusive language about the form of government of the United States, or the Constitution of the United States, or the military or naval forces of the United States, or the flag of the United States, or the uniform of the Army or Navy of the

---

*Bailey v. Drexel Furniture Company, 259 U. S., 20. The opinion of the Court was delivered by Chief Justice Taft.

United States . . . and whoever shall wilfully advocate, teach, defend, or suggest the doing of any of the acts or things in this section enumerated, and whoever shall by word or act support or favor the cause of any country with which the United States is at war or by word or act oppose the cause of the United States therein, shall be punished by a fine of not more than $10,000 or imprisonment for not more than twenty years, or both."

The original Act, though somewhat loose in its phraseology, had merely had in mind the legitimate aim to prevent interference "with the operation or success of the military or naval forces of the United States" and obstruction of "the recruiting or enlistment services"; as amended, it became a much more drastic repetition of the Sedition Act of 1798 (with which its language should be compared), which prevented all criticism of the aims or conduct of the war, while the provisions regarding the flag and uniform seem today a sheer manifestation of Congressional hysteria.*

Then was the time for the Supreme Court to recall its own lofty assertion in the *Milligan Case:* "The Constitution of the United States is a law for rulers and people, equally in war and in peace, and covers with the shield of its protection all classes of men, at all times, and under all circumstances." Then was the time for it to maintain the imperiled First Amendment: "Congress shall make no law . . . abridging the freedom of speech, or, of the press." Instead, the Court, with the exception of Justices Holmes and Brandeis, decided to forget the *Milligan Case* and to forget the First Amendment.

Curiously, the first important free speech case to come before the White Court, that of *Toledo Newspaper Company* v. *United States,* 247 U. S., 402, had nothing to do with the war, though the decision of the Court may have been influenced by the prevailing spirit of war intolerance. The *Toledo News-Bee* had criticized a local court for its capitalistic rulings

*For the tragi-comedy that resulted from the application of this law, particularly by the lower courts, see the author's *This Land of Liberty* (1930) or better, Zechariah Chafee's *Freedom of Speech* (1920).

during a suit to enforce a municipal ordinance against the street railways, to which the local court retaliated by holding the newspaper in contempt proceedings under a Congressional statute forbidding misbehavior "in the presence of the court or so near thereto as to obstruct the administration of justice." The immediate question was that of judicial supremacy, though indirectly the eternal economic issue perhaps entered. The Supreme Court interpreted the language of Congress in a metaphorical sense; "near" meant not spatially near but psychologically so near as to upset a judge's equanimity. "The safeguarding and fructification of free and constitutional institutions," said Chief Justice White solemnly, "is the very basis and mainstay on which the freedom of the press rests, and that freedom, therefore, does not and cannot be held to include the right virtually to destroy such institutions." To this, Justice Holmes replied, in more colloquial English: "A judge of the United States is expected to be a man of ordinary firmness of character. . . . I confess I cannot find . . . in the evidence in the case anything that would have affected a mind of reasonable fortitude."

Economic considerations certainly lurked in the background of the Espionage cases owing to the fact that nearly all the avowed opponents of the war, aside from a few definite pro-Germans, were members of the Socialist or other radical labor organizations.

The first notable victim of the Espionage Acts was the greatly loved leader of the Socialist Party, Eugene V. Debs, who was convicted and sentenced to ten years' imprisonment for a speech delivered in Canton, Ohio, to a party convention, in which he had assailed the "capitalist war" and the terrorization that had already begun to accompany it. The decision was under the earlier and more liberal Espionage Act, but though Debs was certainly not directly interfering with military operations or obstructing enlistment, the Court unanimously held that his words might have led others to do so.

Thomas Jefferson said, at a time when the United States Government was much less firmly established than it was in 1918, "It is time enough for the rightful purposes of civil

government for its officers to interfere when principles break out into overt acts against peace and good order." In substituting for "overt acts" the possible effect of words, the Supreme Court had adopted a principle of obviously indefinite expansion. Realizing the dangers involved, Justice Holmes, in one of the early cases, proposed a compromise formula that was apparently accepted at the time by the Court: "The question in every case is whether the words used are used in such circumstances and are of such a nature as to create a clear and present danger that they will bring about the substantive evils that Congress has a right to prevent." The practical uselessness of this formula as a protection of free speech was demonstrated in all the later cases, wherein the majority of the Court saw "a clear and present danger" in utterances regarded as quite harmless by Justice Holmes and Justice Brandeis.

In *Abrams* v. *United States,* 250 U. S., 616, the Court upheld the sentence imposed upon five ignorant Russians in New York City, who had expressed their resentment at the invasion of their native land by United States troops in a leaflet in which they had quoted a few hackneyed phrases from the Communist Manifesto of 1848. The repetition of Marx's well-worn words was considered by Justice Clarke, speaking for the Court, to have been "clearly an appeal to the 'workers' of this country to arise and put down by force the government of the United States." On the other hand, Justice Holmes, with Mr. Justice Brandeis concurring, asserted: "In this case sentences of twenty years' imprisonment have been imposed for the publishing of two leaflets that I believe the defendants had as much right to publish as the government has to publish the Constitution of the United States now vainly invoked by them."

In the other most notable of the numerous Espionage cases, *Pierce* v. *United States,* 252 U. S., 239, decided in 1920, the majority of the Court summarily solved a problem that has baffled many historians: the cause of American entrance into the World War. A Socialist writer, St. John Tucker, had asserted, like Senator Nye recently, that the Morgan interests had had a good deal to do with it. With regard to this, Justice Pitney in the majority opinion declared:

"Common knowledge [not to mention the President's Address to Congress of April 2, 1917, and the Joint Resolution of April 6 declaring war, which were introduced in evidence] would have sufficed to show at least that the statements as to the causes that led to the entry of the United States into the war against Germany were grossly false; and such common knowledge went to prove also that defendants knew they were untrue."

The issues raised in these cases extended over into the next two Courts, whose attitudes on free speech may best be summarized here. Just as after the Civil War the attack on civil liberties preceded and accompanied a powerful reassertion of special privileges to capitalist industries, so it was in the 'teens and 'twenties. The Taft Court proved even less friendly to free speech than the White Court. The repressive state anti-syndicalist and anti-anarchist laws that came to it were upheld in *Gilbert* v. *Minnesota,* 254 U. S., 325, wherein the Court declared that "a State may punish utterances teaching or advocating that its citizens should not assist the United States in prosecuting or carrying on war with its public enemies"; in *Gitlow* v. *New York,* 268 U. S., 652, wherein the Court held that an avowed belief in proletarian dictatorship was a criminal offense, which brought from Justice Holmes the bold reply, "If in the long run the beliefs expressed in proletarian dictatorship are destined to be accepted by the dominant forces of the community, the only meaning of free speech is that they should be given their chance and have their way"; and in the celebrated *Anita Whitney Case** wherein the principle of "guilt by association" involved in the California anti-syndicalist laws penalizing mere membership in various "subversive" organizations—even though no acts or teachings of violence were charged—was practically upheld by the Court's refusal of jurisdiction on technical grounds.†

---

*Whitney v. *California,* 274 U. S., 357.

†There is no intention, here or elsewhere, to use "technicalities" in a necessarily disparaging sense. In the *Anita Whitney Case,* Mr. Justice Brandeis and Justice Holmes, both presumably in sympathy with the appellant, concurred in the decision. A technical judgment may be strictly necessary or it may be straining at a gnat; in either case, its discussion must be left to lawyers. All that the non-legal historian can do is to

In the vast majority of the cases hitherto decided the denial of free speech (and by implication of free opinion) was based on the argument that certain opinions and utterances, perhaps innocent in themselves, *tended* to produce force and violence. In 1929 an application for American citizenship was denied on the opposite ground that the applicant refused to use force and violence under any circumstances.   In the celebrated "Rosika Schwimmer Case," *United States* v. *Schwimmer,* 279 U. S., 644, the Court reversed the decision of an Illinois circuit court and declined to admit to citizenship an unusually cultured Hungarian woman who had been the motivating power in Henry Ford's "Peace Ship" during the World War.   The basis of the decision, announced by Mr. Justice Butler, was her refusal as a pacifist to bear arms in a hypothetical war, although she testified that she would be willing to act as a nurse and even expose herself to certain death to shield an American soldier; the Court held that it is the duty of every citizen to support the government in war and that this duty is not observed by conscientious objectors.   Justice Holmes, dissenting, said that the applicant was "of superior character and ability, obviously more than usually desirable as a citizen of the United States," and that her view that the Constitution might be improved showed attachment to it rather than the reverse.   "I would suggest," he added, "that the Quakers have done their share to make the country what it is, that many citizens agree with the applicant's belief, and that I had not supposed hitherto that we regretted our inability to expel them because they believe more than some of us do in the teachings of the Sermon on the Mount."*

An exception to this long list of judgments against civil liberties was afforded by the case of *Meyer* v. *Nebraska,* 262

---

record its effects, and if he finds, as he will, that technicalities seem to have a way of multiplying on behalf of the ruling forces in society to indicate that fact also without attempting to decide the vexed question whether the responsibility lies with the courts, the laws, or perhaps the intrinsic nature of the law itself.

*Mr. Justice Brandeis concurred with Justice Holmes, and Justice Sanford wrote a separate dissenting opinion in which he held that the ruling of the circuit court that women could not bear arms anyway should have decided the case.

U. S., 390, in which the Court voided a state law prohibiting the teaching of German in the grades. As if to mark the exceptional character of the decision, it was delivered by Mr. Justice McReynolds, who supported the limitation of civil rights in all the other cases, while Justice Holmes, their chief defender, turned against them, apparently having acquired such a habit of dissent that he was sure the majority must be wrong even when it happened momentarily to be right.

The civil rights decisions of the Hughes Court in 1931-1933 were on the whole considerably more liberal than those of its predecessor, mainly owing to the influence of Chief Justice Hughes himself. But the rejoicings in the public press over these early decisions were somewhat premature: the Court was giving with one hand and withholding with the other. The appeal of Yetta Stromberg,* a California school-teacher convicted of having displayed a red flag at a workers' school in violation of a state law prohibiting the exhibition of any flag as a symbol of "opposition to organized government," was sustained, over the dissent of Mr. Justice McReynolds and Mr. Justice Butler; but the result was merely to invalidate one section of the law because of its vague phrasing rather than to invalidate all such laws as a violation of civil rights. So the "Minnesota Gag Law" preventing from publication, by injunction, any "malicious, scandalous, and defamatory newspaper"—in the case before the Court the scandal was that a certain newspaper had charged the city officials with being in collusion with racketeers—was voided by the Court, but with the distinct reservation that "the protection even as to previous restraint is not absolutely unlimited" but might be enforced in cases of indecency. So that henceforth free speech might be enjoined before utterance if any court suspected that it was going to be "indecent" when uttered. Thus, in the very breath in which it was apparently supporting free speech, the Court placed a fresh limitation upon it. Finally, as regards the citizenship rights of pacifists, the Court, over the dissent of Justices Hughes, Holmes, Brandeis, and Stone, went even beyond the conservatism of the Taft Court: in the case of Rosika Schwimmer, pacifism on non-religious grounds had been de-

*Stromberg v. California, 283 U. S., 359.

clared a bar to citizenship, but in the case of Douglas Macintosh and Marie Bland,* the Hughes Court held that pacifism on religious grounds is equally a bar.†

Even the moderately liberal record of the Hughes Court in regard to civil liberties during its first years was not to be maintained. True, the Court twice intervened to secure a retrial for the nine Alabama Negroes convicted of criminal rape on the flimsiest evidence in the *Scottsboro Case:*‡ once because they had not been allowed adequate legal counsel and again because, contrary to law, Negroes had been excluded from jury panels; but in both instances the decision merely affected irregularities in legal procedure and did not prevent the use of the same flimsy evidence in later convictions of the defendants. Thus it was at best a nominal victory which had little or no effect on the actual legal status of the Negro in the South. It was quite otherwise with an unnoticed decision delivered on the same day with the widely publicized second *Scottsboro* adjudication. In the case of *Grovey* v. *Townsend,* 295 U. S., 45, the Court yielded to the third attempt of the state of Texas openly to debar Negroes from voting in the primaries. Two former efforts of this kind on the part of the state legislature had been declared unconstitutional by the Court, but similar action by the Democratic Party—practically the only political party in Texas—was held not to come under the provisions of the Fifteenth Amendment. Hitherto, the Amendment had been circumvented by educational and other requirements without specific mention of the Negro. The decision in *Grovey* v. *Townsend* was the first to authorize explicit racial discrimination in so many words.

United States v. *Macintosh*, 283 U. S., 605. The import of the decision was aggravated by the fact that the two defendants had served, the one as chaplain and the other as nurse, in the World War and merely declined to serve in some hypothetical future war which their religious conscience might regard as unjust.

†There is no intention on the part of the author to deny that there still exists an amazing amount of freedom of speech in America in happy contrast to Germany, Italy, and Russia. But it exists because of the habit of the people, not because the Supreme Court has intervened effectively to check the excesses of national and state legislatures. Except in the minor instances cited, the Court has not done so. In the light of the past, the reliance of many people on the Supreme Court to prevent fascist movements in the United States seems to be without much foundation.

‡*Powell* v. *Alabama*, 287 U. S., 45; *Norris* v. *Alabama*, 294 U. S., 45; *Patterson* v. *Alabama*, 294 U. S., 600.

In the same 1935-1936 term, the case of *Herndon* v. *Georgia,* 295 U. S., 441, involved a more flagrant violation of free speech than any in the World War itself. Angelo Herndon, for merely possessing socialistic and communistic literature, was convicted of inciting to insurrection under a Georgia pre-Civil War statute passed to prevent slave rebellion. A motion for a new trial on the ground of the insufficiency of the evidence having been denied, Herndon appealed to the Supreme Court on the basis that the state's interpretation of the statute was in violation of the Fourteenth Amendment. The Supreme Court, with Justices Cardozo, Stone, and Brandeis dissenting, held that this point, however well taken, could not be considered because it ought to have been raised in the original motion for a new trial.

The discussion of the decline and fall of the First Amendment has carried us into what was still an unknown future in the period of the White Court. This matters little, however, because since 1918 the transition from one court to another has been, far more than ever before, a merely nominal transition. When Chief Justice White died in 1921 and Chief Justice Taft was appointed in his room, the change from liberalism to reaction in the Court had already taken place. All that remained for the next two courts was to carry out the principles of reaction to their logical conclusion.

CHAPTER X

THE COURT UNDER CHIEF JUSTICE TAFT

1921-1930

WILLIAM HOWARD TAFT, JOSEPH MCKENNA, OLIVER WENDELL HOLMES, WILLIAM R. DAY, WILLIS VAN DEVANTER, MAHLON PITNEY, JAMES CLARK MCREYNOLDS, LOUIS D. BRANDEIS, JOHN H. CLARKE, GEORGE SUTHERLAND, PIERCE BUTLER, EDWARD T. SANFORD, HARLAN F. STONE.

1. The Heaven of Chief Justice Taft

WILLIAM HOWARD TAFT of Ohio, 63 years old at the time of his appointment to the Supreme Court, had the most distinguished career ever achieved by an American citizen—if distinction be judged in terms of the number and importance of the offices held. Governor of the Philippines, Secretary of War, President of the United States, and Chief Justice of the Supreme Court, he regarded the last of his many offices as by far the most desirable. Fifteen years before, he had been virtually offered an appointment as associate justice by Theodore Roosevelt and had reluctantly relinquished it out of deference to Roosevelt's own desire that he should take the presidency rather than the justiceship. In a speech at Pocatello, Idaho, on October 6, 1911, he had declared: "I love judges and I love courts. They are my ideals on earth of what we shall meet afterward in Heaven under a just God." And now for nine years he was to enjoy the boon of presiding over the highest form of this earthly imitation of Heaven.

In addition to the appointment of Chief Justice Taft himself, President Harding had the opportunity to select three associate justices through the successive resignations in 1922 of Justices Clarke, Day, and Pitney. The first two appointments were precisely such as one would have expected from President Harding. George Sutherland of Utah, 60 years old, had since 1896 shared with Reed Smoot the leadership of the

state Republican machine, had served from 1905 to 1917 in the United States Senate where he was noted for his consistent opposition to the policies of Theodore Roosevelt and Woodrow Wilson, had been attached to Harding's personal headquarters during the campaign of 1920, and subsequently as the President's chief political adviser was called "the Colonel House of the Harding Administration." He was considered an authority on international law and he unquestionably knew a great deal about practical politics. On the other hand, Harding's second appointee, Pierce Butler of Minnesota, cared little about politics but knew a great deal about the law—from the viewpoint of a highly successful railroad attorney. His nomination provoked a two months' verbal battle in the Senate, where the opposition was led by Senator Norris of Nebraska, supported by Senator-elect Shipstead of Minnesota, who declared, "The appointment of Judge Gary of the United States Steel Corporation would not in our opinion be more unfitting or improper than the appointment of Mr. Butler." Aside from his corporate connections the chief charge against the nominee was that as regent of the University of Minnesota he had been responsible for the discharge of three faculty members because of their economic views. Attorney-General Daugherty having come to Butler's rescue with a testimonial, "He is a very high-class man . . . a man of very high character, wonderful experience and good health . . . his judicial temperament is 100%," the appointment was at last confirmed by a vote of sixty-one to eight.*

The last of Harding's three appointments aroused less criticism. Edward Terry Sanford of Tennessee, 57 years old, had not been very prominently connected with either party politics or corporate interests; after a single year as assistant attorney-general, he had served for fifteen years as a federal district judge. A man of great social charm and broad culture, he was a conservative with occasional liberal leanings when his humanitarian sympathies were sufficiently aroused.

*For further details regarding the personal background of these and other justices of the contemporary Hughes Court, see the unsigned article by John Chamberlain in *Fortune Magazine,* May, 1936, and the author's articles in the *New Republic,* June 17, July 1, 1936.

The retirement of Justice McKenna at the age of 81 in 1925 made the last change in the Taft Court. In the choice of his successor, President Coolidge, not often accused of originality, introduced a startling innovation by selecting a law professor instead of a politician, practicing attorney, or judge. Harlan Fiske Stone, a native of New Hampshire, 52 years old at the time of his appointment, had been a member of the Columbia law faculty since 1899, and its dean from 1910 to 1923; in 1924 he had been appointed attorney-general—possibly in view of the higher office about to devolve upon him. Almost at once, he aligned himself with Justices Holmes and Brandeis so that the minority of two was henceforth enlarged to a minority of three.

But the presence of two or even three heretics could not seriously disturb the equanimity of the Taft Heaven. With celestial calm, the Court proceeded to exercise its authority on a scale undreamed of hitherto. Enumerated by decades, the number of laws of the United States nullified by the Supreme Court runs as follows:

1790-1800	0
1800-1810	1
1810-1820	0
1820-1830	0
1830-1840	0
1840-1850	0
1850-1860	1
1860-1870	4
1870-1880	9
1880-1890	5
1890-1900	5
1900-1910	9
1910-1920	7
1920-1930	19

The gradual increase of judicial power that had been going on ever since the Civil War had by now gained sufficient momentum to move with accelerating speed.* In less than half

---

*Judged by its record up to date, the Hughes Court will easily surpass even the Taft Court in this matter.

the time, the Taft Court nullified approximately as many laws as did the Fuller Court in its long span of twenty-two years. Furthermore, the conservatism of the Fuller Court was not, at least at first, noticeably behind the sociology and economics of its period, whereas the Taft Court was an anachronism in its attempt to restore the conditions of an earlier generation. A final difference between the two was that the old conflict between state rights and national power, still a real issue in Chief Justice Fuller's time, had become merely nominal by the time of Justice Taft.

The Taft Court was no more favorable to state than to national laws. It mutilated both with equal *sang froid* when they endeavored to control or regulate private industry. The underlying principles of the Court's decisions were the same in each type of case, and the fundamental issues were the same, but since the legal arguments were somewhat different, it will be well for the sake of sweet clarity to divide the cases considered under the heads of national and state legislation.

2. Nullification of National Laws

THE CLAYTON ACT

As a result of its alarm over the Supreme Court's emasculation of the Sherman Anti-Trust Act by its decisions in the *Standard Oil* and *American Tobacco Cases,* Congress after two years' study of the subject passed what was supposed to be a foolproof law in the Clayton Anti-Trust Act of 1914 and at the same time established the bipartisan Federal Trade Commission to carry its provisions into effect. The Commission, a successor to an innocuous Bureau of Corporations, was given wide powers of action in alleged cases of "unfair methods of competition" such as misbranding, adulteration, false advertising, or combinations to fix prices.

During the war the Commission functioned simply as a cost-finding agency in connection with the War Industries Board and other price-fixing organs of the government, but by 1919 it was ready to fulfill its original purposes. At once

it ran afoul of the Supreme Court. The most important cases in the last year of the White Court and the early years of the Taft Court concerned the efforts of the Commission to enforce the Clayton Act. By the end of the decade, as a result of the decisions of the Court, the Clayton Act followed the Sherman Act into the waste-basket.

The first of these decisions was given in the case of *Federal Trade Commission* v. *Warren, Jones & Gratz*, 253 U. S., 421. The firm of Warren, Jones & Gratz was the general selling and distributing agency of both the Carnegie Steel Company and the American Manufacturing Company; for the former it sold steel bands used in baling cotton and for the latter it sold jute bagging likewise used in baling cotton; for itself it required purchasers of steel bands also to buy an equivalent amount of jute bagging and vice versa. The Commission held that this was an "unfair method of competition," but the Supreme Court could not see it.

"The words 'unfair methods of competition,'" it said, "are not defined by the statute, and their exact meaning is in dispute. It is for the courts, not the commission, ultimately to determine as matter of law what they include. They are clearly inapplicable to practices never heretofore regarded as opposed to good morals because characterized by deception, bad faith, fraud or oppression, or as against public policy because of their dangerous tendency unduly to hinder competition or create monopoly. The act was certainly not intended to fetter *free and fair competition as commonly understood and practiced by honorable opponents in trade.*"*

In this case, the Court was merely applying to an agency of Congress the same rule which it applies to Congress itself. Even if Congress does define its terms, the meaning of the definition is still to be decided by the Supreme Court. Thus, Congress can never be sure of its own meaning until this is later determined by the Court. The situation, though somewhat curious, is inevitable once the right of judicial review is granted.

But in the next case, that of *Federal Trade Commission* v.

---

*Italics ours.

Curtis Publishing Company, 260 U. S., 568, the Court went much further. The charge against the Curtis Company (publisher of *Ladies' Home Journal, Saturday Evening Post,* and *Country Gentleman*) was that it sold its publications to news dealers under contracts to exclude all competing magazines from their stands, in violation of the Clayton Act directly prohibiting all such contracts of sale or lease. The case was decided in favor of the company on the ground that their contracts, though admittedly producing the monopolistic practices at which the Clayton Act was aimed, were not technically contracts of sale or lease but "contracts of agency." Decisions on a basis of technicalities were nothing new in the history of the Court; but the assertion of power that accompanied it was:

"Manifestly, the court must inquire whether the commission's findings of fact are supported by evidence. If so supported, they are conclusive. But . . . the court must also have power to examine the whole record* and ascertain for itself the issues presented and whether there are material facts not reported by the commission. If there be substantial evidence relating to such facts from which different conclusions reasonably may be drawn . . . [and] if from all the circumstances it clearly appears that in the interest of justice the controversy should be decided without further delay the court has full power to do so."

Chief Justice Taft, unable to determine the Court's meaning,† filed a half-concurring, half-dissenting opinion, in which Mr. Justice Brandeis joined. If the decision meant, he said, "that where it clearly appears that there is no substantial evidence to support additional findings necessary to justify the order of the commission complained of, the court need not remand the case for further findings, I concur in it. It is be-

---

*A power repeatedly disclaimed by the Marshall and Taney Courts in the Land cases.

†Chief Justice Taney once labored under a similar difficulty. Having dismissed in Circuit Court certain cases on which he was later overruled by the Supreme Court, he explained his earlier decision as follows: "I dismissed them under the impression that I was bound to do so upon the principles upon which this court had decided them in the suits by the trustees. It appears, however, by the opinion just delivered, that I was mistaken, and placed an erroneous construction on the opinions formerly delivered."

cause it may bear the construction that the court has discretion to sum up the evidence pro and con on issues undecided by the commission, and make itself the fact-finding body that I venture with deference to question its wisdom and correctness."

The Federal Trade Commission, however, had no difficulty in understanding the meaning of the decision. In the words of the former chairman of the Commission, Nelson B. Gaskill, "The courts claimed the power both to frame an issue of their own and to support it by their own findings of fact. For all practical purposes the Commission might as well have made no findings of fact whatever."* Without the power to determine either the law or the facts, the Commission might indeed just as well have given up the ghost at once. Instead, it heroically struggled on, trying to find a loophole for the exercise of its authority in the Court's words in the *Gratz Case* condemning "practices . . . opposed to good morals because characterized by deception." An opportunity seemed to be afforded in the case of *Federal Trade Commission* v. *Klesner,* 280 U. S., 19.

It appeared that a popular window-shade store operated for many years in Washington, D. C., under the name, "The Shade Shop," by one W. S. Sammons, who leased the property from one Albert Klesner, was later taken over by the property-owner and operated under the same name, although the manager who had built up the business had been ejected from it. But the Supreme Court held that the name, "The Shade Shop," referred to a general type of business, not to the particular establishment, and hence Klesner had not illegitimately profited from the good will built up by Sammons. According to Mr. Gaskill, "The Commission had found as a fact that Klesner's employees had deliberately deceived customers into the belief that they were dealing with Sammons but the Court said, 'The record is silent as to any attempt on the part of defendant or his employees to deceive or entice Sammons' customers.' "† Since, in the Court's words, it was not a case "of interest to the public" it was "disposed of . . . on its merits."

---

*Nelson B. Gaskill, *The Regulation of Competition* (1936), p. 79.
†*Ibid.,* pp. 84-85.

The Commission made a last attempt, in *Federal Trade Commission* v. *Raladam Company,* 283 U. S., 643, a case which clearly seemed to be of public interest since it concerned the sale of a so-called "obesity remedy" with alleged fraudulent advertising.   But it now turned out that the purpose of the Clayton Act, as interpreted by the Court, was to preserve competition and not to prevent injury to the public through deception.*

"The paramount aim of the Act," the Court decided, "is the protection of the public from the evils likely to result from the destruction of competition or the restriction of it in a substantial degree, and this presupposes the existence of some competition to be affected. . . . It is impossible to say whether, as a result of respondent's advertisements, any business was diverted, or was likely to be diverted, from others engaged in like trade, or whether competitors, identified or unidentified, were injured in their business."   If there were such competitors, the Court pointed out, they were probably to be found among the firms producing other fake remedies for obesity that had been listed some time before by the American Medical Association Bureau.   "It cannot be seriously contended," the Court added, "that the machinery of the Commission was intended to give governmental aid to the protection of this kind of trade and commerce."

Practically, this amounted to saying that one illegitimate business, as defined by the Court itself, could not be prevented unless it were in competition with other illegitimate business, and if it were it still could not be prevented because all these forms of business were equally illegitimate.   It is not surprising that the Federal Trade Commission virtually abandoned the fight after the Raladam decision.   Caught on the horns of the dilemma that when it attempted to check monopoly it found that public deception was the essential consideration and when it attempted to check public deception it found that monopoly was the essential, the Commission decided to sit down between the horns and be as comfortable as possible.†

---

*This case was decided by the Hughes Court.

†One would think the Commission might have gone on to bring up cases in which there was *both* monopoly and public deception, but ap-

THE MINIMUM WAGE CASE

Of much more interest to the general public than the technical rulings which virtually annihilated the Federal Trade Commission was the Supreme Court's five-to-four decision outlawing a minimum wage for women in the District of Columbia in the much-discussed case of *Adkins* v. *Children's Hospital,* 261 U. S., 525. The legal status of minimum wage laws for both men and women was popularly supposed to have been established beyond reversal by the Supreme Court itself in the maximum hours decisions of *Bunting* v. *Oregon* (1917) and *Muller* v. *Oregon* (1908); but the majority opinion, delivered by Mr. Justice Sutherland, without directly overruling those decisions, managed to pass them by at a safe distance and get back by way of *Coppage* v. *Kansas* (1915) and *Adair* v. *United States* (1908) to the good old ground of "freedom of contract" asserted in *Lochner* v. *New York* (1905).

Indeed, the United States Court of Appeals for the District of Columbia, whose decree was affirmed by the Supreme Court of the United States, attempted to force the country backward not only to the period of *Lochner* v. *New York* but a hundred and thirty years further back to the era of Sir William Blackstone. *"The tendency of the times,"* said Judge Van Orsdel of the Circuit Court, *"to socialize property rights under the subterfuge of police regulation is dangerous, and if continued will prove destructive of our free institutions. It should be remembered that of the three fundamental principles which underlie government, and for which government exists, the protection of life, liberty and property, the chief of these is property;* * not that any amount of property is more valuable than the life or liberty of the citizen, but the history of civilization proves that, when the citizen is deprived of the free use and enjoyment of his property, anarchy and revolution follow, and life and liberty are without protection."†

---

parently it couldn't find any or else was too discouraged to make the effort.

*Italics ours.

†284 Federal Reports, 622. Compare the language of Sir William Blackstone, quoted on p. 2 of the present work.

Mr. Justice Sutherland took a longer route to arrive at the same place as Judge Van Orsdel. He prefaced his discussion of the constitutionality of the minimum wage law by a statement that had by this time become traditional with the Supreme Court when it was about to nullify a Congressional statute: "The judicial duty of passing upon the constitutionality of an Act of Congress is one of great gravity and delicacy. The statute here in question has successfully borne the scrutiny of the legislative branch of the government, which, by enacting it, has affirmed its validity;* and that determination must be given great weight. This Court, by an unbroken line of decisions from Chief Justice Marshall to the present day, has steadily adhered to the rule that every possible presumption is in favor of the validity of an Act of Congress until overcome by a rational doubt.† But if by clear and indubitable demonstration a statute be opposed to the Constitution we have no choice but to say so."

He then went on to repeat Hamilton's argument in *The Federalist*, No. 78, and to declare that judicial review was "not the exercise of a substantive power to review and nullify Acts of Congress," but was simply "a necessary concomitant of the power to hear and dispose of a case or controversy properly before the court."‡

Having thus prepared the ground, Mr. Justice Sutherland proceeded with his "clear and indubitable demonstration" that the statute in question was "opposed to the Constitution." That such a law violated the Fifth Amendment, he declared *"is set-*

---

*It had not only borne the scrutiny of Congress, but of twenty-nine state courts of last appeal, twenty-seven of which had upheld the law. Taking all the judges, federal and state, who passed upon the question, thirty-two considered the law constitutional and nine rejected it.

†Taken at its face value, this statement seems a little unkind toward Mr. Justice Sutherland's four dissenting colleagues, as well as toward the majority of the whole judiciary, as plainly implying that their "doubts"— very strongly expressed—must have been "irrational." But probably no such logical implication was intended; in the special vocabulary of the Supreme Court, "a rational doubt" is limited to one entertained by the majority of the Court at the moment of the decision.

‡The question of whether the power was a substantive power or the necessary concomitant of a substantive power is one more interesting to lawyers than to laymen; the practical point was that the Court possessed the power and was about to exercise it.

tled by the decisions of this Court and is no longer open to question."* But what about the Bunting and Muller decisions which were supposed to have settled just the opposite? In the *Bunting Case,* the law, applying to both sexes, had been upheld merely because it was considered necessary to "the health of employees" in specific industries. With regard to the *Muller Case,* where the law applied specifically to women, Mr. Justice Sutherland pointed out that "the ancient inequality of the sexes . . . has continued 'with diminishing intensity.' In view of the great—not to say revolutionary—changes which have taken place since that utterance [the Muller decision], in the contractual, political and civil status of women, culminating in the Nineteenth Amendment, it is not unreasonable to say that these differences have now come almost, if not quite, to the vanishing point."

As to the aim of the law to secure for women in the District of Columbia at least a living wage, Mr. Justice Sutherland, went into more detail:

"What is sufficient to supply the necessary cost of living for a woman worker and maintain her in good health and protect her morals is obviously not a precise or unvarying sum—not even approximately so. The amount will depend upon a variety of circumstances: the individual temperament, habits of thrift, care, ability to buy necessaries intelligently, and whether the woman live alone or with her family. To those who practice economy, a given sum will afford comfort, while to those of contrary habit the same sum will be wholly inadequate. The coöperative economies of the family group are not taken into account though they constitute an important consideration in estimating the cost of living, for it is obvious that the individual expense will be less in the case of a member of a family than in the case of one living alone. The relation between earnings and morals is not capable of standardization. It cannot be shown that well paid women safeguard their morals more carefully than those who are poorly paid. Morality rests upon other considerations than wages; and there is, certainly, no such prevalent connection between the two as to justify a

*Italics ours.

broad attempt to adjust the latter with reference to the former. As a means of safeguarding morals the attempted classification, in our opinion, is without reasonable basis. No distinction can be made between women who work for others and those who do not; nor is there ground for distinction between women and men, for, certainly, if women require a minimum wage to preserve their morals men require it to preserve their honesty. For these reasons, and others which might be stated, the inquiry in respect of the necessary cost of living and of the income necessary to preserve health and morals, presents an individual and not a composite question, and must be answered for each individual considered by herself and not by a general formula prescribed by a statutory bureau.

"It takes no account of periods of stress and business depression, of crippling losses, which may leave the employer himself without adequate means of livelihood. To the extent that the sum fixed exceeds the fair value of the services rendered, it amounts to a compulsory exaction from the employer for the support of a partially indigent person, for whose condition there rests upon him no peculiar responsibility, and therefore, in effect, arbitrarily shifts to his shoulders a burden which, if it belongs to anybody, belongs to society as a whole.

"The feature of this statute which, perhaps more than any other, puts upon it the stamp of invalidity is that *it exacts from the employer an arbitrary payment for a purpose and upon a basis having no causal connection with his business,* or the contract or the work the employee engages to do. The declared basis, as already pointed out, is not the value of the service rendered, but *the extraneous circumstance that the employee needs to get a prescribed sum of money to insure her subsistence, health and morals.* The ethical right of every worker, man or woman, to a living wage may be conceded. One of the declared and important purposes of trade organizations is to secure it. And with that principle and with every legitimate effort to realize it in fact, no one can quarrel; but the fallacy of the proposed method of attaining it is that it assumes that every employer is bound at all events to furnish it. The moral requirement implicit in every contract of employment, viz.,

that the amount to be paid and the service to be rendered shall bear to each other some relation of just equivalence is completely ignored."*

At last, Mr. Justice Sutherland got around to the position of Judge Van Orsdel, though still in different language. "The statute in question," he said, ". . . does not prescribe hours of labor or conditions under which labor is to be done. . . ." It was therefore unconstitutional.

Chief Justice Taft, with Justice Sanford concurring, dissented, chiefly on the ground that the decision practically reversed that in the *Bunting Case*. It is impossible for me," he said, "to reconcile the *Bunting Case* and the *Lochner Case* and I have always supposed that the *Lochner Case* was thus overruled *sub silentio*.† Yet the opinion of the Court herein in support of its conclusion quotes from the opinion in the *Lochner Case* as one which has been sometimes distinguished but never overruled. Certainly there was no attempt to distinguish it in the *Bunting Case*.

"However, the opinion herein does not overrule the *Bunting Case* in express terms, and therefore I assume that the conclusion in this case rests on the distinction between a minimum of wages and a maximum of hours in the limiting of liberty to contract. I regret to be at variance with the Court as to the substance of this distinction. In absolute freedom of contract the one term is as important as the other, for both enter equally into the consideration given and received, a restriction as to one is not any greater in essence than the other, and is of the same kind. One is the multiplier and the other the multiplicand."

Justice Holmes, with whom Mr. Justice Brandeis would presumably have concurred had he been sitting in the case, dissented more fundamentally. "To me, notwithstanding the deference due to the prevailing judgment of the Court, the power

*Italics ours.

†The disastrous result of the Supreme Court's habit of reversing itself only *sub silentio* instead of explicitly is well illustrated by the fact that the Chief Justice himself was uncertain as to the relative standing of two conflicting decisions in one of the most important cases ever brought before the Court.

of Congress seems absolutely free from doubt. *The end, to remove conditions leading to ill health, immorality and the deterioration of the race, no one would deny to be within the scope of constitutional legislation.* The means are means that have the approval of Congress, of many States, and of those governments from which we have learned our greatest lessons. When so many intelligent persons, *who have studied the matter more than any of us can,* have thought that the means are effective and are worth the price, it seems to me impossible to deny that the belief *reasonably* may be held by *reasonable* men.* . . . In the present instance the only objection that can be urged is found within the vague contours of the Fifth Amendment, prohibiting the depriving any person of liberty or property without due process of law. To that I turn.

"The earlier decisions upon the same words in the Fourteenth Amendment began within our memory and went no farther than an unpretentious assertion of the liberty to follow the ordinary callings. *Later that innocuous generality was expanded into the dogma, Liberty of Contract.* Contract is not specially mentioned in the text that we have to construe. *It is merely an example of doing what you want to do, embodied in the word liberty. But pretty much all law consists in forbidding men to do some things that they want to do, and contract is no more exempt from law than other acts."†*

In conclusion, Justice Holmes made short work of Mr. Justice Sutherland's lengthy argument about equivalence of service: "This statute does not compel anybody to pay anything. It simply forbids employment at rates below those fixed as the minimum requirement of health and right living. *It is safe to assume that women will not be employed at even the lowest rates allowed unless they earn them,* or unless the employer's business can sustain the burden. In short the law in its character and operation is like hundreds of so-called police laws that have been upheld. I see no greater objection to using a Board to apply the standard fixed by the Act than there is to the other

---

*"Reasonably" and "reasonable" italicized by Justice Holmes. Other italics are ours.
†Italics ours.

commissions with which we have become familiar, or than there is to the requirement of a license in other cases."*

But it was the opinion of Mr. Justice Sutherland, not that of Justice Holmes and Chief Justice Taft that prevailed. Overruled *sub silentio* by the Hughes Court in the *Nebbia Case,* the Adkins decision would be reaffirmed by the same Court in June, 1936.

THE O'FALLON CASE

After having successively vanquished the Federal Trade Commission and the United States Congress, it was easy for the Court in 1925 to administer a crushing lesson to the Interstate Commerce Commission by its decision in *St. Louis & O'Fallon Railroad* v. *United States, 279* U. S., 461. This celebrated case directly involved only an insignificant railroad nine miles in length, owning but five locomotives and operated largely with second-hand equipment; indirectly, it concerned every railroad in the land. By the Transportation Act of 1920 the government was allowed to recapture one-half of the net earnings of railroads above six per cent upon the value of the property. In determining the latter, the I.C.C. was directed to "give due consideration to all the elements of value recognized by the law of the land for rate-making purposes." The O'Fallon line contended that the I.C.C. had not given due consideration to reproduction costs, which had been repeatedly held by the Court to be an essential element in rate-making, and supported its claim by the Commission's having included in its decision a protest against considering this unearned increment, which had nothing to do with initial capital investment, as a valid factor in rate-making. As to whether, in spite of this argument, the Commission had actually given consideration to reproduction costs in the case in question, there was a sharp difference of opinion between the majority of the Court, represented by Justice McReynolds, which in setting aside the order of the Commission stated that it had not taken these costs into consideration, and the minority of Stone and Holmes, which

*Italics ours.

denied this alleged fact. Justice Stone said, "Had the Commission not turned aside to point out in its report the economic fallacies of the use of reproduction cost as a standard of value for rate-making purposes, which it nevertheless considered and to some extent applied, I suppose it would not have occurred to anyone to question the validity of its order." On this point, the additional comment of Professor R. E. Cushman seems relevant:

"Whatever uncertainties may have been injected into the valuation situation by this decision, we are at least fairly certain that it is unsafe for an administrative commission to try to criticize the economic theory of the Supreme Court, especially when that economic theory has become part of the law of the land."*

TEAPOT DOME

The one important instance in which the Taft Court supported the other branches of the national government was in the cases growing out of the Teapot Dome scandals, which involved no constitutional issues. In the decision† voiding the naval oil leases and compelling the restitution of the property to the government, the Court castigated the fraudulent methods of the oilmen, and in later cases‡ in which it sustained two sentences for contempt of court against Harry F. Sinclair, it inflicted the only punishment (several months in jail) which the chief promoter of the deals ever received. Subsequently in 1930-31 the Hughes Court carried out the same policy by refusing to review the decision of the Circuit Court of Appeals sentencing Secretary of the Interior Albert B. Fall to one year's imprisonment and one hundred thousand dollars fine.

3. Nullification of State Laws

As early as 1921 the Taft Court began drastically to limit the police powers of the states. In *Truax* v. *Corrigan*, 257 U.

---

*"Constitutional Law in 1928-29," *American Political Science Review*, XXIV, 1, Feb., 1930.
†*Mammoth Oil Company* v. *United States*, 275 U. S., 13.
‡*Sinclair* v. *United States*, 279 U. S., 263, 279.

S., 312, it invalidated, over the dissent of Justices Holmes, Brandeis, Clarke, and even Pitney, an Arizona law prohibiting the use of the injunction in labor cases. In the majority opinion delivered by Chief Justice Taft, it was held that peaceful picketing in a Bisbee strike had deprived the plaintiff of property without due process of law by "constituting an unlawful annoyance and a hurtful nuisance in respect of the free access to the plaintiff's place of business." Furthermore, the Chief Justice maintained, the law in question was class legislation; why should ex-employees be specially exempted from restraint by injunction which applied to other groups?

As usual, the dissenting opinion by Justice Holmes was particularly trenchant: "The dangers of a delusive exactness in the application of the Fourteenth Amendment have been adverted to before now. . . . By calling a business 'property' you make it seem like land, and lead up to the conclusion that a statute cannot substantially cut down the advantages of ownership existing before the statute was passed. An established business no doubt may have pecuniary value and commonly is protected by law against various unjustified injuries. But you cannot give it definiteness of contour by calling it a thing. *It is a course of conduct and like other conduct is subject to substantial modification according to time and circumstances."**

As for the argument regarding class legislation, Justice Holmes declared: "Legislation may begin where an evil begins. If, as many intelligent people believe, there is more danger that the injunction will be abused in labor cases than elsewhere, I can feel no doubt of the power of the legislature to deny it in such cases."

Finally, he added, "There is nothing I more deprecate than the use of the Fourteenth Amendment beyond the absolute compulsion of its words to prevent the making of social experiments that an important part of the community desires, . . . even though the experiments may seem futile or even noxious to me and to those whose judgment I most respect."

Then came the extremely important case of *Wolff Packing Company* v. *Industrial Court*, 262 U. S., 522, which raised

---

*Italics ours.

two most vital questions: first, the actual meaning of that favorite phrase of the Supreme Court, "affected with a public interest," and second, the right of a state to enforce compulsory arbitration of industrial disputes. The state of Kansas had instituted an Industrial Court with power to fix prices and wages in the following lines of business: (1) manufacture and preparation of food; (2) manufacture of clothing; (3) production of fuel; (4) transportation of the above; (5) public utilities and common carriers. The Wolff Packing Company, objecting to an increase of wages decreed by the Industrial Court, refused to comply; sued in consequence, it lost its case in the state court and appealed to the Supreme Court on the ground that the Industrial Relations Act of Kansas unconstitutionally interfered with freedom of contract and took property without due process of law.

In delivering the opinion of the Court, which declared the Act unconstitutional, Chief Justice Taft first devoted his attention to the meaning of the disputed term, "affected with a public interest." "The mere declaration by a legislature that a business is affected with a public interest," he declared, "is not conclusive of the question whether its attempted regulation on that ground is justified. The circumstances of its alleged change from the status of a private business and its freedom from regulation into one in which the public have come to have an interest are always a subject of judicial inquiry. . . . One does not devote one's property or business to the public use or clothe it with a public interest merely because one makes commodities for, and sells to, the public in the common callings. . . . It has never been supposed since the adoption of the Constitution, that the business of the butcher . . . was clothed with such a public interest that the price of his product or his wages could be fixed by State regulation."

The Chief Justice here reasserted the traditional *laissez faire* economics of the Supreme Court: that all business was originally private in character and only acquired a public interest when the owner, more or less generously, though still in return for private benefits, devoted it to the public use. The question whether the public "had come" to have an interest in the manu-

facture and production of its food may strike the non-legal mind as slightly ludicrous, but the Chief Justice was quite in accord with Court precedent in declaring that the public had never had any legal interest in its food and still did not have in 1923.

With the question of public interest settled, the rest of the decision followed as a matter of course. Compulsory arbitration, the Chief Justice said, might sometimes be justified, but "it must be where the obligation to the public of continuous service is direct, clear and mandatory and arises as a contractual condition express or implied of entering the business either as owner or worker. It can only arise when investment by the owner and entering the employment by the worker create a conventional relation to the public somewhat equivalent to the appointment of officers and the enlistment of soldiers and sailors in military service. . . . We think the Industrial Court Act, in so far as it permits the fixing of wages in plaintiff in error's packing house, is in conflict with the Fourteenth Amendment and deprives it of its property and liberty of contract without due process of law."

In its immediate application, the decision was, of course, in favor of capital against labor, but it may be considered doubtful whether in its ultimate implications—through its rejection of compulsory arbitration—it was not more favorable to labor than to capital. The case, however, clearly illustrates the inherent powerlessness of the Court to advance any constructive solution of economic problems and its restriction to the method of meeting these by a mere re-affirmation of the *status quo ante*.*

In 1924, in *Burns Baking Company* v. *Bryan*, 264 U. S., 504, the Court declared unconstitutional a Nebraska uniform bread weight law which prescribed a maximum as well as minimum weight because this had been found necessary to protect the customer from such confusion as to standard sizes

___

*It is not here contended that the Court should undertake to suggest constructive solutions of economic problems; such an attempt would merely make the present confusion between legislative and judicial functions more confounded. The case is simply an excellent example of the *impasse* to which the doctrine of judicial review necessarily leads.

as defeated minimum weight provisions. If any question could be purely a matter for legislative discretion it would seem to have been this, but nevertheless the Court speaking through Justice Butler asserted that the law was "not necessary for the protection of purchasers against imposition and fraud by short weights and is not calculated to effectuate that purpose, and it subjects bakers and sellers of bread to restrictions which are essentially unreasonable and arbitrary."

During the next few years the Court made great use, one is tempted to say, an arbitrary use, of this word "arbitrary." In 1925 a Wisconsin law designed to end evasions of inheritance taxes through spurious gifts was found to be arbitrary; in 1926 a Pennsylvania law prohibiting the use of shoddy in comfortables met the same fate; so in 1927 a New York law designed to limit the exorbitant prices charged by theater ticket scalpers; so in 1928 a New Jersey law designed to limit the extortionate fees charged by employment agencies, as well as a Pennsylvania corporation tax law that had been in force for forty years.

State commissions next began to go the way of federal commissions under the Court's rulings. In 1928 the Illinois State Utilities Commission was forbidden to enforce lower rates against the Bell Telephone Company, and the similar New York Public Utilities Commission was forbidden to enforce lower rates against the New York Telephone Company. In 1929-1930 the California Railroad Commission was forbidden to enforce a five-cent fare in the city of Los Angeles and the city itself was forbidden to do so.

Consistent to the last, the Taft Court, just before merging into the Hughes Court, decided in the *Baltimore Railroad Case* that to permit a railroad a return of less than six and twenty-sixths one hundredths per cent on its properties was essentially confiscatory. This was a fitting conclusion to its long series of decisions in favor of private property rights as against both labor and the general public.

APPENDIX ON THE PROHIBITION CASES

The chief significance today of the cases—some two hundred in number—arising out of the Eighteenth Amendment and the Volstead Enforce-

ment Act is that the decisions of the Supreme Court tended to reduce the Fourth and Fifth Amendments to the now emaciated condition of the First Amendment.

In the great majority of instances the Court sustained the most rigorous, not to say ruthless, attempts to force prohibition upon an increasingly unwilling public. The first case to come before its attention, that of *Jacob Rupert* v. *Francis G. Caffey,* 251 United States, 264, involved the constitutionality of the Volstead Act itself under the due-process clause of the Fifth Amendment. The Court held that the right to prohibit intoxicating liquors justified Congress in also prohibiting non-intoxicating liquors, with an alcoholic content of no more than one-half of one per cent, as was done by the Volstead Act, the prohibition of the innocent liquor being regarded as necessary to make effective the prohibition of the guilty liquor.

In *United States* v. *Everett Simpson,* 252 U. S., 465, the Court ruled that the transportation of liquor for personal use into a state where its manufacture and sale had been forbidden was prohibited, such transportation being held to be a form of "interstate commerce."

In *United States* v. *Vito Lanza,* 260 U. S., 377, the question was whether a man who had been punished by a state for selling liquor and later was punished by the federal government for the same sale had not been put in double jeopardy for a single offense contrary to the Fifth Amendment. It was not an instance of double jeopardy, the Court decided, because the Amendment had been aimed at a double punishment by the same authority, whereas here two authorities, federal and state, had been concerned.

In *Charlie Hester* v. *United States,* 265 U. S., 57, the Court held that "the right of the people to be secure in their persons, houses, papers, and effects, against unreasonable searches and seizures," guaranteed by the Fourth Amendment, did not apply to open fields.

In *George Carroll & Kiro* v. *United States,* 267 U. S., 132, it held that the protection of the Fourth Amendment did not extend to automobiles suspected of transporting intoxicating liquor.

In *Sig. Samuels* v. *J. A. McCurdy,* 267 U. S., 188, it decided that the government might, without compensation, seize and destroy liquor lawfully obtained before the passage of the Prohibition Act. This, it insisted, was not ex post facto legislation since it did not apply to the past purchase but to future possession.

The most drastic and dubious of these decisions was in the case of *United States* v. *One Ford Coupe Automobile,* 272 U. S., 321. Here it was adjudged that the automobile of an entirely innocent owner might be legally confiscated if used by another in the transportation of intoxicating liquor—and this in spite of an express provision of the National Prohibition Act guarding the rights of innocent parties. The judgment was given under a Revenue Act of 1918, prior to prohibition, which provided for the forfeiture of automobiles engaged in transporting liquor on which no tax had been paid; although the stamps for such payments were no longer obtainable and there were no officers authorized to receive the payment, the Court asserted that the law was still in full effect.

The effect of these judgments of the Court, given mainly in 1925 and 1926, was that the prohibition officers for a period fairly ran wild in the

exercise of their authority, thereby greatly increasing public hostility toward prohibition. It is interesting that the particular Justices who so stoutly defended the First Amendment in the later Espionage cases offered no defense whatever of the Fourth and Fifth Amendments in these Prohibition cases. The most stringent of the decisions, that in the *One Ford Coupe Case,* was given in the opinion written by Justice Brandeis, while the usually conservative Justices, Van Devanter, Sutherland, and Butler, dissented. The explanation of the apparent anomaly probably lies in a different attitude on the part of the Justices toward the espionage and prohibition issues, Justices Holmes and Brandeis, perhaps to their credit, taking more interest in freedom of speech than in freedom of the stomach. The net result, however, was that the Fourth and Fifth Amendments followed the First Amendment into the discard.

The celebrated "Wire-Tapping Case" *(Olmstead* v. *United States)** raised a slightly different issue. A gigantic conspiracy of rum-runners and bootleggers, owning several ships, underground storage plants, and elaborate offices, with an annual income of over two million dollars, was uncovered by federal prohibition agents who tapped the office telephone wires over a period of five months and thereby collected a mass of conclusive evidence running to seven hundred and seventy-five printed pages. The accused objected to the use of this evidence as having been obtained by crime, wire-tapping being a misdemeanor under the state law, and as constituting an unreasonable search and seizure prohibited by the Fourth Amendment so that the use of the evidence would amount to self-incrimination forbidden by the Fifth Amendment.

By a five-to-four vote the Court held that no constitutional rights of the defendants had been infringed. Chief Justice Taft in the majority decision stated: "There was no searching. There was no seizure. The evidence was secured by the sense of hearing, and that only. There was no entry of the houses or offices of the defendants." There was no analogy between this case and the protection accorded sealed letters in the mails carried by the government, since no such protection had been given to telephone or telegraph messages. Admittedly, the evidence was obtained unethically, but "A standard which would forbid the reception of evidence if obtained by other than nice ethical conduct by government officials would make society suffer and give criminals greater immunity than has been known before."

In this case, Justices Holmes, Brandeis, Stone, and Butler dissented. For Justice Holmes the question was one of weighing goods against evils, there being no precedents to guide the Court. "It is desirable that criminals should be detected, and to that end that all available evidence should be used. It is also desirable that the government should not itself foster and pay for other crimes, when they are the means by which the evidence is obtained. . . . We have to choose, and for my part I think it a less evil that some criminals should escape than that the government should play an ignoble part. If the existing code does not permit district attorneys to have a hand in such dirty business, it does not permit the judge to allow such iniquities to succeed."

---

*Olmstead v. *United States,* 277 U. S. 438.

Mr. Justice Brandeis reinforced the position of Justice Holmes:

"Our government is the potent, the omnipresent, teacher. For good or for ill, it teaches the whole people by its example. Crime is contagious. If the government becomes a law-breaker, it breeds contempt for law; it invites every man to become a law unto himself; it invites anarchy. To declare that in the administration of the criminal law the end justifies the means—to declare that the government may commit crimes in order to secure the conviction of a private criminal—would bring terrible retribution. Against that pernicious doctrine this Court should resolutely set its face."

Chapter XI

THE COURT UNDER CHIEF JUSTICE HUGHES

1930-

. Charles Evans Hughes, Oliver Wendell Holmes, Willis Van Devanter, James Clark McReynolds, Louis D. Brandeis, George Sutherland, Pierce Butler, Harlan F. Stone, Owen Josephus Roberts, Benjamin N. Cardozo.

1. *The Court before the New Deal*

CONTRARY to popular impression, the Hughes Court, as already mentioned, has been essentially a mere continuation of the Taft Court. Aside from the change in the chief justiceship, the slight alterations in the Court's personnel did not modify its general complexion in the least. And with President Hoover to make the appointment, it was certain from the outset that the new Chief Justice, though he might be somewhat more or less conservative than his predecessor, would not be fundamentally different.

When Charles Evans Hughes was nominated for the position, the popular reaction was widely different from what it had been at the time of Mr. Hughes' appointment as associate justice in 1910. He was now 68 years old, instead of 48, and during the fourteen years that had intervened since his resignation from the Court he had been subjected to continuous reactionary influences. As head of the firm of Hughes, Rounds, Schurman and Dwight, with a large corporation practice, he had had frequent occasion to appear before the Supreme Court on behalf of his wealthy clients, among whom had been Truman H. Newberry, Republican Senator from Michigan, who had admitted spending one hundred and seventy-eight thousand dollars on his election in defiance of the Corrupt Practices Act but had been saved from punishment by a decision of the White

Court limiting the application of the Act.* During his term as secretary of state in Harding's Cabinet, aside from his excellent work in the Washington Conference on Limitation of Armaments, he had been chiefly concerned with defending the interests of American capitalists in Mexico and his best known single act had been an arbitrary demand that Count Michael Karolyi, exiled first President of Hungary, pledge himself to make no speeches on political subjects as a pre-condition to his entering the United States—an exaction supposed to be due to the influence of Admiral Horthy, fascist dictator of Hungary.

The appointment of Mr. Hughes was opposed by no less than twenty-six senators led by William B. Borah, then more critical of the Supreme Court than he has since become. Senator Borah said:

"Bear in mind that at the present time coal and iron, oil and gas and power, light, transportation, and transmission have all practically gone into the hands of a very few people. The great problem is, How shall the people of the United States be permitted to enjoy these natural resources and these means of transportation, free from extortion and oppression? I can conceive of no more vital question than this, which has long divided our Supreme Court. It has divided the Court not because one group of justices is less or more conscientious in their views, but because of a wide divergence in viewpoint. I am deeply imbued with the wisdom and justice of the viewpoint of the minority. I do not want to strengthen the viewpoint of the majority."

The younger Senator La Follette exclaimed, "The President is loading down the Federal Judiciary with men whose economic viewpoint is that of the great aggregations of capital," and Senator Norris declared, "No man in public life so exemplifies the influence of powerful combinations in the political and financial world as Mr. Hughes." But the general public, while skeptical of the appointment, was still disposed to give Mr. Hughes enough credit for his earlier liberalism not to put

*Newberry v. United States, 256 U. S., 232. The decision was highly technical, and the judges divided many ways in their opinions. For a brief account of the general bearing of the case, see William Floyd, Social Progress (1925), pp. 85, 152.

sufficient force behind the insurgent senators to make their resistance successful.

The opposition to the appointment of the Chief Justice was as nothing in comparison to the howling tempest of protest that greeted the nomination of Judge John J. Parker in the same year to succeed the recently deceased Justice Sanford. Judge Parker was a North Carolina Republican politician and federal judge who had earned the hostility of the Negroes, by an illiberal speech denying their political capacity, and the animosity of the labor unions, by upholding a second "Gatling Gun Injunction" against strikers in what was known as the *Red Jacket Case.* It was in vain that his defenders pointed out that he had merely followed a precedent established by the Supreme Court; after a seven weeks' battle, the insurgent senators were able to prevent his appointment, by the close vote of forty-one to thirty-nine.

In the state of senatorial exhaustion that followed this prolonged conflict, the appointment of Owen Josephus Roberts of Pennsylvania was accepted almost without discussion. On the score of his relative youth of 55, his having been assistant professor of law at the University of Pennsylvania, and his recent successful prosecution of the Teapot Dome cases for the government, Mr. Roberts was regarded as a liberal. Had the Senate taken time to investigate, it would have learned more about the quality of his liberalism from a speech made by him on February 16, 1923, before the Trust Company Division of the American Bankers' Association, in which after defending the high salaries paid the Standard Oil and other corporation officials, he went on to indicate his political philosophy:

"Are we prepared to go into a frank state of socialism in this country with all that it means in the suppression of ambition, in the deterrence of industry, in the holding back of men who want to arrange their affairs for their good and then for the good of us all—are we to go into a state of socialism, or are you men and men like you prepared to get out, take off your coats, and root for old-fashioned Anglo-Saxon individualism? . . . Everywhere you turn judicial and semi-judicial ad-

ministrative commissions, investigating bodies, inspectors of every known variety are found. The result is that the business man in America today feels that he is doing business with a minion of Government looking over his shoulder with an upraised arm and a threatening scowl."*

The last of President Hoover's appointments, that of Benjamin N. Cardozo to succeed Justice Holmes on his retirement in 1932, met with enthusiastic approval. After a service of eighteen years on the New York Bench, first in the state supreme court and latterly in the state court of appeals, Mr. Justice Cardozo, at the age of 61, had given general satisfaction by the liberality of his decisions and was regarded as certain to carry on the Holmes tradition.

But that tradition had always been a dissenting tradition, and the situation had not changed. Chief Justice Hughes was more liberal than Chief Justice Taft on the question of civil liberties, and was considerably more modern in his views of the law, but fundamentally the pattern was the same. Mr. Justice Roberts was a more forceful and less cultured Justice Sanford. The all-controlling difference of economic viewpoint to which Senator Borah had referred had not been altered; the alignment was still six to three, with the name "Holmes" changed to the name "Cardozo."

Grateful even for the mildly liberal tendency of the new Court in the civil liberties decisions of its first two terms, the country did not look at the implications of its economic decisions. The final blow to the Federal Trade Commission in the *Raladam Case* came in this period. Another defeat was administered to the Interstate Commerce Commission in *United States* v. *Chicago, Milwaukee, St. Paul & Pacific Railroad,* 283 U. S., 840, in which a Circuit Court decision was upheld invalidating an order of the Commission to prevent excessive reorganization fees. The Court stamped the Sherman Act into its grave more firmly in *Standard Oil Company of Indiana* v. *United States,* 283 U. S., 163, by holding that the cross licensing of patents and pooling of royalties were not

---

*It will be noted that Mr. Justice Roberts had thus personally condemned the New Deal ten years before its birth.

instances of "unreasonable" monopoly. Most important of all, a Massachusetts inheritance tax was declared unconstitutional, and the Court began to whittle away the federal gift tax in *Burnet, Commissioner* v. *Nevin*, 283 U. S., 835, by upholding the decision of the Circuit Court that John Wanamaker, Philadelphia millionaire, who at 84 had transferred ninety-five per cent of his estate to his son, could not be held to have done so "in expectation of death."

In its second term, the Hughes Court carried to greater length than had ever been done before a tendency that had long been manifest in the Supreme Court to reverse the decisions of the lower courts when these were favorable to the plaintiffs in cases under the Federal Employers' Liability Act. In most instances the reversal was based on the failure to prove negligence on the railroad's part in the injury or death of its employees.*

In *New State Ice Company* v. *Liebmann*, 285 U. S., 262, generally known as the "Oklahoma Ice Case," the Court nullified an Oklahoma law regulating competition in the ice business on the ground that this business, even in the torrid summer climate of Oklahoma, was not sufficiently "affected with a public interest" to justify the law. The majority opinion delivered by Mr. Justice Sutherland was almost casual, but the dissenting opinion of Mr. Justice Brandeis, three times as long, went into every aspect of the subject and ended with a stern warning to the Court:

"To stay experimentation in things social and economic is a grave responsibility. Denial of the right to experiment may be fraught with serious consequences to the Nation. It is one of the happy incidents of the federal system that a single courageous State may, if its citizens choose, serve as a laboratory; and try novel social and economic experiments without risk to the rest of the country. This Court has the power to prevent an experiment. We may strike down the statute which embodies it on the ground that, in our opinion, the measure is arbitrary, capricious or unreasonable. We have power to

---

*For a summary of the Court's attitude in these cases, see Gregory Hankin, *Editorial Research Report for 1931-32*. Mr. Hankin concludes his observations with the mild remark, "It is apparent that the Supreme Court does not like the Federal Employers' Liability Act."

do this, because the due-process clause has been held by the Court applicable to matters of substantive law as well as to matters of procedure.   But in the exercise of this high power, we must be ever on our guard, lest we erect our prejudices into legal principles.   If we would guide by the light of reason, we must let our minds be bold.

"Mr. Justice Stone joins in this opinion."*

2.   The Court with the New Deal

Never were prophetic words more quickly fulfilled than were those of Mr. Justice Brandeis in the *Oklahoma Ice Case* of 1932.   By the time of the inauguration of President Franklin Roosevelt in 1933, the four years' economic depression hitherto denied by President Hoover as long as that attitude was possible, had at last reached such mammoth proportions that its reality could no longer be overlooked by anyone.   In state after state the banks were closed in order to prevent their crashing; factories and mills were shutting down; debts could not be collected, loans could not be obtained; investment was at a standstill; after ten years of governmental rule by business men, business was on the point of total collapse, and for the first time in American history distress was universal.

With unexampled energy, the Roosevelt Administration attempted to meet the crisis by an enormous amount of emergency legislation which involved "the right to experiment" on a gigantic scale.   The general theory back of this legislation was that the collapse of American industry was due to the forfeiture of its foreign market through foreign retaliatory duties against the excessively high Hoover tariff, and to the simultaneous loss of a domestic market due to such over-concentration of wealth in the hands of a few as left the many without the means to buy either necessities or luxuries once the facilities of easy credit were cut off.   Addressing itself to the more immediate domestic problem, the government attempted "to prime the carburetor" by restoring consumer purchasing power through a series of regulatory Acts designed to extend credit,

---

*Mr. Justice Cardozo took no part in the decision.

maintain wages, and uphold prices. Viewed simply as emergency legislation to put the tottering business world on its feet again, these Acts were momentarily approved even by a great many industrial leaders, who were ready to accept any assistance to save a sinking ship. On the other hand, those who were better situated, bolder, or more far-sighted protested from the first against the whole principle of governmental regulation, seeing in it a fundamental threat to private industry. During the year 1933-1934 the attitude of industry toward the Roosevelt experiments was on the whole that of giving them a temporary trial, provided they could be halted when they had served their immediate purpose, but with a strong minority who objected to having any truck with them at all. This division of opinion was reflected in the Supreme Court.

THE MINNESOTA MORATORIUM CASE

The first important case to bring the general policies of President Roosevelt's New Deal before the Supreme Court, that of *Home Building and Loan Association* v. *Blaisdell,* 290 U. S., 398, involved the constitutionality not of an Act of Congress but of a Minnesota state law extending the period for the redemption of mortgages. The law was fairly conservative in that it protected the interest of the mortgage-holder by providing that during the period of extension the mortgagor should pay the rental value of the premises as ascertained in judicial proceedings, but in spite of this the statute was attacked as an "impairment of contract." The lower court, though practically admitting some impairment, sustained the law as a justifiable exercise of the state police power in an emergency. Had its decision been affirmed by the Supreme Court on the same ground the validation of most of the New Deal legislation would have followed, but though the decision was affirmed, by a five-to-four vote, the majority of the Court, speaking through Chief Justice Hughes, took care to make some fine distinctions.

"Emergency," said the Chief Justice flatly, "does not create power. Emergency does not increase granted power or re-

move or diminish the restrictions imposed upon power granted
or reserved. The Constitution was adopted in a period of
grave emergency. Its grants of power to the Federal Government and its limitations of the power of the States were determined in the light of emergency and they are not altered
by emergency. . . ."

This looked as if it were a preparation for invalidating the
moratorium law. But then came the fine distinctions. "While
emergency does not create power," the Chief Justice went on,
"emergency may furnish the occasion for the exercise of
power. . . . The constitutional question presented in the light
of an emergency is whether the power possessed embraces *the
particular exercise of it in response to particular conditions. . . .*"* Thus the possibility of using the present decision
as a precedent in other New Deal cases was guarded against
in advance.

"Where constitutional grants and limitations of power are
set forth in general clauses, which afford a broad outline," Mr.
Justice Hughes continued, "the process of construction is
essential to fill in the details. . . ." Impairment of contract,
he argued, was not the same thing as "interference with contracts." "The economic interests of the State may justify the
exercise of its continuing and dominant protective power notwithstanding interference with contracts. . . . Undoubtedly,
whatever is reserved of state power must be consistent with the
fair intent of the constitution of that power. . . . This principle
precludes a construction which would permit the State to adopt
as its policy the repudiation of debts or the destruction of contracts or the denial of means to enforce them. But it does not
follow that conditions may not arise in which a temporary
restraint of enforcement may be consistent with the spirit and
purpose of the constitutional provision and thus be found to be
within the range of the reserved power of the State to protect
the vital interests of the community."

Throughout his opinion Mr. Justice Hughes cited many
precedents, of which the most notable was the *Charles River
Bridge Case,* to prove that the decision was in harmony with

*Italics ours.

the traditional policy of the Court. "When we consider the contract clause," he said, "and the decisions which have expounded it in harmony with the essential reserved power of the States to protect the security of their peoples, we find no warrant for the conclusion that the clause has been warped by these decisions from its proper significance or that the founders of our Government would have interpreted the clause differently had they had the occasion to assume that responsibility in the conditions of the later day. The vast body of law which has been developed was unknown to the fathers, but it is believed to have preserved the essential content and spirit of the Constitution. With a growing recognition of public needs and the relation of individual right to public security, the court has sought to prevent the perversion of the clause through its use as an instrument to throttle the capacity of the States to protect their fundamental interests. . . . The principle of this development is, as we have seen, that *the reservation of the reasonable exercise of the protective power of the State is read into all contracts.*"*

In the dissenting opinion of Mr. Justice Sutherland, in which Mr. Justice Van Devanter, Mr. Justice McReynolds and Mr. Justice Butler concurred, objection was taken both to Mr. Justice Hughes' account of the Court's history and to his reasoning. Beginning with the Constitutional Convention and coming on down, Mr. Justice Sutherland cited precedent after precedent to prove the exact opposite of the Chief Justice's contentions, after which he addressed himself to the logical point involved.

The majority opinion, he said, "concedes that emergency does not create power, or increase granted power, or remove or diminish restrictions upon power granted or reserved. It then proceeds to say, however, that while emergency does not create power, it may furnish the occasion for the exercise of power. I can only interpret what is said on that subject as meaning that while an emergency does not diminish a restriction upon power it furnishes an occasion for diminishing it; and this, as it seems to me, is merely to say the same thing by

*Italics ours.

the use of another set of words, with the effect of affirming
that which has just been denied. . . . And so, while, in form,
the suggested distinction seems to put us forward in a straight
line, in reality it simply carries us back in a circle, like be-
wildered travelers lost in a wood, to the point where we parted
with the view of the State court."

But while objecting to the Chief Justice's distinction, Mr.
Justice Sutherland made a fine distinction of his own. The
cases cited in the majority opinion, he said, had nothing to do
with impairment of contract; they were instances of "frustration" of contract—"an essentially different thing." A contract,
he explained, is frustrated when "it disappears in virtue of an
implied condition to that effect read into the contract itself."
But this implied condition was not, as the Chief Justice asserted, read into *all contracts,* but only into those where "the
parties must have made their bargain on the footing that a particular state of things would continue to exist." Clearly this
was not the case in the mortgage issue. The Minnesota law
unquestionably "had the effect of destroying for two years
the right of the creditor to enjoy the ownership of the property, and consequently the correlative power, for that period, to
occupy, sell or otherwise dispose of it as might seem fit." It
was therefore a definite impairment of contract.

Amid all the welter of history, law, logic, and economics
in the opposed opinions, about the only thing really decided
by the decision was that the particular Minnesota law was
constitutional. Any inferences as to other emergency legislation from this decision were extremely hazardous.

THE NEBBIA CASE

Such did not seem to be true of the second important 1934
decision, that in *Nebbia* v. *New York,* 291 U. S., 502, in which
the Court upheld by another five-to-four vote a state law fixing the price of milk, contrary to the many precedents in which
the Court had invalidated similar laws on the ground that
price-fixing was a violation of due process unless the business
concerned was either one "affected with a public interest" or

an attempted monopoly. Mr. Justice Roberts, in the majority opinion, accomplished the difficult feat of both modifying the interpretation of due process and maintaining that his new position was entirely in harmony with precedent.

Quite as if some strange and novel idea had been presented to the Court, Mr. Justice Roberts said, in the majority opinion:

"We are told that because the law essays to control prices it denies due process. Notwithstanding the admitted power to correct existing economic ills by appropriate regulation of business, even though an indirect result may be a restriction of the freedom of contract or a modification of charges for services or the price of commodities, the appellant urges that direct fixation of prices is a type of regulation absolutely forbidden. His position is that the Fourteenth Amendment requires us to hold the challenged statute void for this reason alone. The argument runs that the public control of rates or prices is *per se* unreasonable and unconstitutional, save as applied to businesses affected with a public interest; that a business so affected is one in which property is devoted to an enterprise of a sort which the public itself might appropriately undertake, or one whose owner relies on a public grant or franchise for the right to conduct the business, or in which he is bound to serve all who apply; in short, such as is commonly called a public utility; or a business in its nature a monopoly. The milk industry, it is said, possesses none of these characteristics, and, therefore, not being affected with a public interest, its charges may not be controlled by the state. Upon the soundness of this contention the appellant's case against the statute depends.

"We may as well say at once that the dairy industry is not, in the accepted sense of the phrase, a public utility. We think the appellant is also right in asserting that there is in this case no suggestion of any monopoly or monopolistic practice. It goes without saying that those engaged in the business are in no way dependent upon public grants or franchises for the privilege of conducting their activities. But if, as must be conceded, the industry is subject to regulation in the public interest, what constitutional principle bars the state from correcting

existing maladjustments by legislation touching prices? We think there is no such principle. The due process clause makes no mention of sales or of prices any more than it speaks of business or contracts or buildings or other incidents of property. The thought seems nevertheless to have persisted that there is something peculiarly sacrosanct about the price one may charge for what he makes or sells, and that, however able to regulate other elements of manufacture or trade, with incidental effect upon price, the state is incapable of directly controlling the price itself. This view was negatived many years ago. *Munn* v. *Illinois,* 94 U. S., 113."

PANAMA REFINING COMPANY CASE

But toward the end of 1934 the lower courts, at first favorable to the enforcement of the "codes of fair competition" established under the National Recovery Act, began to show a tendency to invalidate them, until a beautiful test case seemed to be furnished the government by a decision nullifying a provision of the oil code which authorized the President to prohibit the shipment in interstate commerce of oil produced in violation of state proration regulations. The case, *Panama Refining Company* v. *Ryan,* 293 U. S., 388, was carried by the government to the Supreme Court, which, however, avoided the larger issue intended to be raised as to the constitutionality of the whole N.R.A. and invalidated merely the single provision of the single code specifically in question on the ground that it contained an unconstitutional delegation of legislative authority to the President—an entirely new ground for the nullification of Federal activities. Mr. Justice Cardozo alone dissented, pointing out that the invalidated clause contained "no grant to the Executive of any roving commission to inquire into evils and then, upon discovering them, do anything he pleases"; on the contrary, choice had been given him only as to the occasion "but none whatever as to the means."

The implications of both the majority and dissenting opinions were decidedly sinister as regarded the N.R.A. itself, but the government chose to take the decision at its face value as

one concerned with a relatively insignificant matter of detail. Indeed, Secretary Ickes argued that the auspices were most favorable since the Court by invalidating only one section of one code seemed to imply that the other sections of that code and all the sections of all the other codes must be constitutional.

THE GOLD CLAUSE CASE

The *Panama Refining Company Case* was so completely overshadowed by the Supreme Court's Gold Clause decision* that it was soon forgotten.   The United States, after a whole series of steps by the President and Congress, was now definitely off the gold standard, a result that had been easily achieved in England, France, and in other countries whose bonds were usually payable in currency.   But here, since 1896, nearly all bonds, public or private, specified payment in gold coin equal to the standard of weight and fineness as it existed on the date of issuance of the bond.   And in addition to bonds, many leases and other contracts were drawn in similar terms. There were at the date of the Supreme Court's decision some one hundred billion dollars of such obligations, while the total outstanding currency was only about eight billions.   Manifestly, payment in gold was a sheer impossibility.   On the other hand, not only had the Supreme Court explicitly ruled in *Bronson* v. *Rodes,* 7 Wallace, 229, that contracts expressly calling for payment in specie must be paid in specie, but there was no getting around the fact that abrogation of the gold clause would materially impair the value of every contract in which it appeared.

Chief Justice Hughes undertook on behalf of the majority of the Court the delicate task of reconciling law and necessity. With regard to *Bronson* v. *Rodes* and five other decisions based on it, he declared that they "did not deal with situations corresponding to those now presented. . . . The rulings, upholding gold clauses and determining their effect, were made when gold was still in circulation and no act of the Congress pro-

---

Norman v. *Baltimore & Ohio Railroad Company,* 294 U. S., 240. For complete majority and minority opinions, see Doskow, *op. cit.*

hibiting the enforcement of such clauses had been passed. . . . It requires no acute analysis or profound economic inquiry to disclose the dislocation of the domestic economy which would be caused by such a disparity of conditions in which, it is insisted, those debtors under gold clauses should be required to pay one dollar and sixty-nine cents in currency while respectively receiving their taxes, rates, charges and prices on the basis of one dollar of that currency."

Still, the Chief Justice was not ready to give up the Court's traditional assertion that it never considered effects where constitutional rights were involved. "We are not concerned with consequences," he said, "in the sense that consequences, however serious, may excuse an invasion of constitutional right. We are concerned with the constitutional power of the Congress over the monetary system of the country and its attempted frustration. Exercising that power, the Congress has undertaken to establish a uniform currency, and parity between kinds of currency, and to make that currency, dollar for dollar, legal tender for the payment of debts. In the light of abundant experience, the Congress was entitled to choose such a uniform monetary system, and to reject a dual system, with respect to all obligations within the range of the exercise of its constitutional authority. The contention that these gold clauses are valid contracts and cannot be struck down proceeds upon the assumption that private parties, and States and municipalities, may make and enforce contracts which may limit that authority. Dismissing that untenable assumption, the facts must be faced. We think that it is clearly shown that these clauses interfere with the exertion of the power granted to the Congress and certainly it is not established that the Congress arbitrarily or capriciously decided that such an interference existed."

The four dissenting conservatives gallantly stood by their guns. Justice McReynolds, delivering their minority opinion declared:

"Under the challenged statutes it is said the United States have realized profits amounting to $2,800,000,000. But this assumes that gain may be generated by legislative fiat. To

such counterfeit profits there would be no limit; with each new debasement of the dollar they would expand. Two billions might be ballooned indefinitely—to twenty, thirty, or what you will.

"Loss of reputation for honorable dealing will bring us unending humiliation; the impending legal and moral chaos is appalling."

3.   The Court against the New Deal

By the spring of 1935 the effects of the New Deal began to be manifest. Amid a vast amount of confusion, hesitation, and uncertainty, the experiments of the government, mutually inconsistent as many of them were, had actually worked to produce the immediate result desired. Though prosperity was hardly in sight, recovery was clearly on the way. The carburetor had been primed; the machine was ready to start; and the industrial chauffeurs began to get impatient. What if the gasoline tank was still half empty and the road uncharted— in the golden days of Coolidge they had got along without either service stations or road maps. In a word, the New Deal had fulfilled its purpose—or at least their purpose—and it was now time to do away with it.

Coincidentally with this changed attitude of Big Business there came a change in the decisions of the Supreme Court. The first real blow at the New Deal was struck on May 6, 1935, when the Court voided the Railroad Retirement Act by its decision in *Railroad Retirement Board et al.* v. *Alton Railroad Company,* 295 U. S., 330. The Act was a form of compulsory insurance whereby contributions of carriers and their present and future employees were to be pooled to provide an annuity varying according to the length of service for all employees over the age of 65, including those employed at any time during the preceding year and also those employed still earlier who should be re-employed subsequent to the passage of the Act. The one year's retroactive feature was unanimously condemned by the Court; was it not manifestly unjust to compel future employees to contribute toward the support

of past employees who had contributed nothing? In addition, argued a new majority secured by the adherence of Mr. Justice Roberts to the cause of Justices Butler, Sutherland, McReynolds, and Van Devanter, the Act did not come under the power of Congress to regulate interstate commerce since it bore no reasonable relation to the safety, efficiency, and economy of transportation. Here Chief Justice Hughes, and Justices Brandeis, Stone, and Cardozo dissented; the morale of the employees, they thought, did have something to do with the safety, efficiency, and economy of transportation; hence the rest of the Act should have been sustained, apart from its retroactive clause.

THE N.R.A. DECISION

With this guide to what might be the decision of the Court on the N.R.A. itself, the country was hardly surprised by the result of *A. L. A. Schechter Corporation* v. *United States,* 295 U. S., 495. The case which served as a test for the whole N.R.A. was an unfortunate selection for the government in that it concerned the violation of the Live Poultry Code by a local dealer in New York City who was unquestionably not directly engaged in interstate commerce. Yet as Donald Richberg points out,* the Supreme Court in a recent case, *Local 167* v. *United States,* 291 U. S., 293, had decided that those engaged in the live poultry business could be prosecuted under the anti-trust laws because their intrastate activities restrained and burdened interstate commerce, whence it was not unreasonable for the government to expect that it would take the same position in the *Schechter Case.* But the government underestimated the capacity of the Supreme Court to make distinctions.

By an unexpectedly unanimous vote the Court decided against the government. The opinion written by Mr. Justice Hughes was especially interesting when compared with his words in the *Minnesota Moratorium Case.* There he had as-

---

*Richberg, *The Rainbow* (1936), pp. 218-19; for a detailed account of the *Schechter Case,* see pp. 209-41. The Court's opinion is given in full in Doskow, *op. cit.,* pp. 486-521.

serted that "the policy of protecting contracts against impairment presupposes the maintenance of a government by virtue of which contractual relations are worth while—a government which retains adequate authority to secure the peace and good order of society"; here he sharply declared, "extraordinary conditions do not create or enlarge constitutional power" and "it is enough to say that the recuperative efforts of the federal government must be made in a manner consistent with the authority granted by the Constitution."

The distinction from *Local 167* v. *United States,* he said, was very clear. In that case the proved interference with "the free movement of live poultry into the metropolitan area in and about New York City" had directly affected the free movement of interstate commerce, while in the *Schechter Case* the interference charged was wholly indirect. There was "a necessary and well-established distinction between direct and indirect effects," though, as he admitted, the precise line could be drawn "only as individual cases arise," which was tantamount to saying that neither Congress nor the Supreme Court could be sure in advance as to the constitutionality of many laws. After this, the Chief Justice addressed himself to the government's main contention:

"The question of chief importance relates to the provisions of the Code as to the hours and wages of those employed in defendants' slaughterhouse markets. It is plain that these requirements are imposed in order to govern the details of defendants' management of their local business. The persons employed in slaughtering and selling in local trade are not employed in interstate commerce. Their hours and wages have no direct relation to interstate commerce. The question of how many hours these employees should work and what they should be paid differs in no essential respect from similar questions in other local businesses which handle commodities brought into a State and there dealt in as a part of its internal commerce. This appears from an examination of the considerations urged by the Government with respect to conditions in the poultry trade. Thus, the Government argues that hours and wages affect prices; that slaughterhouse men sell at a small margin

above operating costs; that labor represents 50 to 60 per cent. of these costs; that a slaughterhouse operator paying lower wages or reducing his cost by exacting long hours of work, translates his saving into lower prices; that this results in demands for a cheaper grade of goods; and that the cutting of prices brings about a demoralization of the price structure. Similar conditions may be adduced in relation to other businesses. The argument of the Government proves too much. If the federal government may determine the wages and hours of employees in the internal commerce of a State, because of their relation to cost and prices and their indirect effect upon interstate commerce, it would seem that a similar control might be exerted over other elements of cost, also affecting prices, such as the number of employees, rents, advertising, methods of doing business, etc. All the processes of production and distribution that enter into cost could likewise be controlled. If the cost of doing an intrastate business is in itself the permitted object of federal control, the extent of the regulation of cost would be a question of discretion and not of power."

It will be observed that the Chief Justice did not deny that the factors enumerated by the government would have a powerful effect upon interstate commerce; that, indeed, would hardly have been possible; it was enough to show that the effects were indirect and that the effect of recognizing these effects would be to create an amount of centralized authority which the Supreme Court considered unconstitutional.

This disposed of the Live Poultry Code, but it would not have invalidated the far more important codes of the major industries unquestionably engaged in interstate commerce. The latter result was achieved by a more far-reaching opinion, prefixed to the discussion of the commerce power, which virtually held the whole N.R.A. invalid as an unconstitutional delegation of legislative authority to the executive. Considering the number of times that the Supreme Court itself had been accused by its own members of usurping such authority, there was a certain element of sardonic humor in this decision.

As a sort of postlude to the N.R.A. decision, the Supreme Court the next day unanimously invalidated the Frazier-Lemke

Farm Mortgage Act which was virtually a Federal application of the Minnesota moratorium law with the added provisions that it postponed the creditor's redress for five years instead of two and also scaled down the principal by a process supposed to be remarkably advantageous to the creditor. On these two counts the Act was declared to violate the due-process law. But in delivering the Court's opinion, Mr. Justice Brandeis departed from what was literally the oldest tradition of the Court—that of offering no advice or suggestions as to possible future legislation. "If the public interest requires, and permits, the taking of individual mortgages in order to relieve the necessities of individual mortgagors, resort must be had to proceedings by eminent domain; so that through taxation the burden of the relief afforded in the public interest may be borne by the public." How the Old Guard on the Court ever came to concur in an opinion containing this sentence has remained an unsolved mystery; perhaps it trusted to the potency of the little word "if" at its beginning. In any event, Congress did not choose to take advantage of the rather broad hint that was offered.

THE VERMONT INCOME TAX LAW

The session of the Court in 1935-1936 was a dramatic culmination of its long rise in power until the goal of supreme authority over executive, legislative, states, and nation was at last attained. The term opened with a little regarded but highly important case. The state of Vermont had imposed a tax on income derived from interest-bearing securities except in the case of interest received from money loaned within the state. The Supreme Court, in a six-to-three decision, voided the law on the ground that it abridged the "privileges and immunities of citizens of the United States" guaranteed by the Fourteenth Amendment. Why? Because, according to Mr. Justice Sutherland and the majority, those privileges and immunities—undefined in the Constitution—include the right to "trade, buy or sell, contract or negotiate across" state lines. "As citizens of the United States," Mr. Justice Sutherland

maintained, "we are members of a single great community consisting of all the States united and not of distinct communities consisting of the States severally." This nationalistic dogma, though more extreme than anything John Marshall ever uttered, had a patriotic ring, but its devastating implications were pointed out by Mr. Justice Stone,* in that they established an "inexhaustible source of immunities, incalculable in their benefits to tax-payers and in their harm to local governments." Just as when the impairment-of-contract clause had been weakened by contradictory decisions, resort was had to the due-process clause of the Fourteenth Amendment to effect the same purpose, now when the due-process clause had lost its clarity the privileges-and-immunities clause was substituted.

THE A.A.A. DECISION

The new year began with the long awaited decision on the constitutionality of the Agricultural Adjustment Act, the chief pillar of the New Deal after the abolition of the N.R.A. The portions of the Act most relevant to the decision were, first, the statement that it was emergency legislation designed to meet the condition of disparity between the prices of agricultural and other commodities—which had given transactions in agricultural commodities a public interest—by establishing and maintaining "such balance between the production and consumption of agricultural commodities and such marketing conditions therefor, as will re-establish prices to farmers at a level that will give agricultural commodities a purchasing power with respect to articles that farmers buy, equivalent to the purchasing power with respect of agricultural commodities in the base period (1909-1914)"; this being the end in view, the means were provisions for voluntary reduction of acreage or production or both, for "rental or benefit payments in connection therewith," and for the raising of revenue to meet the "extraordinary expenses incurred by reason of the national economic emergency" through processing taxes levied upon

*With the concurrence of Justices Brandeis and Cardozo.

the first domestic processing of the commodity and payable by the processor.

Regardless of the ultimate economic wisdom or unwisdom of the Act, it had admittedly worked much more successfully than the N.R.A., and to the increase in farm purchasing power brought about by it was attributable in large measure the beginnings of economic recovery in the nation.

In the test case of *United States* v. *Butler,* decided on January 6, 1936, the Act was invalidated by another six-to-three decision. In the majority opinion, Mr. Justice Roberts repeated the familiar assertions as to the Court's respect for the Constitution. He declared:

"There should be no misunderstanding as to the function of this court in such a case. It is sometimes said that the court assumes a power to overrule or control the action of the people's representatives. This is a misconception. The Constitution is the supreme law of the land ordained and established by the people. All legislation must conform to the principles it lays down. When an act of Congress is appropriately challenged in the courts as not conforming to the constitutional mandate the judicial branch of the Government has only one duty,—to lay the article of the Constitution which is invoked beside the statute which is challenged and to decide whether the latter squares with the former. All the court does, or can do, is to announce its considered judgment upon the question. The only power it has, if such it may be called, is the power of judgment. This court neither approves nor condemns any legislative policy. Its delicate and difficult office is to ascertain and declare whether the legislation is in accordance with, or in contravention of, the provisions of the Constitution; and, having done that, its duty ends."

Mr. Justice Roberts then continued: "The clause thought to authorize the legislation . . . confers upon the Congress power 'to lay and collect Taxes, Duties, Imposts and Excises, to pay the debts and provide for the common defence and general welfare of the United States.' . . . The Government asserts that warrant is found in this clause for the adoption of the Agricultural Adjustment Act. The argument is that Congress

may appropriate and authorize the spending of moneys for the 'general welfare;' that the phrase should be liberally construed to cover anything conducive to national welfare; that decision as to what will promote such welfare rests with Congress alone, and the courts may not review its determination; and finally that the appropriation under attack was in fact for the general welfare of the United States."

Next, Mr. Justice Roberts entered upon a rather long discussion of the disputed meaning of the words "general welfare," turning in part upon the question as to whether "general" was meant to include "local" or to be distinguished from local; he gave his support to the latter interpretation maintained by Justice Story; and then he ended this section of his opinion rather surprisingly by saying, "We are not now required to ascertain the scope of the phrase 'general welfare of the United States' or to determine whether an appropriation in aid of agriculture falls within it.

"Another principle embedded in our Constitution," he continued, "prohibits the enforcement of the Agricultural Adjustment Act. The act invades the reserved rights of the states. It is a statutory plan to regulate and control agricultural production, a matter beyond the powers delegated to the federal government. The tax, the appropriation of the funds raised, and the direction for their disbursement, are but parts of the plan. They are but means to an unconstitutional end.

"From the accepted doctrine that the United States is a government of delegated powers, it follows that those not expressly granted, or reasonably to be implied from such as are conferred, are reserved to the states or to the people. To forestall any suggestion to the contrary, the Tenth Amendment was adopted. The same proposition, otherwise stated, is that powers not granted are prohibited. None to regulate agricultural production is given, and therefore legislation by Congress for that purpose is forbidden.

"It is an established principle that the attainment of a prohibited end may not be accomplished under the pretext of the exertion of powers which are granted. . . .

"If the taxing power may not be used as the instrument to

enforce a regulation of matters of state concern with respect to which the Congress has no authority to interfere, may it, as in the present case, be employed to raise the money necessary to purchase a compliance which the Congress is powerless to command? The Government asserts that whatever might be said against the validity of the plan, if compulsory, it is constitutionally sound because the end is accomplished by voluntary cooperation. There are two sufficient answers to the contention. The regulation is not in fact voluntary. The farmer, of course, may refuse to comply, but the price of such refusal is the loss of benefits. The amount offered is intended to be sufficient to exert pressure on him to agree to the proposed regulation. The power to confer or withhold unlimited benefits is the power to coerce or destroy. . . .

"Until recently no suggestion of the existence of any such power in the federal government has been advanced. The expressions of the framers of the Constitution, the decisions of this court interpreting that instrument and the writings of great commentators will be searched in vain for any suggestion that there exists in the clause under discussion or elsewhere in the Constitution, the authority whereby every provision and every fair implication from that instrument may be subverted, the independence of the individual states obliterated, and the United States converted into a central government exercising uncontrolled police power in every state of the Union, superseding all local control or regulation of the affairs or concerns of the states.

"Hamilton himself, the leading advocate of broad interpretation of the power to tax and to appropriate for the general welfare, never suggested that any power granted by the Constitution could be used for the destruction of local self-government in the states. Story countenances no such doctrine. It seems never to have occurred to them, or to those who have agreed with them, that the general welfare of the United States, [which has aptly been termed "an indestructible Union, composed of indestructible States,"] might be served by obliterating the constituent members of the Union. But to this fatal conclusion the doctrine contended for would inevitably lead.

And its sole premise is that, though the makers of the Constitution, in erecting the federal government, intended sedulously to limit and define its powers, so as to reserve to the states and the people sovereign power, to be wielded by the states and their citizens and not to be invaded by the United States, they nevertheless by a single clause gave power to the Congress to tear down the barriers, to invade the states' jurisdiction, and to become a parliament of the whole people, subject to no restrictions save such as are self-imposed. The argument when seen in its true character and in the light of its inevitable results must be rejected."

Mr. Justice Stone, in a dissenting opinion in which Mr. Justice Brandeis and Mr. Justice Cardozo concurred, differed with the majority both on the law and the facts. "The pivot on which the decision of the Court is made to turn," he said, ". . . is that a levy unquestionably within the taxing power of Congress may be treated as invalid because it is a step in a plan to regulate agricultural production. . . . It does not deny that the expenditure of funds for the benefit of farmers and in aid of a program of curtailment of production of agricultural products, and thus of a supposedly better ordered national economy, is within the specifically granted power. But it is declared that state power is nevertheless infringed by the expenditure of the proceeds of the tax to compensate farmers for the curtailment of their cotton acreage. Although the farmer is placed under no legal compulsion to reduce acreage, it is said that the mere offer of compensation for so doing is a species of economic coercion which operates with the same legal force and effect as though the curtailment were made mandatory by Act of Congress. In any event it is insisted that even though not coercive the expenditure of public funds to induce the recipients to curtail production is itself an infringement of state power, since the federal government cannot invade the domain of the states by the 'purchase' of performance of acts which it has no power to compel.

"Of the assertion that the payments to farmers are coercive, it is enough to say that no such contention is pressed by the taxpayer, and no such consequences were to be anticipated or

appear to have resulted from the administration of the Act. The suggestion of coercion finds no support in the record or in any data showing the actual operation of the Act. Threat of loss, not hope of gain, is the essence of economic coercion. Members of a long depressed industry have undoubtedly been tempted to curtail acreage by the hope of resulting better prices and by the proffered opportunity to obtain needed ready money. But there is nothing to indicate that those who accepted benefits were impelled by fear of lower prices if they did not accept, or that at any stage in the operation of the plan a farmer could say whether, apart from the certainty of cash payments at specified times, the advantage would lie with curtailment of production plus compensation, rather than with the same or increased acreage plus the expected rise in prices which actually occurred. Although the Agricultural Adjustment Act was put into operation in June, 1933, the official reports of the Department of Agriculture show that 6,343,000 acres of productive cotton land, 14% of the total, did not participate in the plan in 1934, and 2,790,000 acres, 6% of the total, did not participate in 1935. Of the total number of farms growing cotton, estimated at 1,500,000, 33% in 1934 and 13% in 1935 did not participate."

Mr. Justice Stone then called attention to the fact that Congress had set aside intrastate railroad rates through the Interstate Commerce Commission and had destroyed intrastate industries by tariffs. "These results," he went on, "are said to be permissible because they are incidents of the commerce power and the power to levy duties on imports. . . . The only conclusion to be drawn is that results become lawful when they are incidents of those powers but unlawful when incident to the similarly granted power to tax and spend.

"Such a limitation is contradictory and destructive of the power to appropriate for the public welfare, and is incapable of practical application. The spending power of Congress is in addition to the legislative power and not subordinate to it. This independent grant of the power of the purse, and its very nature, involving in its exercise the duty to insure expenditure within the granted power, presuppose freedom of selection

among divers ends and aims, and the capacity to impose such conditions as will render the choice effective. It is a contradiction in terms to say that there is power to spend for the national welfare, while rejecting any power to impose conditions reasonably adapted to the attainment of the end which alone would justify the expenditure.

"The limitation now sanctioned must lead to absurd consequences. The government may give seeds to farmers, but may not condition the gift upon their being planted in places where they are most needed or even planted at all. The government may give money to the unemployed, but may not ask that those who get it shall give labor in return, or even use it to support their families. It may give money to sufferers from earthquake, fire, tornado, pestilence or flood, but may not impose conditions—health precautions designed to prevent the spread of disease, or induce the movement of population to safer or more sanitary areas. All that, because it is purchased regulation infringing states powers, must be left for the states, who are unable or unwilling to supply the necessary relief. The government may spend its money for vocational rehabilitation, March 2, 1934, 48 Stat. at L. 389, chap. 38, but it may not, with the consent of all concerned, supervise the process which it undertakes to aid. It may spend its money for the suppression of the boll weevil, but may not compensate the farmers for suspending the growth of cotton in the infected areas. It may aid state reforestation and forest fire prevention agencies, [June 7, 1934] 43 Stat. at L., 653, chap. 348, U. S. C. A., title 16, § 564, but may not be permitted to supervise their conduct. It may support rural schools, February 23, 1917, 39 Stat. at L., 929, chap. 114, U. S. C. A., title 20, § 11; February 5, 1929, 45 Stat. at L., 1151, chap. 153, U. S. C. A. title 20, § 15a; May 21, 1934, 48 Stat. at L., 792, chap. 324, U. S. C. A. title 20, § 15d, but may not condition its grant by the requirement that certain standards be maintained. It may appropriate moneys to be expended by the Reconstruction Finance Corporation 'to aid in financing agriculture, commerce and industry,' and to facilitate 'the exportation of agricultural and other products.' Do all its activities collapse

because, in order to effect the permissible purpose, in myriad ways the money is paid out upon terms and conditions which influence action of the recipients within the states, which Congress cannot command? The answer would seem plain. If the expenditure is for a national public purpose, that purpose will not be thwarted because payment is on conditions which will advance that purpose. The action which Congress induces by payments of money to promote the general welfare, but which it does not command or coerce, is but an incident to a specifically granted power, but a permissible means to a legitimate end. If appropriation in aid of a program of curtailment of agricultural production is constitutional, and it is not denied that it is, payment to farmers on condition that they reduce their crop acreage is constitutional. It is not any the less so because the farmer at his own option promises to fulfill the condition.

"The suggestion that it must now be curtailed by judicial fiat because it may be abused by unwise use hardly rises to the dignity of argument. So may judicial power be abused. 'The power to tax is the power to destroy,' but we do not, for that reason, doubt its existence, or hold that its efficacy is to be restricted by its incidental or collateral effects upon the states.

"A tortured construction of the Constitution is not to be justified by recourse to extreme examples of reckless congressional spending which might occur if courts could not prevent expenditures which, even if they could be thought to effect any national purpose, would be possible only by action of a legislature lost to all sense of public responsibility. Such suppositions are addressed to the mind accustomed to believe that it is the business of courts to sit in judgment on the wisdom of legislative action. Courts are not the only agency of government that must be assumed to have capacity to govern. Congress and the courts both unhappily may falter or be mistaken in the performance of their constitutional duty. But interpretation of our great charter of government which proceeds on any assumption that the responsibility for the preservation of our institutions is the exclusive concern of any one of the three branches of government, or that it alone can save them

from destruction is far more likely, in the long run, 'to obliter-
ate the constituent members' of 'an indestructible union of indestructible states' than the frank recognition that language,
even of a constitution, may mean what it says: that the power
to tax and spend includes the power to relieve a nationwide
economic maladjustment by conditional gifts of money."

THE LATER DECISIONS

Following the great *A.A.A. Case* came a number of others
that aroused intense interest at the time, but none of them
raised or at any rate settled any new constitutional issues of
importance. On February tenth, the Court unanimously voided
a Louisiana newspaper license tax enacted under the influence
of the late Senator Huey Long for the purpose, so it was con-
vincingly alleged, of controlling the state press. Mr. Justice
Sutherland, whose attitude toward free speech during the
World War may be recalled, was selected to deliver the opinion
of the Court. "The tax here involved is bad," he said, "not
because it takes money from the pockets of the appellees. If
that were all, a wholly different question would be presented.
It is bad because, in the light of its history and its present setting, it is seen to be a deliberate and calculated device in the
guise of a tax to limit the circulation of information to which
the public is entitled in virtue of the constitutional guaranties."
Two months later Justice Sutherland was again selected to
deliver a so-called civil liberties decision, reached this time not
unanimously but with the familiar six-to-three division. The
governmental Securities and Exchange Commission, having
found what it considered to be serious misstatements and omissions in the record submitted by a certain dealer in oil royalty
participation certificates, had issued a subpœna for him to appear before it and explain his statements; the dealer had thereupon withdrawn the statements; the Commission refused to
accept this, and issued a second subpœna. Its action was
roundly condemned by Mr. Justice Sutherland as wholly "unreasonable and arbitrary," smacking indeed of "the intolerable abuses of the star chamber."

Between these two decisions came on February seventeenth one which it had taken the Court sixty days to formulate after the arguments in it had been heard. The case was that of *Ashwander* v. *Tennessee Authority et al.* intended to test the constitutionality of the Tennessee Valley Authority, the last of the three major undertakings of the New Deal. But the case was badly selected in that it directly concerned a contract for the transmission of the energy generated at Wilson Dam constructed during the World War to improve the navigation of the Tennessee River, and involved only indirectly the main question of the government's right to own and sell electric energy in competition with private companies. The Circuit Court, confining its attention to the narrower issue, upheld the government, and the Supreme Court followed its example in the same way. But the Chief Justice in delivering the majority opinion cast an oblique and none too favorable glance at the constitutionality of the T.V.A. itself:

"We limit our decision to the case before us, as we have defined it. The argument is earnestly presented that the Government by virtue of its ownership of the dam and power plant could not establish a steel mill and make and sell steel products, or a factory to manufacture clothing or shoes for the public, and thus attempt to make its ownership of energy, generated at its dam, a means of carrying on competitive commercial enterprises and thus drawing to the Federal Government the conduct and management of business having no relation to the purposes for which the Federal Government was established. The picture is eloquently drawn but we deem it to be irrelevant to the issue here. The Government is not using the water power at the Wilson Dam to establish any industry or business. It is not using the energy generated at the dam to manufacture commodities of any sort for the public. The Government is disposing of the energy itself which simply is the mechanical energy, incidental to falling water at the dam, converted into the electric energy which is susceptible of transmission. The question here is simply as to the acquisition of the transmission lines as a facility for the disposal of that energy. *And the Government rightly conceded at the bar, in*

substance, that it was without constitutional authority to ac-
quire or dispose of such energy except as it comes into being
in the operation of works constructed in the exercise of some
*power delegated to the United States.** As we have said,
these transmission lines lead directly from the dam, which has
been lawfully constructed, and the question of the constitutional
right of the Government to acquire or operate local or urban
distribution systems is not involved.   We express no opinion
as to the validity of such an effort, as to the status of any other
dam or power development in the Tennessee Valley, whether
connected with or apart from the Wilson Dam, or as to the
validity of the Tennessee Valley Authority Act or of the
claims made in the pronouncements and program of the
Authority apart from the questions we have discussed in relation to the particular provisions of the contract of January
4, 1934, affecting the Alabama Power Company."

Mr. Justice Brandeis delivered a separate opinion, in which
Justices Stone and Cardozo concurred, agreeing with the
majority decision and even stating that he did "not disagree
with the conclusion on the constitutional question announced
by the Chief Justice," but holding that "considerations of propriety, as well as long-established practice" should have prevented any discussion of the question in a case in which it was
not involved.   Mr. Justice McReynolds delivered a solitary
dissenting opinion in which he bitterly attacked the T.V.A.
itself :

"The record leaves no room for reasonable doubt that the
primary purpose was to put the Federal Government into the
business of distributing and selling electric power throughout
certain large districts, to expel the power companies which had
long serviced them, and to control the market therein. A government instrumentality had entered upon a pretentious scheme
to provide a 'yardstick' of the fairness of rates charged by private owners, and to attain 'no less a goal than the electrifica-
tion of America.'

". . . If under the thin mask of disposing of property the
United States can enter the business of generating, transmit-

---
*Italics ours.

ting and selling power as, when and wherever some board may specify, with the definite design to accomplish ends wholly beyond the sphere marked out for them by the Constitution, an easy way has been found for breaking down the limitations heretofore supposed to guarantee protection against aggression."

On March 18, 1936, the Guffey Coal Bill was invalidated by the decision in *Carter* v. *Carter Coal Company*. The bill embodied the government's attempt to regulate the notoriously scandalous conditions of both labor and industry in the coal fields by the establishment of a voluntary code empowered to fix minimum prices and maximum hours of labor, while as a gentle persuasive to the adoption of such a code it enacted a coal tax with a drawback of ninety per cent to each coal producer accepting the code. The majority opinion, delivered by Mr. Justice Sutherland, held the law invalid on three counts: the tax was really not a tax but a penalty; coal mining was an intrastate activity and so did not come under the commerce clause; the Act was an illegal delegation of power since it provided that the code should go into effect when adopted by two-thirds of the coal producers and fifty-one per cent of the employees, thereby enabling a part of the industry to legislate for the whole industry. Chief Justice Hughes and Mr. Justice Cardozo, with Justices Stone and Brandeis concurring, filed separate dissenting opinions maintaining that different parts of the Act should have been validated instead of the wholesale invalidation decreed in the majority opinion.

Last of the important decisions of the Court in this epochal 1935-1936 term was its nullification of a New York minimum wage law in the case of *Morehead* v. *State ex rel. Tipaldo*. The law had been expressly framed so as not to come under the *Adkins* v. *Children's Hospital* decision in which, it will be recalled, the Court had invalidated an otherwise similar minimum wage law on the ground that the wages had no relation to the services rendered; the new law prohibited the employment of any women at an oppressive and unreasonable wage, defined as one which is "both less than the fair and reasonable value of the services rendered and less than to meet the

minimum cost of living necessary for health." The Act had been defeated in the lower state court and also in the state court of appeals which insisted that in spite of its wording it still came under the Adkins decision. The change, the state court said, "was a difference in phraseology and not in principle." The majority of the Supreme Court—Justices Butler, Sutherland, McReynolds, Van Devanter, and Roberts—sustained this decision on the ground stated in Mr. Justice Butler's opinion: "This court is without power to put a different construction upon the State enactment from that adopted by the highest court of the State."

Since the highest court of the state had based its own conclusion on *its* construction of a Supreme Court opinion, Chief Justice Hughes dissented and held that the Supreme Court might properly decide upon the applicability of the Adkins rule to the new law, which, he maintained, was substantially different from the former one.

In a more vigorous dissenting opinion, Mr. Justice Stone, with the usual concurrence of Justices Brandeis and Cardozo, pointed out a number of things:

"While I agree with all that the Chief Justice has said, I would not make the differences between the present statute and that involved in the Adkins Case the sole basis of decision. I attach little importance to the fact that the earlier statute was aimed only at a starvation wage and that the present one does not prohibit such a wage unless it is also less than the reasonable value of the service. Since neither statute compels employment at any wage, I do not assume that employers in one case, more than in the other, would pay the minimum wage if the service were worth less.

"The vague and general pronouncement of the Fourteenth Amendment against deprivation of liberty without due process of law is a limitation of legislative power, not a formula for its exercise. It does not purport to say in what particular manner that power shall be exerted. It makes no fine-spun distinctions between methods which the legislature may and which it may not choose to solve a pressing problem of government. It is plain too, that, unless the language of the amendment and

the decisions of this Court are to be ignored, the liberty which the amendment protects is not freedom from restraint of all law or of any law which reasonable men may think an appropriate means for dealing with any of those matters of public concern with which it is the business of government to deal. There is grim irony in speaking of the freedom of contract of those who, because of their economic necessities, give their service for less than is needful to keep body and soul together. But if this is freedom of contract no one has ever denied that it is freedom which may be restrained, notwithstanding the Fourteenth Amendment, by a statute passed in the public interest."

He then quoted, possibly with an ironic satisfaction, the words of Mr. Justice Roberts in the Nebbia decision:

" 'So far as the requirement of due process is concerned, and in the absence of other constitutional restriction, a state is free to adopt whatever economic policy may reasonably be deemed to promote public welfare, and to enforce that policy by legislation adapted to its purpose. The courts are without authority either to declare such policy, or, when it is declared by the legislature, to override it. If the laws passed are seen to have a reasonable relation to a proper legislative purpose, and are neither arbitrary nor discriminatory, the requirements of due process are satisfied, and judicial determination to that effect renders a court *functus officio.*' That declaration and decision should control the present case. They are irreconcilable with the decision and most that was said in the Adkins Case. They have left the Court free of its restriction as a precedent, and free to declare that the choice of the particular form of regulation by which grave economic maladjustments are to be remedied is for legislatures and not the courts.

"In the years which have intervened since the Adkins Case we have had opportunity to learn that a wage is not always the resultant of free bargaining between employers and employees; that it may be one forced upon employees by their economic necessities and upon employers by the most ruthless of their competitors. We have had opportunity to perceive more clearly that a wage insufficient to support the worker does not visit

its consequences upon him alone; that it may affect profoundly the entire economic structure of society and, in any case, that it casts on every taxpayer, and on government itself, the burden of solving the problems of poverty, subsistence, health and morals of large numbers in the community. Because of their nature and extent these are public problems. A generation ago they were for the individual to solve; today they are the burden of the nation. I can perceive no more objection, on constitutional grounds, to their solution by requiring an industry to bear the subsistence cost of the labor which it employs, than to the imposition upon it of the cost of its industrial accidents.

"It is not for the courts to resolve doubts whether the remedy by wage regulation is as efficacious as many believe, or is better than some other, or is better even than the blind operation of uncontrolled economic forces. The legislature must be free to choose unless government is to be rendered impotent. The Fourteenth Amendment has no more embedded in the Constitution our preference for some particular set of economic beliefs, than it has adopted, in the name of liberty, the system of theology which we may happen to approve."

So the term ended.

All the old methods of reducing the power of the Court were once more popularly suggested: Constitutional amendment, abolishing of judicial review, limiting the term of office, and praying for death to make possible the substitution of liberals for conservatives. No man could say at the moment just what changes, if any, would be made.

THE END

THE CONSTITUTION OF THE UNITED STATES

THE CONSTITUTION OF THE UNITED STATES

WE, THE PEOPLE of the United States, in Order to form a more perfect Union, establish Justice, insure domestic Tranquility, provide for the common defence, promote the general Welfare, and secure the Blessings of Liberty to ourselves and our Posterity, do ordain and establish this CONSTITUTION for the United States of America.

ARTICLE I

Section 1. All legislative Powers herein granted shall be vested in a Congress of the United States, which shall consist of a Senate and House of Representatives.

Section 2. [1] The House of Representatives shall be composed of Members chosen every second Year by the People of the several States, and the Electors in each State shall have the Qualifications requisite for Electors of the most numerous Branch of the State Legislature.

[2] No Person shall be a Representative who shall not have attained to the age of twenty-five Years, and been seven Years a Citizen of the United States, and who shall not, when elected, be an Inhabitant of that State in which he shall be chosen.

[3] [Representatives and direct Taxes shall be apportioned among the several States which may be included within this Union, according to their respective Numbers, which shall be determined by adding to the whole Number of free Persons, including those bound to Service for a Term of Years, and excluding Indians not taxed, three-fifths of all other Persons.] The actual Enumeration shall be made within three Years after the first Meeting of the Congress of the United States, and within every subsequent Term of ten Years, in such Manner as they shall by Law direct. The Number of Representatives shall not exceed one for every thirty Thousand, but each State shall have at least one Representative; and until such enumeration shall be made, the State of New Hampshire shall be entitled to chuse three, Massachusetts eight, Rhode-Island and Providence Plantations one, Connecticut five, New York six, New Jersey four, Pennsylvania eight, Delaware one, Maryland six, Virginia ten, North Carolina five, South Carolina five, and Georgia three.

[4] When vacancies happen in the Representation from any State, the Executive Authority thereof shall issue Writs of Election to fill such Vacancies.

[5] The House of Representatives shall chuse their Speaker and other Officers; and shall have the sole Power of Impeachment.

Section 3. [1] The Senate of the United States shall be composed of two Senators from each State, chosen by the Legislature thereof, for six Years; and each Senator shall have one Vote.

[2] Immediately after they shall be assembled in Consequence of the first Election, they shall be divided as equally as may be into three Classes. The Seats of the Senators of the first Class shall be vacated

at the Expiration of the second Year, of the second Class at the Expiration of the fourth Year, and of the third Class at the Expiration of the sixth Year, so that one-third may be chosen every second Year; and if Vacancies happen by Resignation, or otherwise, during the Recess of the Legislature of any State, the Executive thereof may make temporary Appointments until the next Meeting of the Legislature, which shall then fill such Vacancies.

[3] No Person shall be a Senator who shall not have attained to the Age of thirty Years, and been nine Years a Citizen of the United States, and who shall not, when elected, be an Inhabitant of that State for which he shall be chosen.

[4] The Vice-President of the United States shall be President of the Senate, but shall have no Vote, unless they be equally divided.

[5] The Senate shall chuse their other Officers, and also a President pro tempore, in the Absence of the Vice-President, or when he shall exercise the Office of President of the United States.

[6] The Senate shall have the sole Power to try all Impeachments. When sitting for that Purpose, they shall be on Oath or Affirmation. When the President of the United States is tried, the Chief Justice shall preside: And no Person shall be convicted without the Concurrence of two-thirds of the Members present.

[7] Judgment in Cases of Impeachment shall not extend further than to removal from Office, and disqualification to hold and enjoy any Office of honor, Trust or Profit under the United States: but the Party convicted shall nevertheless be liable and subject to Indictment, Trial, Judgment and Punishment, according to Law.

Section 4. [1] The Times, Places, and Manner of holding Elections for Senators and Representatives, shall be prescribed in each State by the Legislature thereof; but the Congress may at any time by Law make or alter such Regulations, except as to the Places of chusing Senators.

[2] The Congress shall assemble at least once in every Year, and such Meeting shall be on the first Monday in December, unless they shall by Law appoint a different Day.

Section 5. [1] Each House shall be the Judge of the Elections, Returns and Qualifications of its own Members, and a Majority of each shall constitute a Quorum to do Business; but a smaller Number may adjourn from day to day, and may be authorized to compel the attendance of absent Members, in such Manner, and under such Penalties as each House may provide.

[2] Each House may determine the Rules of its Proceedings, punish its Members for disorderly Behaviour, and, with the Concurrence of two-thirds, expel a Member.

[3] Each House shall keep a Journal of its Proceedings, and from time to time publish the same, excepting such Parts as may in their Judgment require Secrecy; and the Yeas and Nays of the Members of either House on any question shall, at the Desire of one-fifth of those Present, be entered on the Journal.

[4] Neither House, during the Session of Congress, shall, without the Consent of the other, adjourn for more than three days, nor to any other Place than that in which the two Houses shall be sitting.

Section 6. [1] The Senators and Representatives shall receive a Compensation for their Services, to be ascertained by law, and paid out of the Treasury of the United States. They shall in all Cases, except Treason, Felony, and Breach of the Peace, be privileged from Arrest during their Attendance at the Session of their respective Houses, and in going to and returning from the same; and for any Speech or Debate in either House, they shall not be questioned in any other Place.

[2] No Senator or Representative shall, during the Time for which he was elected, be appointed to any Civil Office under the Authority of the United States, which shall have been created, or the Emoluments whereof shall have been encreased during such time; and no Person holding any Office under the United States, shall be a Member of either House during his Continuance in office.

Section 7. [1] All Bills for raising Revenue shall originate in the House of Representatives; but the Senate may propose or concur with Amendments as on other Bills.

[2] Every Bill which shall have passed the House of Representatives and the Senate, shall, before it becomes a Law, be presented to the President of the United States; if he approve he shall sign it, but if not he shall return it, with his Objections to that House in which it shall have originated, who shall enter the Objections at large on their Journal, and proceed to reconsider it. If after such Reconsideration two-thirds of that House shall agree to pass the Bill, it shall be sent, together with the Objections, to the other House, by which it shall likewise be reconsidered, and if approved by two-thirds of that House, it shall become a Law. But in all such Cases the Votes of both Houses shall be determined by Yeas and Nays, and the Names of the Persons voting for and against the Bill shall be entered on the Journal of each House respectively. If any Bill shall not be returned by the President within ten days (Sundays excepted) after it shall have been presented to him, the Same shall be a Law, in like Manner as if he had signed it, unless the Congress by their Adjournment prevent its Return, in which Case it shall not be a Law.

[3] Every Order, Resolution, or Vote to which the Concurrence of the Senate and House of Representatives may be necessary (except on a question of Adjournment) shall be presented to the President of the United States; and before the Same shall take Effect, shall be approved by him, or, being disapproved by him, shall be repassed by two-thirds of the Senate and House of Representatives, according to the Rules and Limitations prescribed in the Case of a Bill.

Section 8. The Congress shall have Power [1] To lay and collect Taxes, Duties, Imposts and Excises, to pay the Debts and provide for the common Defence and general Welfare of the United States; but all duties, Imposts and Excises shall be uniform throughout the United States;

[2] To borrow Money on the credit of the United States;

[3] To regulate Commerce with foreign Nations, and among the several States, and with the Indian Tribes;

[4] To establish an uniform Rule of Naturalization, and uniform Laws on the subject of Bankruptcies throughout the United States;

[5] To coin Money, regulate the Value thereof, and of foreign Coin, and fix the Standard of Weights and Measures;

[6] To provide for the Punishment of counterfeiting the Securities and current Coin of the United States;

[7] To establish Post Offices and post Roads;

[8] To promote the Progress of Science and useful Arts, by securing for limited Times to Authors and Inventors the exclusive Right to their respective writings and Discoveries;

[9] To constitute Tribunals inferior to the Supreme Court;

[10] To define and punish Piracies and Felonies committed on the high Seas, and Offences against the Law of Nations;

[11] To declare War, grant Letters of Marque and Reprisal, and make Rules concerning Captures on Land and Water;

[12] To raise and support Armies, but no Appropriation of Money to that Use shall be for a longer Term than two Years;

[13] To provide and maintain a Navy;

[14] To make Rules for the Government and Regulation of the land and naval Forces;

[15] To provide for calling forth the Militia to execute the Laws of the Union, suppress Insurrections and repel Invasions;

[16] To provide for organizing, arming, and disciplining, the Militia, and for governing such Part of them as may be employed in the Service of the United States, reserving to the States respectively, the Appointment of the Officers, and the Authority of training the Militia according to the discipline prescribed by Congress;

[17] To exercise exclusive Legislation in all Cases whatsoever, over such District (not exceeding ten Miles square) as may, by Cession of particular States, and the Acceptance of Congress, become the Seat of the Government of the United States, and to exercise like Authority over all Places purchased by the Consent of the Legislature of the State in which the Same shall be, for the Erection of Forts, Magazines, Arsenals, dock-Yards, and other needful Buildings;—And

[18] To make all Laws which shall be necessary and proper for carrying into Execution the foregoing Powers, and all other Powers vested by this Constitution in the Government of the United States, or in any Department or Officer thereof.

Section 9. [1] The Migration or Importation of such Persons as any of the States now existing shall think proper to admit, shall not be prohibited by the Congress prior to the Year one thousand eight hundred and eight, but a Tax or duty may be imposed on such Importation, not exceeding ten dollars for each Person.

[2] The Privilege of the Writ of Habeas Corpus shall not be suspended, unless when in Cases of Rebellion or Invasion the public Safety may require it.

[3] No Bill of Attainder or ex post facto Law shall be passed.

[4] No Capitation, or other direct, tax shall be laid, unless in Proportion to the Census or Enumeration hereinbefore directed to be taken.

[5] No Tax or Duty shall be laid on Articles exported from any State.

[6] No Preference shall be given by any Regulation of Commerce or Revenue to the Ports of one State over those of another; nor shall Vessels bound to, or from, one State, be obliged to enter, clear, or pay Duties in another.

[7] No money shall be drawn from the Treasury, but in Consequence of Appropriations made by Law; and a regular Statement and Account of the Receipts and Expenditures of all public Money shall be published from time to. time.

[8] No title of Nobility shall be granted by the United States:—And no Person holding any Office of Profit or Trust under them, shall, without the Consent of the Congress, accept of any present, Emolument, Office, or Title, of any kind whatever, from any King, Prince, or foreign State.

Section 10. [1] No State shall enter into any Treaty, Alliance, or Confederation; grant Letters of Marque and Reprisal; coin Money; emit Bills of Credit; make any Thing but gold and silver Coin a Tender in Payment of Debts; pass any Bill of Attainder, ex post facto Law, or Law impairing the obligation of Contracts, or grant any Title of Nobility.

[2] No State shall, without the Consent of the Congress, lay any Imposts or Duties on Imports or Exports, except what may be absolutely necessary for executing its inspection Laws; and the net Produce of all Duties and Imposts, laid by any State on Imports or Exports, shall be for the Use of the Treasury of the United States; and all such Laws shall be subject to the Revision and Control of the Congress.

[3] No State shall, without the Consent of Congress, lay any Duty of tonnage, keep Troops, or Ships of War in time of Peace, enter into any Agreement or Compact with another State, or with a foreign Power, or engage in War, unless actually invaded, or in such imminent Danger as will not admit of delay.

ARTICLE II

Section 1. [1] The executive Power shall be vested in a President of the United States of America. He shall hold his Office during the Term of four years, and, together with the Vice-President, chosen for the same term, be elected as follows:

[2] Each State shall appoint, in such Manner as the Legislature thereof may direct, a Number of Electors, equal to the whole Number of Senators and Representatives to which the State may be entitled in the Congress: but no Senator or Representative, or Person holding an Office of Trust or Profit under the United States, shall be appointed an Elector. [The electors shall meet in their respective States, and vote by ballot for two Persons, of whom one at least shall not be an inhabitant of the same State with themselves. And they shall make a list of all the Persons voted for, and of the Number of Votes for each; which List they shall sign and certify, and transmit sealed to the Seat of the Government of the United States, directed to the President of the Senate. The President of the Senate shall, in the Presence of the Senate and House of Representatives, open all the Certificates, and the Votes shall then be counted. The Person having the greatest Number of Votes shall be the President, if such Number be a Majority of the whole Number of Electors appointed; and if there be more than one who have such Majority, and have an equal Number of Votes, then the House of Representatives shall immediately chuse by Ballot one of them for President; and if no Person have

a Majority, then from the five highest on the List the said House shall in like Manner chuse the President. But in chusing the President, the Votes shall be taken by States, the Representation from each State having one Vote; a quorum for this Purpose shall consist of a Member or Members from two-thirds of the States, and a Majority of all the States shall be necessary to a Choice. In every Case, after the Choice of the President, the Person having the greatest Number of Votes of the Electors shall be the Vice-President. But if there should remain two or more who have equal Votes, the Senate shall chuse from them by Ballot the Vice-President.]

[3] The Congress may determine the Time of chusing the Electors, and the Day on which they shall give their Votes; which Day shall be the same throughout the United States.

[4] No Person except a natural born citizen, or a citizen of the United States, at the time of the Adoption of this Constitution, shall be eligible to the Office of President; neither shall any Person be eligible to that Office who shall not have attained to the Age of thirty-five Years, and been fourteen Years a Resident within the United States.

[5] In Case of the Removal of the President from Office, or of his Death, Resignation, or Inability to discharge the Powers and Duties of the said Office, the same shall devolve on the Vice-President, and the Congress may by Law provide for the Case of Removal, Death, Resignation or Inability, both of the President and Vice-President, declaring what Officer shall then act as President, and such Officer shall act accordingly, until the Disability be removed, or a President shall be elected.

[6] The President shall, at stated Times, receive for his Services, a Compensation, which shall neither be encreased nor diminished during the Period for which he shall have been elected, and he shall not receive within that Period any other Emolument from the United States, or any of them.

[7] Before he enter on the Execution of his Office, he shall take the following Oath or Affirmation:—"I do solemnly swear (or affirm) that I will faithfully execute the Office of President of the United States, and will to the best of my Ability, preserve, protect and defend the Constitution of the United States."

Section 2. [1] The President shall be Commander in Chief of the Army and Navy of the United States, and of the Militia of the several States, when called into the actual Service of the United States; he may require the Opinion, in writing, of the principal Officer in each of the executive Departments, upon any Subject relating to the Duties of their respective Offices, and he shall have Power to grant Reprieves and Pardons for Offences against the United States, except in Cases of Impeachment.

[2] He shall have Power, by and with the Advice and Consent of the Senate, to make Treaties, provided two-thirds of the Senators present concur; and he shall nominate, and by and with the Advice and Consent of the Senate, shall appoint Ambassadors, other public Ministers and Consuls, Judges of the Supreme Court, and all other Offices of the United States, whose Appointments are not herein otherwise provided for, and which shall be established by Law. But the Congress may by Law vest the Appointment of such inferior Officers, as they think proper,

in the President alone, in the Courts of Law, or in the Heads of Departments.

[3] The President shall have Power to fill up all Vacancies that may happen during the Recess of the Senate, by granting Commissions which shall expire at the End of their next Session.

Section 3. He shall from time to time give to the Congress Information of the State of the Union, and recommend to their Consideration such Measures as he shall judge necessary and expedient; he may, on extraordinary Occasions, convene both Houses, or either of them, and in Case of Disagreement between them, with Respect to the Time of Adjournment, he may adjourn them to such Time as he shall think proper; he shall receive Ambassadors and other public Ministers; he shall take Care that the Law be faithfully executed, and shall Commission all the Officers of the United States.

Section 4. The President, Vice-President and all civil Officers of the United States, shall be removed from Office on Impeachment for, and Conviction of, Treason, Bribery, or other high Crimes and Misdemeanors.

ARTICLE III

Section 1. The judicial Power of the United States, shall be vested in one Supreme Court, and in such inferior Courts as the Congress may from time to time ordain and establish. The Judges, both of the Supreme and inferior Courts, shall hold their Offices during good Behaviour, and shall, at stated Times, receive for their Services, a Compensation, which shall not be diminished during their Continuance in Office.

Section 2. [1] The judicial Power shall extend to all Cases, in Law and Equity, arising under this Constitution, the Laws of the United States, and Treaties made, or which shall be made, under their Authority;—to all cases affecting Ambassadors, other public Ministers and Consuls;—to all cases of admiralty and maritime Jurisdiction;—to Controversies to which the United States shall be a party;—to controversies between two or more States;—between a State and Citizens of another State;—between Citizens of different States—between Citizens of the same State claiming Lands under Grants of different States, and between a State, or the Citizens thereof, and foreign States, Citizens or subjects.

[2] In all Cases affecting Ambassadors, other public Ministers and Consuls, and those in which a State shall be a Party, the Supreme Court shall have original Jurisdiction. In all other Cases before mentioned, the Supreme Court shall have appellate Jurisdiction, both as to Law and Fact, with such Exceptions, and under such Regulations as the Congress shall make.

[3] The Trial of all Crimes, except in Cases of Impeachment, shall be by Jury; and such Trial shall be held in the State where the said Crimes shall have been committed; but when not committed within any State, the Trial shall be at such Place or Places as the Congress may by Law have directed.

Section 3. [1] Treason against the United States, shall consist only in levying War against them, or in adhering to their Enemies, giving them Aid and Comfort. No Person shall be convicted of Treason unless on the

Testimony of two Witnesses to the same overt Act, or on Confession in open Court.

[2] The Congress shall have Power to declare the Punishment of Treason, but no Attainder of Treason shall work Corruption of Blood, or Forfeiture except during the Life of the Person attainted.

ARTICLE IV

Section 1. Full Faith and Credit shall be given in each State to the public Acts, Records, and judicial Proceedings of every other State. And the Congress may by general Laws prescribe the Manner in which such Acts, Records and Proceedings shall be proved, and the Effect thereof.

Section 2. [1] The Citizens of each State shall be entitled to all Privileges and Immunities of Citizens in the several States.

[2] A Person charged in any State with Treason, Felony, or other Crime, who shall flee from Justice, and be found in another State, shall, on Demand of the executive Authority of the State from which he fled, be delivered up, to be removed to the State having Jurisdiction of the Crime.

[3] No Person held to Service or Labour in one State, under the Laws thereof, escaping into another, shall, in Consequence of any Law or Regulation therein, be discharged from such Service or Labour, but shall be delivered up on Claim of the Party to whom such Service or Labour may be due.

Section 3. [1] New States may be admitted by the Congress into this Union; but no new State shall be formed or erected within the Jurisdiction of any other State; nor any State be formed by the Junction of two or more States, or Parts of States, without the Consent of the Legislatures of the States concerned as well as of the Congress.

[2] The Congress shall have Power to dispose of and make all needful Rules and Regulations respecting the Territory or other Property belonging to the United States; and nothing in this Constitution shall be so construed as to Prejudice any Claims of the United States, or of any particular State.

Section 4. The United States shall guarantee to every State in this Union a Republican Form of Government, and shall protect each of them against Invasion; and on Application of the Legislature, or of the Executive (when the Legislature cannot be convened) against domestic Violence.

ARTICLE V

The Congress, whenever two-thirds of both Houses shall deem it necessary, shall propose Amendments to this Constitution, or, on the Application of the Legislatures of two-thirds of the several States, shall call a Convention for proposing Amendments, which, in either Case, shall be valid to all Intents and Purposes, as Part of this Constitution, when ratified by the Legislatures of three-fourths of the several States, or by Conventions in three-fourths thereof, as the one or the other Mode of Ratification may be proposed by the Congress; Provided, that no Amendment which may be made prior to the Year One thousand eight hundred and

eight shall in any Manner affect the first and fourth Clauses in the Ninth Section of the first Article; and that no State, without its Consent, shall be deprived of its equal suffrage in the Senate.

ARTICLE VI

[1] All Debts contracted and Engagements entered into, before the Adoption of this Constitution, shall be as valid against the United States under this Constitution, as under the Confederation.

[2] This Constitution, and the Laws of the United States which shall be made in Pursuance thereof; and all Treaties made, or which shall be made, under the Authority of the United States, shall be the supreme Law of the land; and the Judges in every State shall be bound thereby, any Thing in the Constitution or Laws of any State to the Contrary notwithstanding.

[3] The Senators and Representatives before mentioned and the Members of the several State Legislatures, and all executive and judicial Officers, both of the United States and of the several States, shall be bound by Oath or Affirmation, to support this Constitution; but no religious Test shall ever be required as a Qualification to any Office or public Trust under the United States.

ARTICLE VII

The Ratification of the Conventions of nine States, shall be sufficient for the Establishment of this Constitution between the States so ratifying the Same.

Done in Convention, by the Unanimous Consent of the States present, the Seventeenth Day of September, in the Year of our Lord one thousand seven hundred and Eighty-seven, and of the Independence of the United States of America the Twelfth.

IN WITNESS whereof We have hereunto subscribed our Names,

G°. WASHINGTON—

Presidt. and Deputy from Virginia

[and thirty-eight members from all the States except Rhode Island.]

ARTICLES IN ADDITION TO, AND AMENDMENT OF, THE CONSTITUTION OF THE UNITED STATES OF AMERICA, PROPOSED BY CONGRESS, AND RATIFIED BY THE LEGISLATURES OF THE SEVERAL STATES, PURSUANT TO THE FIFTH ARTICLE OF THE ORIGINAL CONSTITUTION.

[ARTICLE I]

Congress shall make no law respecting an establishment of religion, or prohibiting the free exercise thereof; or abridging the freedom of speech, or of the press; or the right of the people peaceably to assemble, and to petition the Government for a redress of grievances.

[ARTICLE II]

A well regulated Militia, being necessary to the security of a free State, the right of the people to keep and bear Arms, shall not be infringed.

[ARTICLE III]

No Soldier shall, in time of peace be quartered in any house, without the consent of the Owner, nor in time of war, but in a manner to be prescribed by law.

[ARTICLE IV]

The right of the people to be secure in their persons, houses, papers, and effects, against unreasonable searches and seizures, shall not be violated, and no Warrants shall issue, but upon probable cause, supported by Oath or affirmation, and particularly describing the place to be searched, and the persons or things to be seized.

[ARTICLE V]

No person shall be held to answer for a capital, or otherwise infamous crime, unless on a presentment or indictment of a Grand Jury, except in cases arising in the land or naval forces, or in the Militia, when in actual service in time of War or public danger; nor shall any person be subject for the same offence to be twice put in jeopardy of life or limb; nor shall be compelled in any Criminal Case to be a witness against himself, nor be deprived of life, liberty, or property, without due process of law; nor shall private property be taken for public use, without just compensation.

[ARTICLE VI]

In all criminal prosecutions, the accused shall enjoy the right to a speedy and public trial, by an impartial jury of the State and district wherein the crime shall have been committed, which district shall have been previously ascertained by law, and to be informed of the nature and cause of the accusation; to be confronted with the witnesses against him; to have compulsory process for obtaining Witnesses in his favor, and to have the Assistance of Counsel for his defence.

[ARTICLE VII]

In suits at common law, where the value in controversy shall exceed twenty dollars, the right of trial by jury shall be preserved, and no fact tried by a jury, shall be otherwise re-examined in any Court of the United States, than according to the rules of the common law.

[ARTICLE VIII]

Excessive bail shall not be required, nor excessive fines imposed, nor cruel and unusual punishment inflicted.

[ARTICLE IX]

The enumeration in the Constitution, of certain rights, shall not be construed to deny or disparage others retained by the people.

[ARTICLE X]

The powers not delegated to the United States by the Constitution, nor prohibited by it to the States, are reserved to the States respectively, or to the people.

[ARTICLE XI]

The Judicial power of the United States shall not be construed to extend to any suit in law or equity, commenced or prosecuted against one of the United States by Citizens of another State, or by Citizens or Subjects of any Foreign State.

[ARTICLE XII]

The Electors shall meet in their respective states, and vote by ballot for President and Vice-President, one of whom, at least, shall not be an inhabitant of the same state with themselves; they shall name in their ballots the person voted for as President, and in distinct ballots the person voted for as Vice-President, and they shall make distinct lists of all persons voted for as President, and of all persons voted for as Vice-President, and the number of votes for each, which lists they shall sign and certify, and transmit sealed to the seat of the government of the United States, directed to the President of the Senate;—The President of the Senate shall, in presence of the Senate and House of Representatives, open all the certificates and the votes shall then be counted;—The person having the greatest number of votes for President, shall be the President, if such number be a majority of the whole number of Electors appointed; and if no person have such majority, then from the persons having the highest numbers not exceeding three on the list of those voted for as President, the House of Representatives shall choose immediately, by ballot, the President. But in choosing the President, the votes shall be taken by states, the representation for each state having one vote; a quorum for this purpose shall consist of a member or members from two-thirds of the states, and a majority of all the states shall be necessary to a choice. And if the House of Representatives shall not choose a President whenever the right of choice shall devolve upon them, before the fourth day of March next following, then the Vice-President shall act as President, as in the case of the death or other constitutional disability of the President. The person having the greatest number of votes as Vice-President, shall be the Vice-President, if such number be a majority of the whole number of Electors appointed, and if no person have a majority, then from the two highest numbers on the list, the Senate shall choose the Vice-President; a quorum for the purpose shall consist of two-thirds of the whole number of Senators, and a majority of the whole number shall be necessary to a choice. But no person constitutionally

ineligible to the office of President shall be eligible to that of Vice-President of the United States.

[ARTICLE XIII]

Section 1. Neither slavery nor involuntary servitude, except as a punishment for crime whereof the party shall have been duly convicted, shall exist within the United States, or any place subject to their jurisdiction.

Section 2. Congress shall have power to enforce this article by appropriate legislation.

[ARTICLE XIV]

Section 1. All persons born or naturalized in the United States, and subject to the jurisdiction thereof, are citizens of the United States and of the State wherein they reside. No State shall make or enforce any law which shall abridge the privileges or immunities of citizens of the United States; nor shall any State deprive any person of life, liberty, or property, without due process of law; nor deny to any person within its jurisdiction the equal protection of the laws.

Section 2. Representatives shall be apportioned among the several States according to their respective numbers, counting the whole number of persons in each State, excluding Indians not taxed. But when the right to vote at any election for the choice of electors for President and Vice-President of the United States, Representatives in Congress, the Executive and Judicial officers of a State, or the members of the Legislature thereof, is denied to any of the male inhabitants of such State, being twenty-one years of age, and citizens of the United States, or in any way abridged, except for participation in rebellion, or other crime, the basis of representation therein shall be reduced in the proportion which the number of such male citizens shall bear to the whole number of male citizens twenty-one years of age in such State.

Section 3. No person shall be a Senator or Representative in Congress, or elector of President and Vice-President, or hold any office, civil or military, under the United States, or under any State, who, having previously taken an oath, as a member of Congress, or as an officer of the United States, or as a member of any State Legislature, or as an executive or judicial officer of any State, to support the Constitution of the United States, shall have engaged in insurrection or rebellion against the same, or given aid or comfort to the enemies thereof. But Congress may by two-thirds vote of each House, remove such disability.

Section 4. The validity of the public debt of the United States, authorized by law, including debts incurred for payment of pensions and bounties for services in suppressing insurrection or rebellion, shall not be questioned. But neither the United States nor any State shall assume or pay any debt or obligation incurred in aid of insurrection or rebellion against the United States, or any claim for the loss or emancipation of any slave; but all such debts, obligations and claims shall be held illegal and void.

Section 5. The Congress shall have power to enforce, by appropriate legislation, the provisions of this article.

[ARTICLE XV]

Section 1. The right of citizens of the United States to vote shall not be denied or abridged by the United States or by any State on account of race, color or previous condition of servitude.

Section 2. The Congress shall have power to enforce this article by appropriate legislation.

[ARTICLE XVI]

The Congress shall have power to lay and collect taxes on incomes, from whatever source derived, without apportionment among the several states, and without regard to any census or enumeration.

[ARTICLE XVII]

The Senate of the United States shall be composed of two Senators from each State, elected by the people thereof, for six years; and each Senator shall have one vote. The electors in each State shall have the qualifications requisite for electors of the most numerous branch of the State Legislatures.

When vacancies happen in the representation of any State in the Senate, the executive authority of such State shall issue writs of election to fill such vacancies: *Provided,* That the Legislature of any State may empower the executive thereof to make temporary appointments until the people fill the vacancies by election as the Legislature may direct.

This amendment shall not be so construed as to affect the election or term of any Senator chosen before it becomes valid as part of the Constitution.

[ARTICLE XVIII]

Section 1. After one year from the ratification of this article the manufacture, sale, or transportation of intoxicating liquors within, the importation thereof into, or the exportation thereof from the United States and all territory subject to the jurisdiction thereof for beverage purposes is hereby prohibited.

Section 2. The Congress and the several States shall have concurrent power to enforce this article by appropriate legislation.

Section 3. This article shall be inoperative unless it shall have been ratified as an amendment to the Constitution by the Legislatures of the several States, as provided in the Constitution, within seven years from the date of the submission hereof to the States by the Congress.

[ARTICLE XIX]

The right of citizens of the United States to vote shall not be denied or abridged by the United States or any State on account of sex.

Congress shall have power to enforce this article by appropriate legislation.

[ARTICLE XX]

Section 1. The terms of the President and Vice-President shall end at noon on the 20th day of January, and the terms of Senators and Representatives at noon on the 3d day of January, of the years in which such terms would have ended if this article had not been ratified; and the terms of their successors shall then begin.

Section 2. The Congress shall assemble at least once in every year, and such meeting shall begin at noon on the 3d day of January, unless they shall by law appoint a different day.

Section 3. If, at the time fixed for the beginning of the term of the President, the President elect shall have died, the Vice-President elect shall become President. If a President shall not have been chosen before the time fixed for the beginning of his term, or if the President elect shall have failed to qualify, then the Vice-President elect shall act as President until a President shall have qualified; and the Congress may by law provide for the case wherein neither a President elect nor a Vice-President elect shall have qualified, declaring who shall then act as President, or the manner in which one who is to act shall be selected, and such person shall act accordingly until a President or Vice-President shall have qualified.

Section 4. The Congress may by law provide for the case of the death of any of the persons from whom the House of Representatives may choose a President whenever the right of choice shall have devolved upon them, and for the case of the death of any of the persons from whom the Senate may choose a Vice-President whenever the right of choice shall have devolved upon them.

Section 5. Sections 1 and 2 shall take effect on the 15th day of October following the ratification of this article.

Section 6. This article shall be inoperative unless it shall have been ratified as an amendment to the Constitution by the Legislatures of three-fourths of the several States within seven years from the date of its submission.

[ARTICLE XXI]

Section 1. The eighteenth article of amendment to the Constitution of the United States is hereby repealed.

Section 2. The transportation or importation into any State, Territory, or possession of the United States for delivery or use therein of intoxicating liquors, in violation of the laws thereof, is hereby prohibited.

Section 3. This article shall be inoperative unless it shall have been ratified as an amendment to the Constitution by conventions in the several States, as provided in the Constitution, within seven years from the date of the submission hereof to the States by the Congress.

[ARTICLE XV]

Section 1. The right of citizens of the United States to vote shall not be denied or abridged by the United States or by any State on account of race, color or previous condition of servitude.

Section 2. The Congress shall have power to enforce this article by appropriate legislation.

[ARTICLE XVI]

The Congress shall have power to lay and collect taxes on incomes, from whatever source derived, without apportionment among the several states, and without regard to any census or enumeration.

[ARTICLE XVII]

The Senate of the United States shall be composed of two Senators from each State, elected by the people thereof, for six years; and each Senator shall have one vote. The electors in each State shall have the qualifications requisite for electors of the most numerous branch of the State Legislatures.

When vacancies happen in the representation of any State in the Senate, the executive authority of such State shall issue writs of election to fill such vacancies: *Provided,* That the Legislature of any State may empower the executive thereof to make temporary appointments until the people fill the vacancies by election as the Legislature may direct.

This amendment shall not be so construed as to affect the election or term of any Senator chosen before it becomes valid as part of the Constitution.

[ARTICLE XVIII]

Section 1. After one year from the ratification of this article the manufacture, sale, or transportation of intoxicating liquors within, the importation thereof into, or the exportation thereof from the United States and all territory subject to the jurisdiction thereof for beverage purposes is hereby prohibited.

Section 2. The Congress and the several States shall have concurrent power to enforce this article by appropriate legislation.

Section 3. This article shall be inoperative unless it shall have been ratified as an amendment to the Constitution by the Legislatures of the several States, as provided in the Constitution, within seven years from the date of the submission hereof to the States by the Congress.

[ARTICLE XIX]

The right of citizens of the United States to vote shall not be denied or abridged by the United States or any State on account of sex.

Congress shall have power to enforce this article by appropriate legislation.

[ARTICLE XX]

Section 1. The terms of the President and Vice-President shall end at noon on the 20th day of January, and the terms of Senators and Representatives at noon on the 3d day of January, of the years in which such terms would have ended if this article had not been ratified; and the terms of their successors shall then begin.

Section 2. The Congress shall assemble at least once in every year, and such meeting shall begin at noon on the 3d day of January, unless they shall by law appoint a different day.

Section 3. If, at the time fixed for the beginning of the term of the President, the President elect shall have died, the Vice-President elect shall become President. If a President shall not have been chosen before the time fixed for the beginning of his term, or if the President elect shall have failed to qualify, then the Vice-President elect shall act as President until a President shall have qualified; and the Congress may by law provide for the case wherein neither a President elect nor a Vice-President elect shall have qualified, declaring who shall then act as President, or the manner in which one who is to act shall be selected, and such person shall act accordingly until a President or Vice-President shall have qualified.

Section 4. The Congress may by law provide for the case of the death of any of the persons from whom the House of Representatives may choose a President whenever the right of choice shall have devolved upon them, and for the case of the death of any of the persons from whom the Senate may choose a Vice-President whenever the right of choice shall have devolved upon them.

Section 5. Sections 1 and 2 shall take effect on the 15th day of October following the ratification of this article.

Section 6. This article shall be inoperative unless it shall have been ratified as an amendment to the Constitution by the Legislatures of three-fourths of the several States within seven years from the date of its submission.

[ARTICLE XXI]

Section 1. The eighteenth article of amendment to the Constitution of the United States is hereby repealed.

Section 2. The transportation or importation into any State, Territory, or possession of the United States for delivery or use therein of intoxicating liquors, in violation of the laws thereof, is hereby prohibited.

Section 3. This article shall be inoperative unless it shall have been ratified as an amendment to the Constitution by conventions in the several States, as provided in the Constitution, within seven years from the date of the submission hereof to the States by the Congress.

TERMS OF SERVICE AND AGES OF THE JUSTICES

Dates of Term	Name of Justice	Age at Appointment	Age at Resignation or Death
1789-1795	JOHN JAY (Chief Justice)	43	49
1789-1791	JOHN RUTLEDGE	50	52
1789-1810	WILLIAM CUSHING	57	78
1789-1798	JAMES WILSON	47	55
1789-1796	JOHN BLAIR	57	64
1790-1799	JAMES IREDELL	38	48
1791-1793	THOMAS JOHNSON	59	60
.1793-1806	WILLIAM PATERSON	48	61
1796-1811	SAMUEL CHASE	54	70
1796-1800	OLIVER ELLSWORTH (Chief Justice)	50	55
1798-1829	BUSHROD WASHINGTON	36	67
1799-1804	ALFRED MOORE	44	48
1801-1835	JOHN MARSHALL (Chief Justice)	45	79
1804-1834	WILLIAM JOHNSON	32	62
1806-1823	HENRY BROCKHOLST LIVINGSTON	49	65
1807-1826	THOMAS TODD	42	61
1811-1845	JOSEPH STORY	32	65
1811-1835	GABRIEL DUVAL	58	82
1823-1843	SMITH THOMPSON	54	74
1826-1828	ROBERT TRIMBLE	49	51
1829-1861	JOHN MCLEAN	43	76
1830-1844	HENRY BALDWIN	49	64
1835-1867	JAMES MOORE WAYNE	45	77
1836-1864	ROGER BROOKE TANEY (Chief Justice)	58	87
1836-1841	PHILIP PENDLETON BARBOUR	52	57
'1837-1865	JOHN CATRON	51	79
1837-1852	JOHN MCKINLEY	57	72
1841-1860	PETER VIVIAN DANIEL	56	76
1845-1873	SAMUEL NELSON	52	81
1846-1851	LEVI WOODBURY	56	61
1846-1870	ROBERT COOPER GRIER	52	75
1851-1857	BENJAMIN ROBBINS CURTIS	42	47
1853-1861	JOHN ARCHIBALD CAMPBELL	41	50
1858-1881	NATHAN CLIFFORD	54	77
1861-1881	NOAH HAYNES SWAYNE	57	76
1862-1890	SAMUEL FREEMAN MILLER	46	74
1862-1877	DAVID DAVIS	47	61
1863-1897	STEPHEN JOHNSON FIELD	46	81
1864-1873	SALMON PORTLAND CHASE (Chief Justice)	56	65
1870-1880	WILLIAM STRONG	61	72
1870-1892	JOSEPH P. BRADLEY	57	78
1872-1882	WARD HUNT	62	71

Dates of Term	Name of Justice	Age at Appointment	Age at Resignation or Death
1874-1888	MORRISON RENICK WAITE (Chief Justice)	57	71
1877-1911	JOHN MARSHALL HARLAN	44	78
1880-1887	WILLIAM BURNHAM WOODS	56	62
1881-1889	STANLEY MATTHEWS	56	64
1882-1902	HORACE GRAY	53	74
1882-1893	SAMUEL BLATCHFORD	62	73
1888-1893	LUCIUS QUINTUS CINCINNATUS LAMAR	62	67
1888-1910	MELVILLE WESTON FULLER (Chief Justice)	55	77
1889-1910	DAVID JOSIAH BREWER	52	73
1890-1906	HENRY BILLINGS BROWN	54	70
1892-1903	GEORGE SHIRAS JR.	60	71
1893-1895	HOWELL EDMUNDS JACKSON	60	63
1894-1921	EDWARD DOUGLASS WHITE	48	75
1895-1909	RUFUS WILLIAM PECKHAM	57	70
1898-1925	JOSEPH MCKENNA	54	81
1902-1932	OLIVER WENDELL HOLMES	61	91
1903-1922	WILLIAM RUFUS DAY	53	73
1906-1910	WILLIAM HENRY MOODY	52	56
1909-1914	HORACE HARMON LURTON	65	70
1910-1916	CHARLES EVANS HUGHES	48	54
1910-	WILLIS VAN DEVANTER	51	77*
1910-1916	JOSEPH ROCKER LAMAR	53	58
1912-1922	MAHLON PITNEY	54	64
1914-	JAMES CLARK MCREYNOLDS	52	74*
1916-	LOUIS DEMBITZ BRANDEIS	59	79*
1916-1922	JOHN HESSIN CLARKE	58	65
1921-1930	WILLIAM HOWARD TAFT (Chief Justice)	63	73
1922-	GEORGE SUTHERLAND	60	74*
1922-	PIERCE BUTLER	56	70*
1923-1930	EDWARD TERRY SANFORD	57	65
1925-	HARLAN FISKE STONE	52	63*
1930-	CHARLES EVANS HUGHES (Chief Justice)	68	74*
1930-	OWEN JOSEPHUS ROBERTS	55	61*
1932-	BENJAMIN NATHAN CARDOZO	61	66*

*Present age.

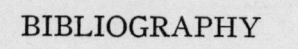

BIBLIOGRAPHY

BIBLIOGRAPHY

I. Books

BATES, ERNEST SUTHERLAND, *This Land of Liberty* (1930)
The Story of Congress (1936)

BEARD, CHARLES AUSTIN, *The Supreme Court and the Constitution* (1912)
An Economic Interpretation of the Constitution of the United States (1913)

BECK, JAMES M., *The Constitution of the United States, with a Foreword by the late W. T. Harding* (1923)

BEVERIDGE, ALBERT J., *The Life of John Marshall* (4 vols.) (1919)

BIDDLE, GEORGE W., *Constitutional History of the United States as seen in the Development of American Law* (1889)

BOUDIN, LOUIS B., *Government by Judiciary* (1932)

BOWERS, CLAUDE G., *The Party Battles of the Jackson Period* (1922)

BRADLEY, CHARLES (editor), *Miscellaneous Writings of the Late Joseph P. Bradley* (1902)

BRANDEIS, LOUIS DEMBITZ, *The Social and Economic Views of Mr. Justice Brandeis* (1930)

BRANT, IRVING, *Storm over the Constitution* (1936)

BRENTANO, L., *The Relation of Labor to the Law of Today* (1891)

CARDOZO, BENJAMIN N., *The Nature of the Judicial Process* (1928)

CARSON, HAMPTON L., *History of the Supreme Court of the United States* (1902)

CLARK, F. B., *Constitutional Doctrines of Justice Harlan* (1915)

CLARK, L. D., *The Law of the Employment of Labor* (1911)

CLIFFORD, P. G., *Nathan Clifford* (1922)

CORWIN, EDWARD SAMUEL, *National Supremacy* (1913)
The Doctrine of Judicial Review (Princeton, 1914)
John Marshall and the Constitution (1919)
The Twilight of the Supreme Court (Yale Press, 1934)

COUNTRYMAN, EDWIN, *The Supreme Court and its Appellate Power under the Constitution* (1913)

DAVIS, HORACE A., *The Judicial Veto* (1914)

DOSKOW, AMBROSE, *Historic Opinions of the United States Supreme Court* (1935)

ELLIOTT, WILLIAM YANDELL, *The Need for Constitutional Reform* (1935)

ESTEY, J. A., *The Labor Problem* (1928)

ETTRUDE, DORMIN, JR., *Power of Congress to Nullify Supreme Court Decisions* (1924)

FLACK, HORACE E., *The Adoption of the Fourteenth Amendment* (1908)

FRANK, JEROME, *Law and the Modern Mind* (1930)

FRANKFURTER, FELIX, and LANDIS, J. M., *The Business of the Supreme Court* (1927)

FREUND, ERNST, *The Police Power, Public Policy, and Constitutional Rights* (1904)

GASKILL, NELSON B., *The Regulation of Competition* (1936)

GOODNOW, F. J., *Social Reform and the Constitution* (1911)

GREGORY, C. N., *Samuel Freeman Miller* (1907)

GROAT, G. G., *An Introduction to the Study of Organized Labor in America* (1919)

HAINES, CHARLES GROVE, *The American Doctrine of Judicial Supremacy* (1914)
    The Revival of Natural Law Concepts (1930)

HANEY, LOUIS H., *History of Economic Thought* (1930)

HANKIN, GREGORY and CHARLOTTE A., *Progress of the Law in the United States Supreme Court, 1929-30* (1930)
    The United States Supreme Court, 1928-29 (1929)

HART, A. B., *Salmon Portland Chase* (1899)

HENRY, JOHN M., *Nine above the Law* (R. T. Lewis, 1936)

HOCKING, W. E., *Man and the State* (1926)

HOLMES, OLIVER WENDELL, *Collected Legal Papers* (1921)
    The Dissenting Opinions of Mr. Justice Holmes (1929)

HUGHES, CHARLES EVANS, *The Supreme Court of the United States* (1928)

JEVONS, W. S., *The State in Relation to Labor* (1887)

JOHNSON, ALLEN, and ROBINSON, WILLIAM A., *Readings in Recent American Constitutional History* (1927)

JOHNSON, EMILY, ed., *Limitation of Power of the Supreme Court* (1935)

KLAUS, SAMUEL, ed., *The Milligan Case* (1929)

KOCOUREK, ALBERT, *An Introduction to the Science of Law* (1930)

KONKLE, BURTON ALVA, *Life of James Wilson* (1934)

LASKI, HAROLD J., *Authority in the Modern State* (1927)
    Studies in Law and Politics (1932)
    The State in Theory and Practice (1935)

LAWRENCE, DAVID, *Nine Honest Men* (1936)

LEWIS, W. D., *Great American Lawyers* (1909)

MAINE, HENRY SUMNER, *Ancient Law* (1888)

MARTIN, C. E., *An Introduction to the Study of the American Constitution* (1928)

McGEHEE, L. P., *Due Process of Law Under the Federal Constitution* (1906)

MERRIAM, C. E., *A History of American Political Theories* (1903)

MOSCHZISKER, ROBERT VON, *Judicial Review of Legislation* (1923)

MOTT, RODNEY L., *Due Process of Law* (1926)

MYERS, GUSTAVUS, *History of the Supreme Court of the United States* (1912)

O'CONNOR, JOHN JOSEPH, *The Supreme Court and Labor* (1932)

POLLOCK, SIR FREDERICK, *Essays in the Law* (1922)

POUND, ROSCOE, *Outlines of Lectures on Jurisprudence* (1920)
The Spirit of the Common Law (1921)
An Introduction to Philosophy of Law (1922)
Law and Morals (1926)

POWELL, THOMAS REED, *The State Police Power of 1922-30* (1932)

REED, THOMAS H., ed., *The Constitution in the Twentieth Century* (1936)

RICHBERG, DONALD, *The Rainbow* (1936)

RODELL, FRED, *Fifty Five Men* (1936)

RYAN, JOHN A., *A Living Wage* (1906)
Declining Liberty and Other Papers (1927)
Distributive Justice (Revised edition, 1927)
The Supreme Court and the Minimum Wage (1932)

SMITH, CHARLES W., *Roger B. Taney: Jacksonian Jurist* (1936)

SMITH, J. ALLEN, *The Growth and Decadence of Constitutional Government* (1930)

STIMSON, F. J., *Labor in its Relations to the Law* (1895)

SWIFT, MORRISON ISAAC, *The American House of Lords* (1911)

SWISHER, CARL B., *Stephen J. Field, Craftsman of the Law* (1892)
Roger B. Taney (1936)

TAFT, WILLIAM H., *The Anti-Trust Act and the Supreme Court* (1914)

WARREN, CHARLES, *The Supreme Court in United States History* (1922, rev. ed. 1926)
The Supreme Court and Sovereign States (1924)
Congress, the Constitution and the Supreme Court (1925, rev. ed. 1935)
The Making of the Court (1928)

WILLOUGHBY. WESTEL WOODBURY, *The Supreme Court of the United States* (1890)
Social Justice (1900)
The Constitutional Law of the United States (1910), rev. ed. 1929)

II. Magazine Articles on Recent Cases

"AAA Abolition: excerpts from Supreme Court decision." *Time*, Vol. 27, pp. 12-13, Jan. 13, 1936

"AAA Decision," *Christian Century*, Vol. 53, pp. 134-6, Jan. 22, 1936

ADAMS, JAMES TRUSLOW, "Crises and the Constitution," *Scribner's Magazine*, Vol. 98, pp. 326-30; Vol. 99, pp. 1-6, 63-9, 135-9, Dec.,1935—March, 1936

"Agricultural Adjustment Act Declared Unconstitutional," *Catholic World*, Vol. 142, pp. 620-1, Feb., 1936

AIKMAN, DUNCAN, and JONES, HAWLEY, "Bogey of Regimentation," *Harper*, Vol. 169, pp. 641-50, Nov., 1934

"Al Smith's Speech," *New Republic*, Vol. 85, pp. 352-4

ARNOLD, T., "New Deal Is Constitutional," *New Republic*, Vol. 77, pp. 8-10, Nov. 15, 1933

"Battle Lines of '36," *Collier's*, Vol. 93, p. 54, Feb. 17, 1934

BAYLE, J. E., "AAA: An Epitaph," *Atlantic*, Vol. 157, pp. 217-25, Feb., 1936

BEARD, C. A., "Social Change and the Constitution," *New Republic*, Vol. 83, pp. 116-18, Jan. 12, 1935

"Republican Hopes," *Current History*, Vol. 43, pp. 519-20, Feb., 1936

"AAA and the Supreme Court," *Current History*, Vol. 43, pp. 516-18, Feb., 1936

"Challenge to the New Deal by Organized Industry and Business," *Current History*, Vol. 43, pp. 513-16, Feb., 1936

BLAIR, E. F., "Has the Supreme Court Doomed the New Deal?" *Fortune*, Vol. 12, pp. 63-6, Sept., 1935

BLIVEN, B., "What's on the People's Mind," *Current History*, Vol. 43, pp. 449-54, Feb., 1936

BORAH, W. E., "Supreme Court," *Readers' Digest*, Vol. 28, pp. 1-6, March, 1936

BOUDIN, L. B., "Government by Judiciary," *Political Science Quarterly*, Vol. 26, p. 238

BROGAN, D. W., "American Constitutional Crises," *Fortnightly*, Vol. 144, pp. 1-11, July, 1935

BROUN, H., "Loose Construction," *Nation*, Vol. 142, p. 130, Jan. 29, 1936

BUEHLER, A. D., "Taxation of Business Enterprise, Its Theory and Practice," *Annals of American Academy of Political and Social Science*, Vol. 183, pp. 96-103, Jan., 1936

BURNS, E. M., "Court and the T.V.A.," *New Republic*, Vol. 86, p. 60, Feb. 26, 1936

DARVALL, F., "Supreme Court versus the New Deal," *Contemporary Review*, Vol. 148, pp. 31-7, July, 1935

DAWSON, MITCHELL, "The Supreme Court and the New Deal," *Harper's*, Nov., 1935

"Decision of Supreme Court on the National Industrial Recovery Act; with text," *Monthly Labor Review*, Vol. 40, pp. 1466-83, Jan., 1935

DENNIS, LAWRENCE, "The Planless Roosevelt Revolution," *American Mercury*

EISNER, L. P., "Constitution vs. New Deal," *Review of Reviews*, Vol. 93, pp. 41-43, Jan., 1936

ESSARY, J. F., "Long Live the King—Roosevelt and Dictator," *American Mercury*, Sept., 1933

"Finding Men to Find a President," *Literary Digest*, Vol. 121-5, March 7, 1936

FINKKELSTEIN, M., "Dilemma of the Supreme Court; Will It find the N.R.A. and the A.A.A. Unconstitutional?" *Nation*, Vol. 137, pp. 428-30, Oct. 18, 1933

FLYNN, J. T., "Justice Roberts and Justice Stone: Dialog based on the opinion and the dissenting opinion of the Supreme Court in the AAA case," *New Republic*, Jan. 22, 1936

"Free to print without taxation; Supreme Court's Outlawry of Louisiana levy on newspaper earnings," *Literary Digest*, Vol. 121, p. 17, Feb. 22, 1936

FRANKFURTER, F., "Social Issues before the Supreme Court," *Yale Review*, Vol. 22, pp. 476-95, March, 1933

GARRISON, L. K., "Constitution and the Future, with a Suggested Amendment," *New Republic*, Vol. 85, pp. 328-30, Jan. 29, 1936

HAINES, C. G., "Shall We Remake the Supreme Court? The Practice of Other Countries," *Nation*, May 14, 1924

"High Spots in the Campaign," *New Republic*, Vol. 80, pp. 356-8, Nov. 7, 1934

HOUGHTON, W. M., "Open Letter to Mr. Jefferson," *American Mercury*, Vol. 37, pp. 273-6, March, 1936

HUTCHINSON, P., "Final Verdict on Recovery: Will the Supreme Court Support Mr. Roosevelt?" *Forum*, Vol. 90, pp. 141-7, Sept., 1933

LASKI, H. J., "Englishman Looks at the Constitution," *Living Age,* Vol. 350, pp. 85-7, March, 1936

LERNER, M., "John Marshall's Long Shadow," *New Republic,* Vol. 84, pp. 148-52, Sept. 18, 1935

"Where Does the Supreme Court Stand?" *Nation,* March 4, 1936

LIPPMANN, WALTER, "Challenge to the Constitution," *American Mercury,* Vol. 119, pp. 44-5, Jan., 1935

LORANCE, J., "Law and the Supreme Court," *Commonweal,* Vol. 21, pp. 499-501, March 1, 1935

"Packing the Supreme Court," *Christian Century,* Vol. 52, pp. 38-9, Jan. 9, 1935

MALLON, P., "Party Line-up for 1936," *Current History,* Vol. 42, pp. 337-44, July, 1935

McBAIN, H. L., "Constitution and the New Deal," *Yale Review,* Vol. 25, pp. 114-30, Sept., 1935

MONTAGUE, G. H., "New Deal Upheld in TVA Test-case; Supreme Court's Eight-to-one Decision," *Literary Digest,* Vol. 121, p. 5, Feb. 22, 1936

"New Soil Conservative Act, Substitute for AAA; with Test of Act, Pro and Con Arguments, and Glossary of Terms," *Congressional Digest,* Vol. 15, pp. 62-96, March, 1936

ODEGARD, P. H., "Future of States' Rights," *North American Review,* Vol. 240, pp. 238-63, Sept., 1935

OPPENHEIM, J. H., "Supreme Court Grows up," *American Mercury,* Vol. 36, pp. 273-84, Nov., 1935

OWENS, J. W., "Between the Devil and the Democrats," *Atlantic,* Vol. 156, pp. 641-50, Dec., 1935

POLLARD, J. F., "Wake Up, Supreme Court, The 18th Amendment Violates the Constitution," *Forum,* Vol. 88, pp. 213-19, Oct., 1932

POWELL, T. R., "Common Sense and the Constitution," *Current History,* Vol. 43, pp. 484-9, Feb., 1936

RATNER, S., "Was the Supreme Court Packed by President Grant?" *Political Science Quarterly,* Vol. 50, pp. 343-58, Sept., 1935

"Scottsboro, What Now?" *New Republic,* Vol. 82, pp. 270-1, April 17, 1935

"Should the Powers of the United States Supreme Court be Modified? With Pro and Con Arguments," *Congressional Digest,* Vol. 14, pp. 289-320, Dec., 1935

"Supreme Court and Farm Relief, Outlawing the Frazier-Lemke Act," *New Republic,* Vol. 83, pp. 154-5, Jan. 19, 1935

"Supreme Court Makes the New Deal more Secure: Decision upholding the Minnesota Mortgage Moratorium Law," *Literary Digest,* Vol. 117, p. 45, Jan. 20, 1934

"Supreme Court Rules out Security in Railroad Retirement Act Decision," *Nation,* Vol. 140, p. 588, May 22, 1935

REYNOLDS, W. L., "Constitution vs. Socialism," *National Republic,* Vol. 21, pp. 23-4, Oct., 1933

SHAW, BERNARD, "Freedom and Government," *Nation,* July 10, 1935

SOKALSKY, G. E., "Supreme Court Swings the Ax: AAA Decision," *Nation,* Vol. 142, p. 61, Jan. 15, 1936

"Psychology of the New Deal," *Atlantic Monthly,* Vol. 157, pp. 369-78, March, 1936

SOULE, GEORGE, "Back to State's Rights," *Harper's,* Vol. 171, pp. 484-91, Sept., 1935

TAYLOR, M., "TVA Decision," *Christian Century,* Vol. 55, pp. 318-20, Feb. 26, 1936

"TVA Decision, a Trojan Horse," *Nation,* Vol. 142, pp. 236-7, Feb. 26, 1936

"The Lawless Supreme Court," *Nation,* Feb. 19, 1936

"The Riddle of the Supreme Court," *Nation,* Jan. 29, 1936

"The T.V.A. Decision," *Nation,* Feb. 26, 1936

TUCKER, R., "Court of the Lost Guess," *Collier's,* Vol. 94, p. 32, July 7, 1934

TUGWELL, R. G., "United States Supreme Court Declares AAA Illegal," *Congressional Digest,* Vol. 15, p. 74, March, 1936

WARREN, C. W., "Shall We Re-make the Supreme Court? Origin of Its Powers," *Nation,* May 7, 1924.

WARREN, V. A., "Decision," *Christian Century,* Vol. 53, pp. 318-20, Feb. 26, 1936

"What to do with the Supreme Court," *Nation,* July 10, 1935

WHITTLESEY, W. L., "Back to the Constitution," *Survey Graphic,* Vol. 24, pp. 325-7, July, 1935

"Will the Supreme Court Decisions Elect Next President?" *Nation,* July 27, 1935

YARROS, V. S., "Senator Borah and Monopolies," *Christian Century,* Vol. 52, pp. 262-3, Feb. 12, 1936

"Yellow Light; Supreme Court Lets Government Proceed with Caution on Power Program," *Business Week,* p. 7, Feb. 22, 1936

LIST OF CASES CITED

LIST OF CASES CITED

356   THE STORY OF THE SUPREME COURT

INDEX

INDEX

A.A.A. decision
  see *United States* v. *Butler*
Ableman v. *Booth*, 166
Abrams v. *United States*, 255
Act of July 13, 1861, 169
Adair, 236, 237
Adair v. *United States*, 236, 238, 249, 269
Adams, Abijah, 78
Adams, John, 16, 27, 43, 44, 45, 62, 72, 74, 75, 77, 80, 81, 82, 87
Adams, John Quincy, 102, 106, 108, 110, 129, 131, 143, 148
Adams, Samuel, 16, 45
Adamson Act, 245, 247
Adkins v. *Children's Hospital*, 269-275, 314, 315, 316
Africa, 129, 148, 163
Agricultural Adjustment Act, 303-311
Alabama, 65, 147, 259
Alabama Power Co., 313
Alaska, 229
Alien Act, 73, 213
Allgeyer v. *Louisiana*, 225, 226
Altgeld, Gov., 218
Aluminum Co. of America v. *Ramsey*, 248
Amendments
  see Constitution
America, 54, 56, 58, 259, 287
American Bankers' Assn., 286
American Citizen, 94
American Doctrine of Judicial Supremacy, The
  by Charles G. Haines, 15, 25-26
American Express Co., 232
American Law Review, 184
American Medical Assn. Bureau, 268
American Revolution, 16, 17, 18, 20, 24, 43, 44, 45, 50, 64, 68, 85, 107, 112, 132, 162
American Sugar Refining Co., 223-224
American Tobacco Case
  see *United States* v. *American Tobacco Co.*
Ames, Fisher, 37, 40

Annapolis, 67, 139
Antelope, The, 128
Anti-Federalists, 51, 58, 77, 80
Anti-slavery agitation, 139
Areopagitica
  by John Milton, 74
Arizona, 158, 248, 277
Arizona Copper Co. v. *Hammer*, 248
Armour, Philip D., 209
Arredondo, F. M., and Son, 134
Arredondo Case, the
  see *United States* v. *Arredondo*
Arthur, Chester A., 195
Articles of Confederation, 17-18, 20, 61
Ashmore, Margaret, 149
Ashwander v. *Tennessee Authority et al.*, 312-314
Atkin v. *Kansas*, 228
Atlanta, 249
Atlantic, the, 72
Aurora, 94
Austin, 147
Australia, 15

Bache, Benj. Franklin, 51, 52
  Aurora, 75
Bailey v. *Drexel Furniture Co.*, 252
Baldwin, Abraham, 37
Baldwin, Henry, 84, 131, 135, 137, 146, 151
Baltimore, 67, 68, 129, 141
Baltimore & Ohio R. R., 211
Baltimore Railroad Case, 280
Bank of Augusta v. *Earle*, 148
Bank of Maryland, 120
Bank of North America, 45, 66
Bank of the United States, 136, 141, 173
Bank of the United States v. *Primrose*, 148
Bankruptcy, 185
Bankruptcy laws, 118, 119, 129-130
Barbier v. *Connolly*, 203
Barbour, Philip, 137, 143, 150
Barlow, Joel, 74
Bartemeyer v. *Iowa*, 206
Baruso, 111

359

DATE DUE

TERMS OF SERVICE AND AGES OF THE JUSTICES

C0-AWV-289

intt

To my friend,
    Roy T. Ambert,

            Geo. P. Alt.

Christmas, 1936.